May God himself, the God of peace,
sanctify you through and through.
May your whole spirit, soul and body be kept blameless
at the coming of our Lord Jesus Christ.
The one who calls you is faithful
and he will do it.

I THESSALONIANS 5:23-24 (NIV)

WHERE ALL HOPE LIES

Sermons for the Liturgical Year

James R. Van Tholen

Edited by
Susan Dykstra-Poel
Eileen Borduin Vanderzwan
Edward Wierenga
and
Joseph Wright

WILLIAM B. EERDMANS PUBLISHING COMPANY
GRAND RAPIDS, MICHIGAN / CAMBRIDGE, U.K.

Wm. B. Eerdmans Publishing Co.
255 Jefferson Ave. S.E., Grand Rapids, Michigan 49503 /
P.O. Box 163, Cambridge CB3 9PU U.K.
www.eerdmans.com

Printed in the United States of America

07 06 05 04 03   7 6 5 4 3 2 1

Library of Congress Cataloging-in-Publication Data

Van Tholen, James R.
Where all hope lies: sermons for the liturgical year /
James R. Van Tholen; edited by Susan Dykstra-Poel . . . [et al.]
p.   cm.
Includes bibliographical references.
ISBN 0-8028-0970-7 (pbk.: alk. paper)
1. Church year sermons.   2. Christian Reformed Church — Sermons.
3. Sermons, American — 20th century.   I. Dykstra-Poel, Susan.   II. Title.

BX6827.V36   2003
252′.05731 — dc21

2003040765

Contents

EPIPHANY

LENT

EASTER

PENTECOST

ORDINARY TIME

Sermons from the Minor Prophets

Sermons from the Book of Daniel

Sermons from the Book of Revelation

Title Sermon

Sermons for Various Occasions

Foreword

Let's say that Christian preaching is the presentation of God's word at a particular time to particular people by someone authorized to do it. Like telling others of one's spiritual experiences (some Christians call it "sharing" or, in intellectually chaste moods, "just sharing"), good preaching is personal and concrete. A sermon is not a lecture. But even a highly personal and concrete preacher, such as Jim Van Tholen, did not create his message from scratch. He worked out of the Bible, which was his community's book. And how he (and Rachel) personally felt about his message mattered, but it mattered less than how faithfully Jim brought the message. After all, the preacher himself is addressed by his message, just as his listeners are. In fact, the sermon's message ultimately comes only through, and not from, the preacher, and it centers on the same God who sends it. "For we do not proclaim ourselves," as St. Paul put it; "we proclaim Jesus Christ as Lord" (2 Cor. 4:5).

To follow St. Paul in this task, a preacher selects a biblical text and then does in other words what the text does, always with an eye on the text's ultimate relation to Christ. Thus, depending on the text, Jim Van Tholen warned people one Sunday and comforted them the next. He prophesied, counseled, taught, or rebuked. Sometimes he provoked people if his text was provocative enough. Occasionally he began by challenging a popular opinion and ended up by reinforcing it, but only after moving this opinion inside a biblical view of the world. Once in a while he reproduced an interrogative text by turning a big part of his sermon into a repeated question.

As every faithful preacher knows, the life, death, and resurrection of Jesus Christ occupy the center of human history and the center of Christian preaching. This is especially clear when sermons follow the liturgical year, as do those in this volume. In the life of Christ we find "the Word made flesh." The gospel is full of the words of God, but the words need to have a face so that we can recognize them. So the words became flesh. Because they did, we can recognize the fierceness of God's determination. We can read it in the face of Jesus Christ — the face he sets like flint as he turns toward Jerusalem, the city of his death. God-in-the-flesh shows us humility, courage, self-giving love. The feet of God take him to the hovel of a leper, and the hands of God reach to a body that is otherwise untouchable. The knees of God bend in front of disciples so that God can wash the feet of men who hadn't dreamed of doing this for each other. The arms of God, stretched and nailed to a crossbeam by his own creatures, open to embrace a world. The voice of God speaks peace to faithful women who have showed up at the tomb on Easter morning.

In the death of Christ, God adopts a "like-cures-like" strategy of defeating death by way of another death. Then God follows up with a similar strategy for passing along the death benefits of Christ to his followers. Remarkably, God elects to salvage human beings by deputizing other human beings to preach Christ to them — other human beings who are just as damaged and foolish as their audience. In 2 Corinthians 4:7 Paul compares the preacher (he has himself especially in mind) to a baked clay jar. To find the flame of love in such homely ware, to find the flame of God's glory in human hearts, is to find a kind of miracle.

Paul's illustration reminds us that the preacher's job is not just to repeat a text but also to outfit it for the hearing of a congregation. The preacher not only does in other words what the text does. He also says in other words what the text says — dressing it up or down, shaping and coloring and amplifying it in such a way that when people hear the preached text they hear God's Word to them. For example, they might hear a warning that sin is not only an offense against God and neighbor but also a form of self-abuse. They might hear that we do not belong to ourselves, that we are not our own authors or centers, and that, surprisingly, this is a comfort. They might hear that idolaters want to carry their gods around with them, but that the God of Scripture carries us, and that a central question of religion is therefore "Who is carrying whom?"

When preaching works well, the result is eventful. People feel pierced, or assured, or blessed. They sense that they are somehow joined to God by this religious event, just as they are in baptism or the Lord's Supper. Indeed, Christians think of a preached and heard sermon as "an audible sacrament," to use a phrase attributed to Augustine. Sacraments are ligaments of the covenant between God and believers — covenant "binders," we might say. So preaching naturally binds believers to God by making God audible to them. But a sermon may also take hold of others. A well-designed sermon may make God audible to unbelievers, or to seekers, or to people who are so consciously ambivalent about God that they would hardly know what to call themselves.

In fact, we may generalize: one of the main functions of preaching is to make God real to listeners, including to the preacher, who is always a sermon's "pioneer listener," as Roger Van Harn once put it. Of course God is real whether people in church think so or not. Presuming to "activate" God by preaching a sermon would be a prime piece of arrogance.

But in another way, sermons do render God actual to listeners. In healthy preaching God's grace and power come home to people: these qualities are brought to mind, raised up in consciousness, affirmed by the heart. A Godly life is at least a God-conscious life, and the preacher stimulates such a life by re-presenting God to listeners. When this is effectively done — that is, when the preacher's good efforts are energized and focused by the power of the Holy Spirit (the unpredictable variable or "x-factor" in preaching) — then once more God seems large and luminous to people who are listening.

The sermons in this volume represent the work of a young preacher who understood and accepted the urgency of rendering God real to listeners. In these honest, gritty, sometimes desperately deep sermons, we find a faith beyond doubt, but not beyond question. Jim Van Tholen didn't preach his doubts; he preached the gospel. But he preached the gospel as a human being, complete with its puzzles, questions, and pain. That's a good deal of what made Jim a believable preacher. Always starting from Scripture, but then drawing as well upon the riches of Flannery O'Connor, Frederick Buechner, Annie Dillard, Kathleen Norris, and others, Jim showed us the turns and twists in a serious Christian life. He showed us that God is great in large part because God is good — good to sinners, to questioners, to people who turn their back on God and walk toward the darkness. (Jesus washed Judas's feet too.) But whatever path Jim followed in his sermons, he preached the Word of God in all its tragedy and victory. He preached Christ around the year from Advent through Easter and Pentecost to the ordinary rhythms of ordinary life. He did it with intelligence and power, and sometimes he did it with beauty.

Jim's friends and congregations do not understand why God saw fit to receive Jim so early. What would this man have sounded like at full maturity? But our pain is mixed with gratitude for what Jim was able to do for us with a Bible in his hand, and our gratitude may now attach to this permanent record of some short, golden years.

Cornelius Plantinga, Jr.

Preface

In May 1999, *Christianity Today* published "Surprised by Death" (here reprinted in its entirety and under its original title, "Where All Hope Lies"), the first sermon James Van Tholen preached to his congregation in Rochester, New York, after his return to the pulpit following surgery and chemotherapy for cancer. Close friends of Jim, seeing his sermon in print, recognized an opportunity to share more of his sermons with a larger audience. Jim reluctantly acquiesced so that his congregation could have a collection of his sermons and a role in selecting them. Sadly, Jim died a few weeks later. A memorial fund was established to support this project.

The Council of the Rochester Christian Reformed Church appointed a committee to collect and edit a compilation of Jim's sermons for a book. That committee decided to arrange the book according to the liturgical year, the framework within which Jim had organized worship. As Jim had wanted, the committee solicited suggestions of especially meaningful sermons from members of the congregation. The committee then tried to incorporate as many of these suggestions as possible. Another goal was to keep intact several series of sermons, not only for Advent and Lent, but also a series on the minor prophets and on two books of the Bible: Daniel and Revelation. After comparing manuscripts, audio tapes, and computer files, the committee endeavored to establish a text that was faithful to Jim's voice and intent. All Scripture passages are taken from the New Revised Standard Version unless otherwise noted.

Thanks are due to the many who contributed to the memorial fund, to members of the congregation for thoughtful suggestions of sermons to include, and to the William B. Eerdmans Publishing Company.

We are grateful to God for the opportunity to hear his gospel as clearly as Jim preached it, with a gift for fresh insight into a text, evincing grace, honesty, and prophetic boldness, and demonstrating as well as demanding faithfulness.

Susan Dykstra-Poel
Eileen Borduin Vanderzwan
Edward Wierenga
Joseph Wright

ADVENT

That We Might Have Hope

Text: Romans 15:1-6

We who are strong ought to put up with the failings of the weak, and not to please ourselves. Each of us must please our neighbor for the good purpose of building up the neighbor. For Christ did not please himself; but, as it is written, "The insults of those who insult you have fallen on me." For whatever was written in former days was written for our instruction, so that by steadfastness and by the encouragement of the scriptures we might have hope. May the God of steadfastness and encouragement grant you to live in harmony with one another, in accordance with Christ Jesus, so that together you may with one voice glorify the God and Father of our Lord Jesus Christ.

Romans 15:1-6

In her striking book *Dakota*,[1] Kathleen Norris writes about life on the plains: life in a harsh and unforgiving climate; life under constant economic pressure; life within a small town that is getting smaller by the year. And in this life, says Kathleen Norris, there is something the people do to help them persevere: they remember and hold on to and tell the stories of the past, the stories of survival, and from them they take hope. And this isn't just an activity for senior citizens, but one for the whole community. So a high school student will choose to write about how his North Dakotan family has always been there and will always remain. The assurance, the promise, the hope for the future comes from those descriptions of survival in the past. In whatever weakness they find themselves, they can rely on these people and places and events from their history to provide hope.

This is similar to Paul's idea for the church concerning what we have from our history. In our present weakness, says Paul, we have something to say to each other, too. We have something to rely on, to count on, to re-

---

1. Kathleen Norris, *Dakota: A Spiritual Geography* (New York: Ticknor & Fields, 1993).

member — and from it we can take hope. And it is, of course, the Scriptures. "For whatever was written in former days was written for our instruction, so that by steadfastness and by the encouragement of the scriptures we might have hope" (v. 4). Paul is not speaking here of just anything that was written in former days, but rather anything that belonged to the Scriptures, to the Old Testament — that's the only Scriptures he knows. And anything that was written there, he says, no matter how long ago, no matter what part of it, was written for us, was written for our instruction so that we might have hope.

We've walked in on the middle of a conversation here in Romans 15, because for more than a chapter Paul has been talking about an issue concerning the church of Rome, the issue of religious regulations regarding food and special days. Some in the church think that Christians have to observe the old Jewish regulations very carefully, while others feel free to ignore them. That's the conversation in chapter 14. Now in chapter 15 Paul's wrapping that up, and he's talking about how important it is that we in the body of Jesus Christ get along, that we are able to live together. And the way to do that, he says, is to treat each other the way Christ treated us. He says in verse 3, "For Christ did not please himself; but, as it is written, 'The insults of those who insult you have fallen on me.'"

Paul is using a statement from a psalm that applies to Jesus Christ, and that brings him to this marvelous declaration about the Scriptures, to this general truth about the Scriptures. Why can Psalm 69 carry weight, make a difference, say something today? Because "whatever was written in former days was written for our instruction, so that by steadfastness and by the encouragement of the scriptures we might have hope." It was written for us, for the Romans as they considered belonging to Jesus Christ on the western side of the Italian peninsula in the middle of the first century, and for us as we consider belonging to Jesus Christ on the southern shore of Lake Ontario at the end of the twentieth century. Wherever we are, and whenever we are, we in the body of Jesus Christ possess a gift, and the gift is whatever belongs to these ancient words of the Old Testament, because they were written for our instruction, that we might have hope.

Notice that Paul doesn't say the Scriptures were written to provide information, that they're there to give us history or that they're there to teach us science. No, that's not what they're there to do. And, though there's certainly information there to be gained, when we make that what they're about, when we treat the Scriptures as an encyclopedia or a history book or a science text, then we miss them. We miss them, not because they don't provide any information, and not because they're unrelated to history or science; we miss them because that's not their purpose; they're there so that we might have hope. And the terribly sad thing about the people trying to prove or disprove certain statements of the Scriptures is that they tend to forget what those Scriptures are first of all about: they're not about the information they possess or the facts they provide; they're about hope. "For whatever was written in former days was written for our instruction, so that by steadfastness and by the encouragement of the scriptures we might have hope."

That is the gift we who are in Christ possess: we have a source of hope. And there is nothing of greater value as we work our way through a broken, misguided, diseased world. "Hope," says John Timmer, whose own sermon on this text revealed its beauty to me, "is like oxygen. Take oxygen away and people suffocate. Take hope away and people perish. The Scriptures keep us breathing."[2] The Scriptures keep us breathing, not because they fill us with facts, but because they fill us with hope. They keep us breathing because they speak of a God who is the same yesterday and today and forever. They keep us breathing because they give us a new way of seeing. Whatever hope we have in this world, Paul says, comes to us through the pages of Scripture.

And what do we find there? What do we find in those Scriptures Paul's talking about? We find Jonah. The story of Jonah is not a pick-me-up. It's not a good American story at all, really. It's not a keep-your-chin-up-God-will-reward-you kind of passage. Jonah is a story of disobedience. And not just Nineveh's disobedience, but Jonah's disobedience, too. Nineveh is a terribly wicked city, says the Lord. And he wants Jonah to announce that he's going to do something about it. But Jonah doesn't listen. "Jonah, go east to Nineveh," said the Lord. And Jonah boards the first boat he can find heading west. He has no interest in prophesying against Nineveh. Well, we know what happens to Jonah. He has to exit the ship a little early, because you can run, but you can never run far enough from the Lord. And he ends up buried in the belly of a fish.

So in Jonah we read of a terribly wicked city that God has had it up to here with, and we read of a prophet who refuses him, whom God chases down on the high seas and dumps into some sea creature's tummy. No heroes, nobody in the book of Jonah who's made their own way, who's got a future all worked out — no success stories. But the book of Jonah contains something for us more precious than success; it contains hope. Success can fail just like the world's greatest city failed and just like the Lord's

2. John Timmer, "Keep Hope Alive," May 21, 1993.

prophet failed; hope comes from somewhere else. "Let all know that sure deliverance comes from God the Lord alone."[3] That's the story of Jonah. So at the end of the day, both the wicked city and the cowardly prophet are alive — not because of what they are but because of what they know: deliverance comes from God the Lord alone.

But hope is found elsewhere, too, as in the story of Joseph. This story at the end of Genesis is fascinating, because it's a story we know, a story whose parts we have lived out in our own lives at times. It's about a family, a terribly hurting family, not too different from most families at one time or another. Here's a father who loves foolishly and unequally, a young boy Joseph who naively celebrates his role as the favorite, and his ten brothers who just hate him and want to hurt him and never think about the consequences. So Joseph ends up sold into slavery, Jacob a heartbroken old man, and their family filled with pain. No heroes here, either. No Father's Day sermons about Jacob come out of this; no solutions to sibling rivalry here. They're all human beings who are a lot to blame for the messes they've found themselves in. It's a desperate situation.

But it's not a desperate story. It's a story that's full of hope. When the brothers end up in Egypt and run across Joseph again in the pharaoh's palace, they realize that he can now do to them what they did to him, and they're terrified. But Joseph says, "Do not be afraid! Am I in the place of God? Even though you intended to do harm to me, God intended it for good, in order to preserve a numerous people, as he is doing today" (Genesis 50:19-20). And there is hope, because even within his people's rivalries and dysfunctionalities and self-absorption, even there God is at work, using it for good, preserving lives. That gives us hope.

And that's a different kind of hope than Kathleen Norris describes. It's different because it's real. The things of the past, those examples of survival that the people around her like to hold on to, are made up, or at best they're only part of the truth. The truth is that failure and devastation are a large part of the past there, and the future holds no guarantees. That high school student who says so confidently that his family has always been on the plains and is sure to stay there — actually, his family's been there less than seventy-five years, and the likelihood of his own staying is very low. That's the truth; but they don't pay attention to that part, says Kathleen Norris. They take their hope from lies, lies that hard work and perseverance can overcome all obstacles, and that there's always a happy ending.

3. From the hymn, "Song of Jonah," text © 1982, Calvin Seerveld.

The astounding thing about the Scriptures that Paul's talking about — and the thing that we can forget when we treat them too religiously — is that there's no pretense whatsoever, no lies. Whether it's Jonah or Joseph or Ecclesiastes or Jeremiah, these Scriptures recognize life's realities. They recognize failure and sin and pain and injustice and death. The Scriptures from which we gain hope don't give us that hope because somebody hung in there or because each family was perfect or because every good person is given money and health and children or because no one ever got worse than they deserved. These Scriptures know better than that, and they don't pretend otherwise. What we find here are real people in real situations, and in their words, their experiences, their failure, their obedience, their prayer, even their sin, we see the presence of God and have hope. Now. Today.

This Advent season we're going to consider three of those experiences, three moments of painful reality, and from them, remembering the words of Paul, we will be instructed, that by their encouragement we might have hope. If the coming of Jesus Christ doesn't speak to the most real and difficult of situations, then it is not worth celebrating, and then our hope is not much different from those whose hope rests on lies and myths. But our hope *is* different, because it rests on truth, because it rests on a suffering Savior.

In the twenty-first chapter of Numbers the people of Israel are journeying toward their new land when fatigue and impatience get the best of them, and they start complaining against Moses and against God. God sends poisonous snakes among them, and the snakes bite the people, and a large number of them die. But then they cry out to the Lord, and he has Moses make a bronze snake and put it on a pole. When a snake bites someone, the person looks at the bronze snake and is healed. The reason that story is there, and the reason why the stories of Jonah and Joseph are there, is the same: it is that we might have hope, that we might find Jesus.

That's right; it's Christ we're directed to in Jonah, because he's the one who received what Nineveh and Jonah deserved. And it's Christ we're pointed to in Joseph's narrative, because in no more amazing way did God bring good out of evil than he did in the crucifixion of his Son. And it's Christ we're shown in Numbers 21, because we hear him say, "As Moses lifted up the serpent, so I will be lifted up, that you can look at me and be healed" (John 3:14).

That's Advent: believing that Christ is coming into every experience of our lives, and it makes all the difference. Advent is seeing, as the writers of the books of Jonah and Genesis and Numbers saw, that God's weakness is stronger than human strength, that his plan of salvation is going forward, that the Messiah is coming. And that is why we turn now to Joseph and Jonah and Jeremiah, because whatever was written about them in former days was written for our instruction, that by the encouragement of their stories we might have hope.

Umpire

Text: Job 9:25-35

For he is not a mortal, as I am, that I might answer him,
that we should come to trial together.
There is no umpire between us,
who might lay his hand on us both.
If he would take his rod away from me,
and not let dread of him terrify me,
then I would speak without fear of him,
for I know I am not what I am thought to be.

Job 9:32-35

It's all so leisurely and low-key — God and his prosecuting attorney talking things over in heaven. Job chapter 1: On a day when all God's angelic deputies have come in to make their reports, one of them is singled out: Satan, the "Accuser," the district attorney, gets debriefed. "Where have you been?" asks the Lord. "Where I'm supposed to be," says the accuser, "east and west, north and south, ranging across the earth, walking up and down in it. I've been observing; I've been taking notes."

"Say," God responds, "I wonder if you've noticed my man Job. Have you seen how God-fearing he is, how supremely righteous? Have you noticed how blamelessly he serves me and turns away from evil?"

It's almost as if God is nudging Satan, twitting him about how un-

---

Based on a sermon by Cornelius Plantinga Jr., which was based on a sermon by Douglas E. Nelson.

necessary prosecuting attorneys are where law-abiding citizens are concerned. "Have you considered my servant Job?" asks God.

Well, the prosecutor's job has made Satan cynical. "Sure," he says. "Sure, I've seen Job." And then Satan returns volley with a question that threatens all godliness in the world: Does Job fear God for nothing? "Sure," says Satan. "I've seen Job. But you've made him rich. You send him a check every time he says his prayers. Of course he'll serve you. Does Job fear God for nothing?"

With a smirk on his face the accuser surveys Job's wealth and happiness. Does Job fear God for nothing? "Look," says Satan, "you've bought Job's faith. He's got vital health, a quiver full of children, pens bursting with livestock, granaries bulging after harvest. He's got an unlimited supply of natural gas, snowmobiles for the desert sands, and health insurance with no deductibles.

"Of course he'll serve you," says Satan. "He's no fool. This man's faith is for hire — and so far you've been the highest bidder. But suppose we change the rules. Suppose you stretch out your hand and touch all that he has. He'll curse you to your face!"

"You're on," says the Lord. "I bet he won't."

And with that the curtain rises and the drama that is the book of Job begins. So Job is thrown out there on the game board to be moved around by God's Satan — a powerful adversary, a crafty and devastating accuser, a minister of permitted evil — but always under God's control.

Job for his part knows nothing of this. He's not in on any of it. All he knows is that the sun begins to set on his happiness. Suddenly, inexplicably, Job's world turns cold and dark. His possessions are stolen. Lightning strikes his sheep. His servants fall victim to a terrorist attack. And then, one day, a tornado comes across the wilderness, and the roof collapses on Job's seven sons and three daughters. Finally Job himself is sickened and laid low. And Job is left sitting on a dung heap, nursing his case of shingles and cursing the day of his birth.

The friends of Job come to comfort him. It is so much more fun to talk about pain than to suffer it, and Job's friends are talkers. They look at his oozing sores and tell him it is all for the best. "Happy is the one whom God reproves," says Eliphaz. "Hear this and know it is for your own good."

Job does not believe it. He does not believe that the loss of his home and the sores on his body and the death of his family can be explained so simply. He does not believe that God would attack him, hurt him, destroy him. Something has suddenly gone wrong with the God Job knows. Some wire in him has gotten crossed. Some terrifying character change has come over him. And pious cliches don't make any difference. Pat answers, proof texts, somebody trying to figure out the sin you committed to deserve this, none of it is any help.

We've heard that sort of thing, you and I — people who somehow cannot resist trying to explain our suffering to us. God is testing you. God is toughening you. God is disciplining you! God gave you your throat cancer, but never mind: "All things work together for good to those who love God, who are called according his purpose" (Romans 8:28).

We've heard it all. And Job hears it — yard upon yard of conventional wisdom from his friends. It's one of the most maddening parts of his suffering that Job has to sit there listening to all this. Job's friends stuff him to the teeth with all the orthodox phrases until at last Job begs them, pleads with them, to do him one favor: Shut up.

Job doesn't go for easy answers. He demands from *God* the reason for his suffering. Job refuses to believe that the evil lies in himself, that he must have done something to deserve this. He keeps protesting his innocence. "I have not denied the words of God," says Job. "I do not understand how I've offended God." And Job returns to his brooding. He can't figure it out. The greatest of all the men in the East sits on the town garbage heap, scraping his sores with a bit of limestone and wondering *why*.

Why? Why must this come to him? How has he mistreated God? For what purpose does he suffer so much? What has gone wrong with *God?* On and on through the chapters Job asks and keeps on asking till he is unable to speak. Job keeps hunting for the God who used to be good but has gone sour, who had once blessed but now has inexplicably begun to curse.

There's a powerful passage in Elie Wiesel's autobiography, *Night.* In that passage we find something much like Job's struggle. Wiesel escaped Auschwitz as a boy, escaped with his life but not without experiencing the horror of that place. He saw "his mother, a beloved little sister and all his family except his father disappear into a furnace fed with living creatures." He writes,

> Never shall I forget that night, the first night in the camp, which has turned my life into one long night, seven times cursed and seven times sealed. Never shall I forget that smoke. Never shall I forget the little faces of the children, whose bodies I saw turned into wreaths of smoke beneath a silent blue sky.
>
> Never shall I forget those flames which consumed my faith forever.
>
> Never shall I forget that nocturnal silence which deprived me,

for all eternity, of the desire to live. Never shall I forget those moments which murdered my God and my soul and turned my dreams to dust. Never shall I forget these things, even if I am condemned to live as long as God Himself. Never.[4]

Wiesel goes on to tell how some of the pious Jews around him began to recite the Kaddish, the Hebrew prayer for the dead: "*Yitgadal veyitkadach shmé raba. . . .* May God's name be blessed and magnified."

And Wiesel turns to shout at God. *Where is God* in all of this? Why is the all-powerful one silent? "I did not deny God's existence," he says, "but I doubted his absolute justice. I felt revolt rising up in me. I became the accuser and God the accused!"

Job is Elie Wiesel's archetype. Like believers of all ages who find tragedy exploding their world to bits, Job keeps hunting for God. At times he accuses. At times he shouts. But he will not let go. He keeps knocking and pounding at the door of heaven until his knuckles are smashed and his hands are running with blood.

But Job never gets an answer. Finally, at the end of the book, God speaks, but he does not respond. Job is given no explanation; instead he is overwhelmed by the mystery and greatness of God. In the end Job finds God — more God than he had ever known or could ever grasp. He finds God, but God comes with no explanations.

Well, here in chapter 9 we see Job searching for ways to fix the problem himself, to do something that will make his problem of evil go away and be resolved. If God won't come to Job, then maybe Job can get to God; maybe Job himself can make things right.

Maybe he just needs to put this nasty affair behind him, put it out of his mind, forget that any of it ever happened, and he and God will be able to go on like they were before. Ah, but that won't work. "If I say, 'I will forget my complaint, I will put off my sad countenance and be of good cheer,' I become afraid of all my suffering, for I know you will not hold me innocent" (vv. 27-28).

But maybe there's another way, maybe Job can make himself clean, make himself innocent, cleanse himself of whatever it is that has set off God. But that, too, is destined to fail. "If I wash myself with soap and cleanse my hands with lye, yet you will plunge me into filth," says Job to God (vv. 30-31). No, there is no making things right with God unless God is in on the discussion, part of the peacemaking himself.

4. Elie Wiesel, *Night* (New York: Bantam, 1982), p. 32.

But how is that going to be? "For," as Job says in verse 32, "he is not a mortal, as I am, that I might answer him, that we should come to trial together." If only Job could somehow see God, lay hold on God, get God into court to answer the charges against him. But there you are. There isn't any way to do that. There isn't any bridge between us and everlasting God. No subpoena, no lawsuit can be brought, because there is no court that will hear the case.

And that is Job's only real ray of hope. Ignoring the problem won't work; cleansing himself is out. But God and human being coming together, confronting each other — that could be something. "If only there were an umpire between us," says Job. It's a wish he's making in verse 33, more than a statement. If only there could be a third party to this quarrel, someone to get the silent, confusing God and the suffering, tormented human being together. An *umpire*, no less.

Forget for a moment the idea of a man in a blue suit who calls balls and strikes and who occasionally has to put his chest protector up against Lou Piniella. No, the word here *(mizpach)* has a far more general meaning than that. Job is thinking of someone to *judge* between two parties.

Job wants his day in court. He wants someone to judge between them, someone neither God nor man, an arbitrator, an umpire. This umpire, says Job, could "lay his hand upon us both." He would decide this terrible dispute. He would bring us together again. He could say: Job, here is where you have spoken what you did not understand. You have been rash and foolish in your charges against God. And then the umpire could turn to God and might say: God, you too have some adjustments to make in your tormenting of this poor man and your silent refusal to explain yourself. "If only there were an umpire between us," says Job, with, so to speak, one hand on God's shoulder and one on mine.

Ah, but the very thought is silly, of course. And Job knows wishing won't make a thing come true. No use sighing and supposing. Back he goes to his realities. God has declared war on him without warning and without reason. All the meanings that tie his life together have been slashed to ribbons. For some incomprehensible reason he has become not God's son, but God's target. Back he goes to his groping and complaining. More lectures from his friends. More hopeless questions from Job himself. He has had one flash of insight — one inspiration, we might call it — and then it's gone. One word of light in Job's darkness — a word about a mediator, a word about an umpire; but the word does not become flesh.

And yet, the need for Job's umpire remains, long after Job's case has been settled. For Job is not the only faithful one to suffer inexplicably. Job is not the only servant of God to have felt like a divine punching bag. The truth is that some terrible suffering, some of *your* suffering, is not explainable, at least not in any language we speak. The truth is, faithful lives get torpedoed by cancer and abandonment and depression and loss and vendetta even now, and we wonder, Why?

An umpire is needed still. Someone, we would say, who will be both divine and human, both judge and victim. François Mauriac writes in the foreword to Elie Wiesel's book about a day when the young Wiesel watched the hanging of another child in Auschwitz. This child, he tells us, had the face of a sad angel. The young Wiesel heard someone behind him groan, "Where is God?" *Where* is God in all of this? And a voice within Elie Wiesel answered: "Where? He is here — he has been hanged on these gallows."

I think Job helps us to see a deeper way to take that. What child is this who could be both victim and judge of evil? Who on earth, who in heaven's name could be a mediator to lay his hand upon us both? Who could reconcile a fallen and hopeless human race with a high and inexplicable God? Who could be hanged on the gallows of human evil but in that evil bring all heaven to do battle with it?

Someone to lay his hand upon us both — one nail-torn hand upon the broken humanity there on the garbage heap, one mangled hand upon the King of Heaven. "If only there were an umpire between us, who might lay his hand upon us both." There is our hope, but, unlike Job, we know it is not fleeting.

God and humanity reconciled because of the coming of a person — what an advent that must be. What an advent that is.

— THIRD SUNDAY OF ADVENT —

The Sacrifice

Text: Genesis 22:1-19

When they came to the place that God had shown him, Abraham built an altar there and laid the wood in order. He bound his son Isaac, and laid

him on the altar, on top of the wood. Then Abraham reached out his hand
and took the knife to kill his son. But the angel of the Lord called to him
from heaven, and said, "Abraham, Abraham!" And he said, "Here I am."
He said, "Do not lay your hand on the boy or do anything to him; for now
I know that you fear God, since you have not withheld your son, your only
son, from me." And Abraham looked up and saw a ram, caught in a
thicket by its horns. Abraham went and took the ram and offered it up as
a burnt offering instead of his son.

Genesis 22:9-13

Kali Poulton. In Northern California, it's Polly Klaas. It always seems to
be the same horrific story, just told each time with a new name in a new
place a few months or just weeks after the last one — a child ripped away
from her home, a little boy lost forever to his loving parents. It's those stories that have made me recognize the gravity of this story about Abraham
and Isaac and God. Those real-life events, those events that I can't dis-
count or turn into myth because I know they're real, because I know they
happened — those events make me appreciate this event, this situation in
which it's not some sick stranger looking for the child but the Lord God
himself.

Up until a few years ago Genesis 22 didn't bother me much, didn't disturb me, and the reason it didn't disturb me is because I softened it. Even
though I wouldn't have called it that, I thought of it as a sort of myth, as
some sort of object lesson — after all, our God would never ask for a boy's
sacrifice, and he would never need to conduct a test, because he knows everything, anyway. Genesis 22 doesn't fit that neat, easy-to-follow God and
faith that I like to have, so I pretended it was something else. But reading
it against the background of Kali Poulton and Polly Klaas, reading it in
order to preach it, reading it as it stands here in Genesis doesn't allow you
to do that. Because it's not presented as an exercise; it's not some lesson
about offerings; it's there because it's one more chapter in the relationship between God and his servant, Abraham. And in this chapter God is
not negotiating over Sodom or following Abraham to Egypt; this time
God wants something. And this time it's not just some strange idea like
packing everything up and leaving home or having all the men circumcised. This time what God wants from Abraham is the most difficult,
painful, crazy thing he could ever ask for: Isaac. He wants the son that he
promised to give, the son that Abraham waited his whole life to have.

And he knows that. God knows what he's asking for. Literally he says
to Abraham, "Take your son, your only son, whom you love, Isaac." He

knows exactly what he's asking, and he's even careful how he asks it. In Hebrew there's a little two-letter word that we don't translate into English, the word *na*. That word is a polite word, a kind word, a word that almost adds something like "please." And that's what God adds here: "Take your son, your only son, whom you love, Isaac. Take Isaac, *if you will*, to Mount Moriah and offer him as a sacrifice there."

We must remember that, as difficult and strange and even gruesome as this story is, it is not the story of God the Abductor, God the Stranger, God the One who capriciously rips a child from the arms of loving parents. Abductors never say *na*, and parents never go along. But Abraham and God are not strangers; they know each other well. And it's *after* all that they've been through together, after the journeys and the covenants and the blessings and the confrontations and the truth-telling and the negotiations between them, that God tests Abraham in chapter 22. It's after these things that God comes to Abraham kindly and says, "Take your son, your only son, whom you love, Isaac, and offer him as a burnt offering." It's after all these other things that God says that, and it's after all these other things that Abraham gets up early the next morning to do what God has asked.

That doesn't mean that it makes sense, or that it's easy. Abraham, after all, doesn't know what's behind this; he doesn't know that it's a test. He can't know, or the test is over. So he's left wondering. It's hard to imagine what he was going through as he packed his gear and cut the wood. What was in his mind as he walked for three days with nothing else to think about but the sacrifice of the son he had waited a century for? How frustrated, how scared, how tearful was he as he built the altar upon which he would slaughter his child?

But Abraham never wavers. We have to be careful not to exaggerate the other side of it. What God asked of Abraham is the greatest sacrifice Abraham could make, and it had to be devastating even to think about. But our text doesn't spend time there. It doesn't focus on Abraham's anguish or his fear. It doesn't tell us what he felt; it tells us what he did. And what he did was get up early the next morning and saddle the donkey. Abraham obeyed; Abraham showed his faith, even though he didn't know it was a test, even though he could have no idea at all why God would want to take the son that he'd promised him for so long, even though he had no possible explanation.

And of course we don't get much more than Abraham. We have that one sentence to help us, that "after these things God tested Abraham." But we don't really understand it, of course. The perception of God we walk around with doesn't include things like this — he doesn't need to test because he knows everything anyway, and he doesn't do tests like this because this is hard and ugly and painful, and he's a nice god. That's why we have to let Genesis 22 re-mold that perception of God.

William Willimon says that once he showed a church group a video that dramatized the sacrifice of Isaac. He says that the group watched silently as the superb Israeli actor, Topol, playing Abraham, struggled up the windswept mountain with a knife under his coat and his son trudging silently behind him. After it was over, Willimon led the adults in a discussion.

One of the first to speak was a middle-aged man. "I'll tell you the meaning this story has for me," he said. "I've decided that I and my family are looking for another church." "What?" asked Willimon in astonishment. "Why?" "Because when I look at that God, the God of Abraham, I feel I'm near a real God, not the sort of dignified, business-like, Rotary Club God we chatter about here on Sunday mornings. Abraham's God could blow a man to bits, give and then take a child, ask for everything from a person and then want more. I want to know *that* God."

He's right. That God, the God of Genesis 22, is not the god we often talk about. He's not the god that turns up in campaign speeches and on sober moments of situation comedies. He's not the god that we pray to before sessions of Congress or football games. That god is simple, transparent, with obvious allegiances and easy-to-follow rules of conduct, a god who always provides but never tests. But that god doesn't exist.

The God of the Bible, the God of the heavens and earth, the God of Abraham is a God who is God, a God who does not explain himself, a God who does not sit upon some heavenly throne tirelessly blessing patriots, quarterbacks, and practitioners of some bit of religion. This God is not so simple. This God is God. This God tests.

And so the way through our own difficulties with this request of God in Genesis 22 is not to diminish it or to insist on understanding it; the way through the difficulties is to do what Abraham does: obey and put your faith in the God you know. Abraham rises early the next morning and saddles that donkey not because it's easy, not because he understands everything, not because he knows the outcome. He does it because he knows his God. And he trusts him. So, even on his way up that mountain, with knife in hand and the blade sharpened for his own son, Abraham can say, "God will provide the lamb for the offering, my son." God will provide. *God will provide.* That's how Abraham can obey even now, because he believes that, no matter what, God will provide.

And there's the gospel in this story, because the God of Abraham is the God of us. He won't be calling for the sacrifice of our children, not like he did Isaac, but he's still that same God. He's still a God who tests. He's still a God who can seem to throw his whole plan in reverse, to act exactly opposite of a way for his promises to be fulfilled and his kingdom to come. He's a God who can let a holocaust take place and slavery become an American institution for a while. He'll allow an infant to be born with disease and a parent to die tragically and a racist to kill a stranger of another color at a bus stop in the name of Jesus Christ. And sometimes I think he tests, even now. Sometimes he calls us to take a hard and painful path, so he may learn something of our faith, and those tests can be painful and difficult and impossible, too. And they can cost something we love as much as Abraham loved Isaac.

I don't know when he's testing today. We can't know, just as Abraham couldn't. What I know is what we are to remember in all those impossible, difficult, painful moments: we are to remember that we know this God. He is not a stranger, not an adversary, not an abductor. We remember that, even though he is not predictable or transparent or domesticated, he's still the God of Abraham, he's still *our* God. And *our* God may be a God who tests, but he is also a God who will provide.

And we must believe this not only when we bring the knife up, but even if we have to bring it down. *God will provide.* That's how Abraham overcame his fear and his anguish and his despair. Because *God will provide.* Walter Brueggemann says, "Faith is nothing other than trust in the power of resurrection against every deathly circumstance. Abraham knows beyond understanding that God will find a way to bring life even in this scenario of death. That is the faith of Abraham."

So, with the knife at Isaac's throat, the voice comes all the way from heaven: "Abraham! Abraham! Do not lay your hand on the boy; for *now I know* that you fear God, since you have not withheld your son, your only son, from me." God tested Abraham to find out something that he didn't know. Now he does, because Abraham believed, because Abraham trusted that, even in this horror, God would provide, God would live up to his promise.

That's what we share with Abraham — the promise. That's why gatherings of God's people are really gatherings of Abrahams. They're gatherings of people who have been asked to give up and to suffer and to hurt, and yet they keep going up the mountain, telling their children, telling themselves, "God will provide." That's the faith that allowed Abraham to keep going up the side of Mt. Moriah, and it's our faith, too. Because the testing, confusing God whom we cannot understand or explain, whose plan we don't see, who demands from us absolute obedience, who demands everything that we have, he is the God who has given us a promise that we can count on. *We* know, God will provide.

And that's why that ram in the thicket means so much. Because God provides the very offering he has required. And the only thing Abraham had to do was believe he would. There's a Jewish scholar, Yeshayahu Leibowitz, who hates Christianity because he says it's all backwards. The basic symbol of Judaism, he says, is Abraham's binding of Isaac, a human being giving up his son for God. The basic symbol of Christianity is the crucifixion, God giving up his son for human beings.

But that's not right. God has always been providing the lamb. He did it on Mt. Moriah. And he did it once and for all in Bethlehem. Remember what John the Baptist said the first time he saw Jesus? "Here is the lamb of God who takes away the sin of the world!" (John 1:29).

It is a beautiful thing that Abraham did not withhold his son, his only son, from God. But how much more beautiful, how divine, that for Abraham and Isaac and every other one who looks to him to provide, God did not withhold his Son, his only Son, from us. He took Isaac off the altar and put Jesus there, so that in all of our testing, in all of our pain, in all of our questions, we could know that God will provide. God has provided the lamb.

That's what we know; that's what we celebrate. Not simply that there's a beautiful divine infant in a manger, but that the Lamb of God came down from heaven for us and our salvation. In the words of Frederick Buechner: "It is the Resurrection and Life [Mary] holds in her arms. It is the bitterness of death he takes at her breast."

No Christmas in Jerusalem

Text: 2 Kings 25

All the army of the Chaldeans who were with the captain of the guard broke down the walls around Jerusalem. Nebuzaradan the captain of the guard carried into exile the rest of the people who were left in the city and the deserters who had defected to the king of Babylon — all the rest of the population. . . . In the thirty-seventh year of the exile of King Jehoiachin of Judah, in the twelfth month, on the twenty-seventh day of the month, King Evil-merodach of Babylon, in the year that he began to reign, released King Jehoiachin of Judah from prison; he spoke kindly to him, and gave him a seat above the other seats of the kings who were with him in Babylon. So Jehoiachin put aside his prison clothes. Every day of his life he dined regularly in the king's presence.

2 Kings 25:10-11, 27-29

In his novel *The Gold Coast,* Nelson DeMille tells the story of John and Susan Sutter. The Sutters have it all — wealth, leisure, happiness, passion — and they live on one of those glorious estates on the gold coast of Long Island. That's at the beginning; the story that DeMille goes on to tell is the decline and fall of John and Susan Sutter, how they come to have little money, no meaning, deep regret, and a broken marriage. The problem begins when the mansion next to theirs is purchased by Frank Bellarosa, a notorious figure, one of the last mafia dons, a king of organized crime. The rest of the story tells how this gangster unravels their lives, how they are destroyed by getting too close to him, how their personal kingdom is brought down by an evil they allowed to enter their world. The narrator of these events is John Sutter himself. And so, as he tells us, he's a bit embarrassed by them, and regretful, and saddened, because this is *his* story, after all. And it should never have happened this way.

The author of Kings is in much the same position as he narrates the events in the text before us, because they are also the result of an evil that started out next door but eventually caused his people to lose everything. And so I think he is embarrassed by it all, and saddened, because this is *his* story, after all, and it, too, is a story of going from the top to the bottom, losing everything in just a little while. But the big difference between him and that character in the Nelson DeMille novel is that he's speaking to people who experienced the crash themselves. He's telling these people their own story, so that they will always know why they lost their land and their king and their temple and their God.

It was so very different at the beginning. At the beginning of Kings, Israel is living on the Gold Coast themselves. Solomon has taken over the throne from his father David. He's walking with the Lord, and the Lord is blessing him with wealth and honor and wisdom. And Solomon builds the most luxurious temple anyone in Israel has ever heard of, so that the

Lord may have glory and honor as the only God of the Jewish people. Solomon goes on to build a palace for himself, his own Taj Mahal. And Israel possesses most of the eastern coast of the Mediterranean Sea. Everything is just like it's supposed to be.

And the Lord tells Solomon: "If you will walk before me . . . , with integrity of heart and uprightness, . . . I will establish your royal throne forever. . . . But if you turn aside from following me, you or your children, then I will cut Israel off from the land that I have given them" (1 Kings 9:4-7). And everything is glorious, until we turn a few pages and get our first hint that Solomon's commitment is not everything that it could be: "King Solomon loved many foreign women . . ." (11:1).

So ten of the twelve tribes are taken from Solomon's son and become Israel; David's line is left to rule only Judah, with Jerusalem as its capital. Israel's kings abandon the Lord and give the people idols to worship. Then even in Judah and Jerusalem, the author of Kings tells us, they put altars to other gods "on every high hill and under every green tree," and the people "committed all the abominations of the nations that the Lord drove out before the people of Israel" (1 Kings 14:23-24).

And from there it only gets worse. The kings in Judah, the descendants of David, do all kinds of evil in the sight of the Lord. Sometimes a king comes along who cleans things up, but none of them gets rid of that evil next door, and few of them even try. Finally, there is a king so evil that the Lord will take no more, and he vows that he "will wipe Jerusalem as one wipes a dish, wiping it and turning it upside down" (2 Kings 21:13).

And that is the story of Kings. It's the story of four hundred years of flirting with evil. It's the story of forty-one kings, most of whom care only about power and wealth and women and little about anything else, especially God. It's the story of a people seduced by a different and exciting way to live till they hardly remember who they are. And because of all this, the only people of God who are left, the nation of Judah, is hurtling toward destruction, toward collapse, toward apocalypse. And by the time of 2 Kings 24-25 the apocalypse is now. It lasts too long for us even to read it all in one sitting.

In its dying moments, Jerusalem's kings are a dime a dozen. Except they're not worth even that. Jehoahaz rules for three months, is taken prisoner by Egypt, and dies in chains. Jehoiakim dies with Jerusalem surrounded by the Babylonian army. His son Jehoiachin, or Jeconiah, rules for three months before the Babylonians get through and chain him up in Babylon for the next forty years. They're running things now, so they put Zedekiah on the throne. But he thinks he can make it on his own. Which brings us to our passage this morning: Zedekiah has rebelled, and Nebuchadnezzar's army is coming after Jerusalem one last time.

This Advent we've dealt with some difficult situations, situations in which hope was at a premium, but it doesn't get much worse than this, because the Jewish people who know the Lord know him only in one place — in Jerusalem, in that beautiful temple put together by Solomon. So when they're taken 400 miles away to Babylon, they're also taken 400 miles away from the Lord. That's why we read in Psalm 137, "By the rivers of Babylon we sat and wept when we remembered Zion." It's not just their home that they're losing; it's their faith, it's their people, it's their future, it's their *God*.

And this chapter makes that perfectly clear. The last three legitimate kings are either killed by other nations or jailed by them. The fourth, Zedekiah, is forced to watch the murder of his sons, the ones who are supposed to sit on his throne, before his eyes are put out, and he's carried off to Babylon. But it doesn't stop there. This destruction is absolute.

The walls of Jerusalem are torn down. The leaders of the people, the best of the priests, and the nobles of the city are executed by the king of Babylon. The rest are shipped off to exile. The only ones left are the very poor, who will farm the area for the Babylonians. The city is gutted by fire, the temple is completely destroyed, and the beautiful items set there by Solomon — the bronze pillars, the wick trimmers, the dishes, the sprinkling bowls — are carried off by soldiers of another god in their backpacks. The vessels of the Lord end up decorating the pawn shops of Babylon — scrap metal. After twenty-one verses of detailed description of the destruction, the narrator sums it all up for us: "So Judah went into exile out of its land."

There is no more Judah. All the treasures of Solomon — the temple, the palace, the riches, the land, the people — all of it is gone. There is no more Judah, there is no more people of God. And our author makes that clear, even in his calendar. Up until now everything in the book has been dated in terms of the Jewish kings: "In the tenth year of King Hezekiah of Judah. . . . In the fifteenth year of Ahab king of Israel." But now, in verse 8, we're told that it's "In the fifth month, on the seventh day of the month — which was the nineteenth year of Nebuchadnezzar king of Babylon — " that they came to Jerusalem and set fire to the temple of the Lord. Now we're on Babylonian time. Judah is gone.

And the last report from Jerusalem in the book of Kings makes that abundantly clear: "Then all the people, high and low and the captains of the forces set out and went to Egypt; for they were afraid" (v. 26). The unimaginable has happened: the exodus that put them in this land has been undone. They're back on their way to Egypt, running for their lives, without their land, their freedom, their hope. Because they abandoned the God who had brought them out of their slavery a thousand years before, they're going back to their slavery.

And that's what Kings is about. It's a description of how the people of God lost everything they had, how they went from the glory of Solomon to the shame of Zedekiah. The writer of Kings wants his people to know that it wasn't Babylon or Egypt or anybody else who took it all away. It wasn't Egypt or Babylon; it was the Lord their God.

God is behind this exile. It has been clear from God's warning to Solomon, "If you turn from me, I will cut off Israel," to the days of the evil king Manasseh, when the Lord declares, "I am bringing upon Jerusalem and Judah such evil that the ears of everyone who hears of it will tingle" (2 Kings 21:12), to the end of 2 Kings 24, where it says, "Indeed, Jerusalem and Judah so angered the Lord that he expelled them from his presence." The one responsible for the fall of Jerusalem, the destruction of Judah, is God himself.

And that's what Kings is about. It's about a God who will not wait forever, a God who will defend his honor and defeat his enemies, a God who will punish sin. The God who refuses to explain himself to Job and the God who tests Abraham is also the God who judges his people when they turn away from him, when they fail him.

Once again God proves himself to be something other than the nice, easy-going, just wanting to get along with everybody sort of God that's so popular in our land. Once again he proves himself to be truly God, and that is not something we can ever take lightly. Because this God is our God; the God of 2 Kings 25 is the God of Luke 2. And we fool ourselves if we think frolicking with evil, sending our devotion elsewhere, giving him just a part of us, doesn't matter to him. He brought Israel out of the house of slavery, out of Egypt — but when they abandoned him, he sent them back. Our God is a God who judges his people.

Back in Deuteronomy 28:47, the Lord had warned that if these people did not serve him completely, they would then serve their enemies, and they would suffer as they did it. Kings proves the truth of that warning. It describes how, when the people did not serve him, the Lord sent them to serve others. So that's where it should end. That was the deal: if the people serve him, the Lord is with them. They failed. So he abandoned them. End of story.

But it's not. It's not the end of the story. It doesn't end with verse 26, with the rest of the Jews fleeing to Egypt in fear. It doesn't end with that day in Jerusalem. Instead, Kings ends thirty-some years later, and hundreds of miles from Jerusalem. It ends not with the destruction of the entire nation, but with the release of one person.

It seems that old King Jehoiachin, the last legitimate ruler of Judah, is still alive. And after being kept in a cell for thirty-seven years, Jehoiachin is released and given a place of honor at the king's table. He trades in his prison clothes for a fancy robe, and the king of Babylon supports him for the rest of his life. And *that's* how Kings ends — not with a description of the rest of the Jewish nation, how they're either in chains or in exile or in slavery or dead. It ends by saying that one of them still eats like a king.

And that, too, is a word about our God. It seemed certain — if they abandoned him, he would abandon them. He would destroy their nation, empty their cities, remove their kings. But he doesn't leave it that way. He never leaves it that way. Instead, the last thing we read is that the future that disappeared completely in Jerusalem has popped up again in Babylon, of all places. And that's the future, manufactured solely by the grace of God, that we celebrate here today, the future that extends somehow even all these years later, even here.

King Jehoiachin reigned for three short months but still found time to do what was evil in the sight of the Lord. But by the grace of God destruction is not the last word on him. Even the last verse of 2 Kings isn't the last word on Jehoiachin. Matthew will see to that. *His* is the last word on King Jehoiachin, and he tells us that Jehoiachin was the father of Salathiel, and Salathiel was the father of Zerubbabel, who was the ancestor of Jacob, the father of Joseph, the husband of Mary, of whom was born Jesus, who is called Christ (Matthew 1:12-16). And that, of course, is the last word on all of us sinners, who earn only God's judgment but still, somehow, receive his Son.

CHRISTMAS

Meditation

Text: Luke 2:14

"Glory to God in the highest heaven,
and on earth peace among those whom he favors!"

Luke 2:14

Perhaps the best writer the Christian Reformed community has ever produced is Peter DeVries. I enjoy his novels partly because so much of what he writes from his life reminds me of my life. But Peter DeVries's life was much darker than mine; his was too familiar with disease and death. We see that clearly in his book *The Blood of the Lamb*. *The Blood of the Lamb* is really about the life of Peter DeVries, even though the character's name is not DeVries; it is Wanderhope, Don Wanderhope, from the Dutch word *wanhoop*, which means "despair." And there is plenty for Don Wanderhope to despair over — his childhood tuberculosis, his struggle with faith, and the deaths over the years of his brother, wife, and daughter — all of it from the real life of Peter DeVries. Early in the book, when his brother dies young, Don turns to heaven and asks, "Why don't you pick on somebody your own size?"

That's a question that's been near us this Advent season, as we've considered harder depictions of God than we prefer: as we've thought about Job devastated, because God is proving something with him; as we've seen Abraham taking a knife to the son he's waited for his whole life, because God is testing him; as we've watched the residents of Jerusalem hightailing off to Egypt, back to the land of slavery, because God is angry with them. And as we've thought about the troubling, enigmatic God of those stories, we could imagine one of the people involved blurting out, "Why don't you pick on somebody your *own* size?" Or, at least, why don't you explain yourself? Why don't you shed some light on how my suffering or my giving up my son or my seeing my nation destroyed fits into your plan? Why don't you ask my opinion once in a while? Why *don't* you pick on somebody your own size?

The texts that we've looked at while waiting for the Messiah this year are difficult texts, texts that raise questions, that make us wonder about getting along in a world with an almighty, eternal God who doesn't let us in on all of his secrets. And — I want to be clear about this — we haven't come up with any answers these last three weeks, not to those questions. And if it seems like we have, then I've misled you. We haven't. Concerning those questions — the questions about why this pain and what God's thinking and where he is exactly — concerning *those* questions what we've learned is not answers but humility. Because we've learned that God is God.

He's not that simple divinity who's more like a pal than a god — someone we call on when we need a hand with a sporting event or a trip or a war, but who doesn't bother us much otherwise. This God is not like that; this God is God. He is silent, he tests, he judges, and he doesn't give us the blueprint to understand it all. As he himself said, he is God and no mortal (Hosea 11:9). And he leaves it to us to trust him — even when we don't know what's going on, even when it all falls apart, even when it's all so hard.

Toward the end of *The Blood of the Lamb,* the leukemia in Don Wanderhope's daughter seems to be in remission, just in time for her birthday, so he buys her a cake. On the way to the hospital, he stops in a nearby church to offer a prayer for her. Just then he's met by one of the nurses who tells him that an infection has caught her. Wanderhope rushes to the hospital only in time to say goodbye. For, at three o'clock, a few minutes after he gets there, Carol dies.

After a few drinks, Don remembers the cake he left on a pew in the church. He gets it and steps out of the sanctuary onto the sidewalk outside. He then notices the statue of Christ on the cross hanging over the entrance to the building. So, afflicted by grief and affected by alcohol, Don Wanderhope takes the cake carefully out of the box, balances it on his hand, and throws it with all of his might in the face of Jesus Christ. A perfect shot, he says, landing just under the crown of thorns. And so, Don lives up to his name — he is in despair over a child's death and a God who will not answer.

I feel for Don Wanderhope; I feel for Peter DeVries. I understand that accusing question, Why don't you pick on somebody your own size? I understand the despair, the anger over great suffering and no answers. But that's not all there is, otherwise cake would be the only response. It's not, because what we know, what we're really singing about today, is that God has answered.

He has answered every claim that he enjoyed the distance between himself and his people, that he is unaffected by their suffering, that he could have prevented it but didn't want to. This is God's answer: a child, an infant, wrapped in bands of cloth and lying in a manger. Now he *has* taken on someone his own size — not by turning away from us, but by becoming one of us.

"I am God and no mortal," he declared. Until today. From this day forward, from Christmas Day on, it can never again be said with complete truth that God is God and not a human being. Because the God who is God, the God who is at times silent and testing and judging, that almighty, incomprehensible God has become mortal, has become human. He has taken on bones and parents and vulnerability and troubles and questions of his own.

And that is his answer. That is his answer to Job and Abraham and the people of Jerusalem and Don Wanderhope and every other one who has looked to him from their pain and yearned for a response. This is his answer. It's not an explanation; it's not an apology. And it's not an undoing of the pain or a promise that there will never be another child taken down by leukemia.

And we should say that out loud. There's too much about this holiday that's artificial comfort, sentimentality with no theology. We of all people have to be honest about Christmas and about the difference it makes. We have to admit that the Don Wanderhopes exist and that sometimes our suffering is a lot like theirs, and our reaction also might be to heave pastry and faith together in the face of God. Except that we know something: we know that he *hasn't* kept his distance. We know that he *hasn't* left us without a word. In fact, his Word became flesh and lived among us. He has come down to our size.

So there is indeed "Glory to God in the highest heaven, and on earth peace among those whom he favors." Not because we now understand everything that's going on — the diagnoses and the divorces and the deaths — but because God himself has spoken — indelibly, permanently, astoundingly. He didn't explain; maybe he *couldn't* explain, since he is God and we are not. But to bring us peace he did something more than explain it: he participated in it. He took it on himself — the pain, the trials, the judgment for sin. And so he watched his own child die one day at three in the afternoon.

And so the peace we have warrants the voices of angels because it is a peace first of all with God. The God who judges sin placed the weight of that judgment on his own child. The peace we have is genuine peace because, in spite of the battles and the casualties around us, in spite of the wounds we bear right now, we know that God himself — almighty and mysterious as he is — came down to our size to lessen them and finally to remove them. That's the gift he brings, peace of soul and spirit and faith, because we know that he took our curse upon himself, and we know that, whatever we go through and however alone we feel, the God of the world did not leave us to ourselves but joined us in the place of our suffering. And that night he sent his angels to all of the misfits and the sufferers with one piece of news: "to you is born this day in the City of David, a Savior, who is the Messiah, the Lord." And we say, Glory to God in the highest, and on earth, right now, right here, for us whom he has favored — there is peace.

— FIRST SUNDAY AFTER CHRISTMAS —

Jesus, God with Us

Text: Matthew 1:18-25

". . . She will bear a son, and you are to name him Jesus, for he will save his people from their sins." All this took place to fulfill what had been spoken by the Lord through the prophet: "Look, the virgin shall conceive and bear a son, and they shall name him Emmanuel," which means, "God is with us." When Joseph awoke from sleep, he did as the angel of the Lord commanded him; he took her as his wife, but had no marital relations with her until she had borne a son; and he named him Jesus.

Matthew 1:21-25

Well, I'm glad we didn't start here this year — even though every time I can remember that I've read from the Gospel of Matthew for Christmas, this is exactly where I started. Skip all the names; get right to the story. So I don't want to pretend that I've done much differently than most of you on that score; genealogies are not exactly filled with fascinating, helpful material, not at first glance, anyway. And that's why we need to take another glance; that's why, at least every so often, when we do Christmas from Matthew, we should do it from verse 1 and not verse 18. Because even what we read this morning, even the *story* of Mary and Joseph and Jesus, is not supposed to be read all by itself; Matthew wanted us to read all the names first.

In the names we learn some things, or are reminded of some things, about God. We're reminded that God didn't just get into the Messiah business when Mary met Joseph, or when the Romans took over Judea; he's been aiming for this day all along. For God, according to Matthew, the whole Old Testament takes place in Advent, the whole Old Testament has to do with Christmas. And we're reminded in Matthew's names that this Messiah is a human being in the very line of Abraham and Rahab and Solomon and Joseph himself, but that he's also something new, something very different. In the names we see that, as far as his people may wander from God, he still remembers them. In spite of all they do to cut off the line of David, this God quietly, usually invisibly, keeps it going, keeps it moving toward Christmas, keeps it heading toward the Christ.

And that very God of the Old Testament, and of Matthew's genealogy, is the God of this story of the virgin Mary and Joseph and Jesus. The God who kept moving toward Christmas by arranging impossible births to some woman in her nineties and to a foreigner who's just trying to make sure she and her mother-in-law have enough to eat, and even to a king and another man's wife, that same God is at it again here — stepping in to make sure that the line of David leads to the Christ, his Christ. So now Mary is found to be with child from the Holy Spirit. And it's the same Spirit, the same God, that has been at work through all those centuries — watching over the line of David, staying faithful to his promise, bringing to us a Messiah who is from both the man Abraham and the Spirit of God. That's the Messiah Matthew wants you to meet in our passage this morning, the Messiah whom all of history has aimed at, the Messiah who is the result of a promise God refused to let die.

His name is Jesus. Actually, it's *Joshua* — Jesus is the Greek version of the Hebrew name Joshua. It's not a strange name in first-century Judah, not unique. There are other Joshuas running around Nazareth. It's a special name, but it's not a new name, not at all. In fact, Mary and Joseph might have come up with it all on their own.

But that's the thing — Mary and Joseph didn't come up with it. The angel of the Lord came up with it. "You are to name him Jesus," he tells Joseph, "for he will save his people from their sins." There's the difference — every little Joshua or Jesus in Judea is running around with a name that means, in Hebrew, "the Lord saves," "God saves," and in one sense this Jesus is just like they are. He's the son of people named Joseph and Jacob and Matthan and Eleazar — regular people, normal people, just like the parents and grandparents of all those other Joshuas. But this one wasn't named by a parent or grandparent; this one was named by the Lord. And this one is going to live up to his name.

On the one hand, he's Joshua, the son of Joseph, the son of Jacob, a real human being like the rest of us; but, on the other hand, he's not just Joshua, he is *God-saves*. He's the one all those centuries have been leading up to, the one who is God's promise in person, the one who is the new Genesis in history — Joshua son of Joseph, but also *God-saves*. His name not only *means* God saves; he *is* God saving; he himself *will* save his people from their sins. So this is your Messiah, says Matthew, his name is Joshua, Jesus, the son of Mary and Joseph, and the descendant of all these other people, but the one whose name comes from the Lord, the one whose name is not only Joshua, but *God-saves*.

That's his name, that's what the birth certificate reads, but that's not all that he'll be called. They'll call him Emmanuel, says Matthew, which means "God is with us." They shall name him Emmanuel — but Matthew doesn't mean Mary and Joseph this time. He's not referring to his real name, the one on his driver's license. No, that's *Jesus*. But "they" are going to call him Emmanuel; not Mary and Joseph, but people. People who know him, people who experience him, people who understand him and touch him and see him and hear him and worship him and seek him — people, all kinds of people, are going to call him Emmanuel. They're going to say, "In that man Jesus, God is with us." They shall name him Emmanuel.

This is not the Messiah everybody was expecting. You know, they were expecting a Son of David who would act a lot more like David — create a kingdom of the Jewish people, win territory, get rid of enemies like the Romans, sit in a palace. That's what they thought the Messiah would be, but he's not. Not this Joshua. He doesn't save his people from their *enemies;* he saves them from their *sins*. This Messiah doesn't save them from others — other people, other nations, other sins. He saves them from *their* sins; he saves them from themselves.

So people won't be naming him "robed-in-glory" or "majestic-in-power," at least not at first they won't. They're not going to call him the Conqueror of Gentiles or the Lord of Warfare, because he's not going to save them from the things they hate, the things that keep them from power or money or fame. He will save his people from their sins; he will save his people from what's on the inside, not the outside. And when they understand that, when they experience this Messiah, they will name him Emmanuel, which means "God is with us."

John Timmer tells of an essay, composed many years ago by an English schoolboy, in which the boy wrote: "Why are so many twins born into the world today? I believe it is because little children are afraid of entering the world alone." Timmer says that's deep thinking for a schoolboy, because he's put his small finger on a big problem, on what some have called the chief problem of our time: loneliness. Amid all of our technological advancement, all of the ways we have to be more and more independent, we struggle with loneliness, the kind of feeling that sends death rates and suicide rates up right now, in the middle of the holiday season, because people now are a little more aware of the emptiness. And we all share that feeling to some extent, we all share the fear that perhaps we will not be loved, perhaps we will not be cared about, perhaps we will be left alone.

And the Messiah whom Matthew wants you to meet, the one who does not save us from our enemies but from ourselves, that Messiah is a Messiah for our loneliness. In him God commits himself. He commits himself to be our twin forever; to be with us always. He is the one people are going to call Emmanuel.

"That name," says John Timmer, "is Matthew's first and last word about Jesus. Quite literally! For Matthew mentions it [here] in the opening chapter of his Gospel . . . and Matthew mentions it in the closing chapter, where he quotes these words of Jesus: *I am with you always, to the end of the age.*"

Timmer goes on to say, "Loneliness is not seeing a loved face. Loneliness is not experiencing the warmth and wonder of a loving heart. What every person ultimately needs is a loved face, is the warmth and wonder of a loving heart. And because God knows this better than anyone else, he sent his Son into our world — to be that face, to be that heart. His name will be Emmanuel, which means God's loved face with us; God's loving heart with us. From now on, in Jesus, God's face is always there. From now on, in Jesus, the warmth of God's loving heart is always there."

That's what those who know this Jesus will understand. They will experience him not only as Jesus, as the one his parents named Joshua, but also as the one whom the angel of the Lord named *God-saves.* And he will save them from their sins, from floundering through life on their own, from watching the generations roll along and believing they don't mean anything or lead anywhere. He will save them from themselves — from their failures, from their emptiness, from their loneliness. And they, *they,* will name him Emmanuel, because in him, they know, God is with us.

The Messiah Matthew introduces to us in his first chapter doesn't come the way most messiahs would be expected. He doesn't reside in the clouds of heaven, lofty and majestic, too great to soil himself with the human race. He's not that sort at all. Instead he comes through a line of people who are thoroughly human — not from pure blood or great righteousness but through sin and shame and failure and foreigners. He comes not in the clouds but in a young woman nobody's ever heard of.

From the human perspective, when you compare him to the other gods of the other religions in the world, you have to say, Our God is really sort of odd. He uses the most common of people, people that aren't any different from any of us here; he comes in the most common of ways, when by his Spirit an anonymous young woman is found to be with child. And the strangest thing is that he comes at all — he's not the Above-Us-God, too holy to come down. This God's love is so immense that he *wants* to come down. And he has proven his love by the fact that he *did* come down and touch our ground. It's a strange, surprising, remarkable story about the Messiah who comes in such a way, who comes through such ordinary people, who comes to such ordinary lives that he ends up with the name, with the very *name*, God-With-Us. That's how his people know him; that's how he brings his salvation.

And we can reject that, because it is so common, and so odd, and so human — this Joshua. Or, we can recognize that a Messiah who comes right to us, a Messiah who is truly human, a Messiah who saves us from our sins is the most important kind. And then we can follow the way of Joseph — that silent, righteous man — and trust the word of the Lord, that in this Jesus the whole Old Testament is being fulfilled, in this Jesus the Lord has faithfully kept his promise, and in this Jesus we can know — in our own hearts, our own lives — that God is with us, forevermore.

EPIPHANY

After Christmas

Text: Matthew 2:1-18

Then Herod secretly called for the wise men and learned from them the exact time when the star had appeared. Then he sent them to Bethlehem, saying, "Go and search diligently for the child; and when you have found him, bring me word so that I may also go and pay him homage." When they had heard the king, they set out; and there, ahead of them, went the star that they had seen at its rising, until it stopped over the place where the child was. When they saw that the star had stopped, they were overwhelmed with joy. On entering the house, they saw the child with Mary his mother; and they knelt down and paid him homage. Then, opening their treasure chests, they offered him gifts of gold, frankincense, and myrrh. And having been warned in a dream not to return to Herod, they left for their own country by another road.

Matthew 2:7-12

"And having been warned in a dream not to return to Herod, they left for their own country by another road." So the magi go home. They spend two years on the road, chasing a star. They come this close to a run-in with one of the all-time nuts of Middle East dictatorships. Finally, they find the infant king they're looking for. They fall on their knees and worship him. They drop off their Christmas presents. And they go home.

It's an amazing story that we remember at Epiphany: God invites Gentiles — magicians, astrologers, from as far away from Jerusalem as you can get — to his Son's baby shower. Magi from the east, from another world really, bow before the Jewish Prince of Peace. It is worth our attention, because these strangers have paved the way for the rest of us who come from so far to worship in Bethlehem, whose roots don't lie in David and Abraham but in O'Malleys and Vanderhydes. The King of the Jews is for us, too. God wants us there, too, says Matthew. Nothing can speak of the love of Christmas more than this: God's gift is for all people. And so this birth *is* one that brings joy to the world. It's one that transforms the world.

That's why that last line about these wise men is kind of strange: they go home. Rather pedestrian, isn't it? They spend two years in Advent, Christmas comes, they do their thing and go home. It feels like it should be more than that, but it isn't. Not for magi, not for shepherds, not for Jesus himself. Not for us. Christmas may have changed the world, but it doesn't stop it. It doesn't stop it at all.

So, now Christmas is over. And, strangely enough, life is back to normal, and not just for the folks from out of town. The angels have returned to the realms of glory. The shepherds are back in the fields. The inn has a few vacancies. Christmas has come; Jesus is born; but Joseph and Mary are still the same people with the same problems. They aren't living with this Prince-of-Peace son of theirs in a palace or a mansion. They still have that census to take care of and bills to pay and a wedding coming up and now a child to raise. And, on top of those things, all because the magi had to stop for directions, now they've got Herod on their backs as well.

And that's the part, of course, that really doesn't fit: the Savior of the nations has come, but before the nations even have time to read about it in the morning paper, their new Savior is high-tailing it off to Egypt to save his skin. The long-awaited Messiah is here, but the King of kings and Lord of lords is heading out of town to avoid King Herod's hit men. The angels have proclaimed him, the shepherds have seen him, the magi have worshiped him, yet some two-bit semi-king is still able to chase him off to Africa. The Savior is born today, but tomorrow he's running for his life. The Savior is born today, but tomorrow there's a voice heard in Ramah, wailing and loud lamentation, Rachel weeping for her children, refusing to be consoled, because they are no more. The Savior is born today, but tomorrow innocent children are dying in the place of the Messiah. That's what happened — after Christmas.

This is the difficult part of the story, the part that we don't care to think about, the part about Herod's brutal slaughter of babies in his attempt to kill Jesus. And this part of the story raises a tough question for us who have spent the better part of a month singing carols about joy to the world and peace on earth: If Jesus Christ is the long-promised Messiah of the Jews, why is Rachel still weeping? If he is the Son of David who will establish his kingdom forever, why does she refuse to be comforted? If he is the Mighty God and Prince of Peace, what's he doing in Egypt?

That's the difficult part about proclaiming the birth of the Messiah, and it's as difficult for us as it was for Matthew. You have to wonder: If the angels are right that the Savior has come, where is the salvation? If Jesus Christ is the genuine article, how can there be such weeping after Christmas?

And of course that question is personal for each of us right now. Our hams are eaten, our programs are given, our carols are sung, our presents are opened, our families are gone — the celebrations are over, and tomorrow life returns to normal. We go back to work and to school and to the daily routine of our lives, most of us without missing a beat from where we left off a few days ago. And, in spite of all our proclamation that Jesus Christ is born today, we know all too well, just as clearly as Matthew describes it, that the aches and pains of our lives are still with us after Christmas.

After Christmas this year many of us will face the death of someone we love — we may be prepared for it, but very likely we won't. After Christmas some of us will continue to deal with the family problems that have nearly worn us out in the past or have brought us to the point of breaking relationships that we thought would never end. After Christmas some of us will be involved in accidents or illnesses that drag us down and present us with challenges that we never thought we'd see. After Christmas we still live in a violent world, a world of terrorism and crime, a world of famine and racism, a world that is at war in spite of the birth of the Prince of peace. And so we too belong to Matthew chapter 2: after Christmas we go home and try to avoid our Herods.

And of course there's another kind of weeping that goes on, one that is perhaps even more difficult to explain than the weeping over our aches and pains, and that is the weeping over sin. If he is the Savior, if he is *my* Savior, the one who saves me from my sin, then why am I sinning after Christmas? How come the story of Jesus' advent, a story that I believe, hasn't made more of a difference for me, more of a dent in my fallibility? It's one thing to weep over Herod's killing the children and trying to kill the Christ, to weep over *Herod's* denying the Savior; it's another matter all together to weep over *my* denying the Savior.

It would be nice if the response to Christmas was more than just going home again. It would be so much simpler if Christmas made things so clean that everything stopped at Matthew 1, so clean that Matthew 2 couldn't happen, not after Christmas. But that, of course, is not how it works. It's not simple; it's not simple at all.

That's why Herod is so easy to understand, so easy to relate to — easier than the magi, really. You know, if the magi really are three kings, then they're about the strangest kings anybody's ever known. They hear that a new, special king has come onto the scene, so they round up the best gifts they've got and take a chance that they can find him, so that they can fall at his feet. That's not the kind of attitude that gets most kings their jobs. Herod is much more typical as far as that goes.

You know, this isn't Herod's first brush with violence. One time he killed three of his sons because they were a threat to his crown. That prompted Caesar Augustus to quip, It is better to be Herod's pig than his son. And he's right about that, because a pig doesn't threaten you, a pig doesn't frighten you, a pig doesn't take away your kingdom. But a Messiah does.

"Where is the child who has been born king of the Jews?" asked the magi. "When King Herod heard this, he was frightened." You bet he's frightened. There's room for only one king in town. So Herod sends his goons to Bethlehem — better to lose a few toddlers than a whole kingdom.

And that's how it goes with Jesus Christ: from the moment he's born he's a threat to all the ones with the power, all the kings who don't bow down to children. So there is weeping after Christmas precisely because of Christmas, because the birth of a king is not something you can take lightly. You either fall on your knees or you pull out your sword. Herod didn't have to think twice.

So, if all we have are romantic ideas about Christmas, about the world being a nicer place because of it, then we're really missing the point, and we need to read Matthew's second chapter a little better. The truth is that life goes on after Christmas just as those magi go on their way home. The truth is that the suffering isn't over just because Jesus has arrived. The truth is that some of it is even worse now, because Jesus' coming means the whole world has a decision to make — to bow down and worship or to try to kill. And the truth is that sometimes that decision comes hard even for us who *have* worshiped him, because we would prefer running our own kingdoms, just like Herod. And sometimes we resent another king in town, and we want to kill him, too. There are all kinds of pain, after Christmas.

But after Christmas something is dramatically different. It has to be, or Matthew wouldn't take such pains in all of chapter 1 to introduce us to the Messiah — a Messiah, says Matthew, who's not only for Bethlehemites and Jerusalemites but for magi, for people from Iraq and Nigeria and Texas. You see, once you give yourself, once you worship this Messiah, you never come away the same. Just like the magi, after Christmas you go home a different way.

After Christmas we go home a different way, because God is with us, and we have seen him. Because the King of the earth is here, and, even if he brings suffering now, he will bring peace in the end. Because this king is nothing like Herod — he doesn't kill to protect himself; he dies to protect his people. This king knows what suffering is like, and he came to take ours away.

It is true: after Christmas life goes on, for everyone. So the magi go home to explain where they've been, and shepherds go back to the fields and try to figure all of this out, and Joseph and Mary head off to Egypt so that the king of the Jews will make it to age three. And we go on, too. We go on to lives that are overwhelming and temptations to forget all about Bethlehem. We go on to lose loved ones and face cancer and grow old; we go on to commit sins that tear us up and try to kill the Messiah all over again; we go on, and going on means pain.

But we remember as we go on. We remember that we do not weep alone. Rachel weeps, too, says Matthew, whenever her children suffer. And we remember that our Messiah became part of this same painful, broken, suffering world. And he was a sufferer the whole time he was here, from day one, just so that Rachel will stop weeping one day, just so that our suffering will end. And all that the Jews, and the magi, and even the Herods have to do to be part of that is let him live, let him be king, bow before him and then go home a different way.

That's what's supposed to happen after Christmas: we go home with a new king, who suffers with us, who suffers for us; we go home knowing that, as we follow him, even now, we do not walk in darkness but have the light of life.

— SECOND SUNDAY AFTER EPIPHANY —

God at Work

Text: Psalm 146

Do not put your trust in princes,
    in mortals, in whom there is no help.
When their breath departs, they return to the earth;
    on that very day their plans perish.
Happy are those whose help is the God of Jacob,
    whose hope is the Lord their God,
who made heaven and earth,
    the sea, and all that is in them;

who keeps faith forever;
  who executes justice for the oppressed;
  who gives food to the hungry. . . .
The Lord will reign forever,
  your God, O Zion, for all generations.
Praise the Lord!

                                          Psalm 146:3-7, 10

In 1936 Charlie Chaplin made a film called *Modern Times,* sort of a commentary on modern life. In one classic scene Charlie is working on a factory assembly line. In typical assembly-line fashion, his job is to stand in
front of a conveyor belt, which takes a steady stream of rectangular
thingamajigs past him. What they are is unclear — and unimportant —
but each thingamajig is exactly the same, a small rectangular box. And
Charlie's job is to tighten two bolts on the top of each one as it goes by.
Two quick turns of the wrist for every thingamajig, one thingamajig every
two seconds for ten hours a day.

   Well, at the end of one long day of bolt-tightening, some wire gets
crossed in Charlie: the assembly line has driven him over the edge. And,
long after the conveyor belt has stopped, he's still twisting his wrist. He's
still looking for thingamajigs. So he stumbles around the factory tightening everything in sight: the bolts on other machines, his co-workers' but-
tons, his supervisor's nose. Endless hours of monotonous assembly-line
living have turned the little tramp into a mindless cog, a human ratchet
set, unable to break the habit, running from item to item and person to
person tightening all the would-be bolts.

   In 1936 that was Charlie Chaplin's take on modern times. And he has
a point. Although the assembly line doesn't look quite the same anymore,
modern times still are full of thingamajigs calling for attention, calling
for our action within a few seconds before the next one will roll by. My
friend Peter Jonker, whose own work with Psalm 146 has been especially
helpful to me, reminded me of that. He says that it's very easy to see what
we do "as a long series of disconnected deadlines and meetings, laundry
and grocery lists, tests and papers, lesson plans and staff meetings . . . little turns of the wrist." Just one more installation service, one more term
in office, one more council meeting.

   So in modern times we all run the risk of finding ourselves on the assembly line, believing that we have to keep up with some conveyor belt,
that life itself is two turns of the wrist for every thingamajig coming at us
every two seconds for eighteen or twenty hours a day. We tighten, we sleep,

we tighten, we sleep, until we die. That's the assembly-line life: it's meaningless; it's just one thing after another; it's possessed by the desire to get through. And of course that's what modern times are all about, that's what they can do to us: there's so much to do today, there's so much we *have* to do today, that we can get lost in the details, lost in our own lives, lost in getting all the thingamajigs tightened.

That's why pausing to hear the Word of God is so important, because God's Word brings us away from the assembly-line mentality; it lifts our gaze from the thingamajigs in our lives and puts our focus on the Lord. That's certainly what Psalm 146 does. Don't put your trust in princes, don't invest your life in mortals, in human beings, in factories, because you won't find any meaning there, there's nothing that will last there. "When their breath departs, they return to the earth; on that very day their plans perish." To redeem your life, to redeem your world, to redeem these modern times you must look beyond these things. To redeem your everyday life you must look to God. So, says the psalmist, "Happy are those whose help is the God of Jacob, whose hope is in the Lord their God" — because the one whose hope is in the Lord is not living on an assembly line. The one who hopes in the Lord sees beyond all the thingamajigs.

And what that person sees is God at work. What we see is the Lord with his sleeves rolled up, the Lord down on his hands and knees, maybe sweat on his brow or a broom in his hand — God on the job. Now, of course, that's not how we usually think of the activities of God. Divinity in our minds is a white-collar occupation, a management position. So God is a king or a judge or, in these modern times, a CEO.

But that's not the idea in Psalm 146. In Psalm 146 we get a look at God's date book, his to-do list. It's a peek at what he does with his time. So in the second half of this psalm, we see the name of God over and over again — the Lord, the Lord, the Lord, in all capital letters. And each time it's used, it's the subject of a different verb; each time it says something else about what the Lord is doing:

[The Lord] executes justice for the oppressed;
    [he] gives food to the hungry.
The Lord sets the prisoners free;
    the Lord opens the eyes of the blind.
The Lord lifts up those who are bowed down;
    the Lord loves the righteous.
The Lord watches over the strangers;

he upholds the orphan and the widow,
but the way of the wicked he brings to ruin.

It seems the Lord has a pretty full calendar. You would think just ruining the way of the wicked would be a full-time job, but he's got a lot more in the works than that: he's looking after children without parents and parents without sight. He's firming up the cause of people living under dictators or forced into poverty. He's looking for justice in the prisons and feeding the hungry. And, on top of all that, he's keeping a close eye on the righteous, because they have a special place in his heart.

The Lord is king. He reigns forever, says the psalm. But he's a king who can look a lot like a carpenter, a king who puts his hands on the shoulders of a child and the bedpost of a dying person and over the stove for the hungry. The God we have is busy — but not with assembly-line work, not twisting his wrist over an endless supply of thingamajigs. The Lord's job is to restore the world, to take its broken parts and put them back together. This king wears overalls and has dirt under his fingernails and calluses on his hands. He works hard; that's how he remains faithful forever.

And recognizing that, and putting our hope there, makes all the difference for us who live in these modern times. And the difference between assembly-line living and real living comes down to Psalm 146. It comes down to where our hope is. It comes down to whether we believe that God is here, working.

Because everything we do, whether as recreation or on our jobs or in church ministries, all of it can be assembly-line-standing, wrist-twisting, bolt-tightening, one-thing-after-another dreariness. And that goes for the things we do with the word "church" on them as much as those things we spend our lives at every day. It's amazing, but even working as an elder, or spending an evening as a family preparing meals at the Open Door Mission, or worshiping — even that part of life can be something to get through, something on the assembly line, something that doesn't matter. Or it can be something else.

Because when we hear this psalm, when our eyes are lifted and we look beyond ourselves and upon the work of the Lord, when we throw open his calendar and see what he's got planned, when we look upon his commitment to putting the pieces back together again, then we know that what we do can make a difference, too. We can be part of what counts, part of upholding the cause of the oppressed, part of lifting up those who are bowed down, part of giving food to the hungry. Then our work will not be meaningless, then what we do will last — because it begins with God. It begins where this psalm begins: putting our hope in the Lord who is faithful forever; knowing that all these little jobs — the conversations and bus rides, the greeting of a stranger and the taking of an offering, the interest in a student and the phone call to the sick — all of them have a much bigger place than we'd ever know by looking at them. Because God is at work here. And what we do fits into what he does. Often, we are *how* God is at work.

But that's hard to see, isn't it? Amid stories of discarded children and drug-addicted infants, or reports of slaughter-filled civil wars and senseless terrorism, or evidence of the success of wickedness, it's hard to see that God is at work, that he is making a difference, and that we are, too.

The film *Smoke* is centered around a neighborhood tobacco shop. The owner of this shop, Auggie Wren, has a strange habit. Every morning, for the last twelve years, at exactly 8:00, he stands at the corner of 3rd Street and 7th Avenue in New York City, and he takes a picture, always the same picture at the same time, a picture of his tobacco shop. It's his "project." One day, Paul Benjamin, a writer who lives in the neighborhood, expresses interest in Auggie's photography. So Auggie shows him an album. Paul's startled to find that all of the pictures are of the exact same place. He flips through the first volume, and Auggie immediately puts the next one in front of him, with the comment that he has four thousand photos of that street corner.

Well, Paul begins turning the pages of the next album. And that's when Auggie says, "You'll never get it if you don't slow down, my friend." "What do you mean?" asks Paul. "You're going too fast," says Auggie, "you're hardly even looking at the pictures." "They're all the same," Paul says. "They're all the same," says Auggie, "but each one is different from every other one. You got your bright mornings and your dark mornings, you got your summer light and your autumn light, you got your weekdays and your weekends, you got your people in overcoats and galoshes and your people in t-shirts and shorts." "Slow down, huh?" "That's what I'd recommend."

For most of us life is the same picture over and over again, and if we don't slow down, if we don't stop just twisting and tightening and going from one thing to the next, we'll never get it. We'll never see that each one is different. Because in those pictures, right before our very eyes, God is at work. He's feeding, he's setting free, he's giving sight, he's lifting up — right in front of our eyes, right in our own lives, right in our own ministries. That's what we see when we know where to begin. And when we do that, it makes a difference.

I experienced that in a striking way last summer. I was to meet a doctor whose work might offer me real hope with my cancer. But, within fifteen seconds of his walking into the room, it was obvious that there was no such hope — which was difficult to hear, which did not seem to be God at work. But in the next ninety minutes, God was at work, because in that person's good humor and kindness and patience and concern, the hard fact of death was overshadowed by the overwhelming reality of life, the overwhelming power of love. And so I left his office with less hope for me but more hope in God.

So we return to school and work and church with our own schedules and plans and things to do, but we begin with Psalm 146 — God's schedule. Here's God's to-do list. The carpenter's out working with his hands again. It's tough work, frustrating the wicked and standing up for the weak. It makes you wonder if he can pull it off. But when you read a little farther than Psalm 146, when you think about how he's used his hands since then, you see not only calluses but nailprints, and you realize that whatever he has left to do will get done, and whatever he's doing will last forever.

In this year and in your ministries, may our work belong to God's work. And may we never go too fast to see it.

— THIRD SUNDAY AFTER EPIPHANY —

Strength of Another Kind

Text: Psalm 46

There is a river whose streams make glad the city of God,
the holy habitation of the Most High.
God is in the midst of the city; it shall not be moved;
God will help it when the morning dawns.
The nations are in an uproar, the kingdoms totter;
he utters his voice, the earth melts.
The Lord of hosts is with us;
the God of Jacob is our refuge.

Psalm 46:4-7

About ten years ago, when my sermon-writing days were in their infancy, I wrote a sermon on this psalm. Soon after that, I, along with two other seminarians, had the opportunity to submit a sermon and then meet with John Timmer, who as many of you know is a preacher I greatly admire. Well, I gave him the sermon I had recently written on Psalm 46. While I expected that he would not fawn over it as a homiletic masterpiece, I figured my sermon had some strengths, some good points — until I got it back from him. I remember it well. He used a red pen, and it looked as though in my absence my manuscript had received multiple stab wounds.

In that sermon I took Psalm 46 apart. I found out when it might have been written. I took some author's idea about some battle in Chronicles that this psalm could fit, and I talked about that. I analyzed it. But John Timmer's comments taught me that psalms do not need to be analyzed as much as they need to be imbibed, lived out, prayed. That's what the people of Israel did with them: they prayed them. Because the poetry of the psalms, like all great art, all great cultural expression, fails if it doesn't keep speaking, if it doesn't still have a voice later, if it doesn't address the human condition of all times. "So," said John Timmer, "don't tell me what battle Psalm 46 may have come from; tell me what Psalm 46 goes through. Tell me what it means. Tell me what it's about. To me it's about vulnerability."

And he's right, though I was probably a little too depressed to see it at that moment. He's right about the psalms and living them, breathing them, using them to address our circumstances and our days and our fears. And he's right about Psalm 46 — it's not about a battle from Chronicles; it's about vulnerability. And my sermon from all those years ago — which I looked for and was unable to find this week — missed that. It missed it completely.

Psalm 46 is about vulnerability. And it's hard for me to think about vulnerability right now without thinking of this congregation and its current circumstances. Because, from my recent experience, I would say, "Vulnerability, thy name is cancer. Thy name is chemotherapy." It has a lot of other names, too, of course — AIDS, loneliness, poverty, bipolar disorder. We are vulnerable, in our difficult circumstances, because it's so much more than we expected, so much more that we bargained for. Now, in such a context, what does this psalm have to say to us who are so very vulnerable?

Well, first off, Psalm 46 is a psalm for times like these. "A Mighty Fortress Is Our God," which Martin Luther took from this psalm, is best sung not on Reformation Day but on the day of a funeral, the day of a diagnosis, the day of grief or pain or divorce or persecution. That's when Luther sang it; it was his favorite psalm. And it's best sung on those hard days, because this psalm is a statement of faith, and faith looks beyond what we see, beyond what's happening around us right now, beyond the pain and difficulty, and says that God himself is with us. This psalm is about vulnerability because the writer and pray-ers of these words know that there is so much to make us vulnerable in this world, so much that can go wrong, so much that can collapse everything we count on in one terrible day or even in one deadly minute. The pray-ers of this psalm know that the things we like to rest in — like family and exercise and military power and money — those things are all so tenuous, so ready to be turned upside down without a moment's notice.

Psalm 46 is a statement of faith — but not one that says that war and disease and failure and grief will not come near us as long as we believe, that God is on our side and therefore nothing will be against us. The psalms are too honest for that, too real. What this statement of faith says is that even if those things come near, even if the pain or failure or catastrophe go to the very center of our lives, even if everything is chaos, even then "the Lord of hosts is with us; the God of Jacob is our refuge."

In the days of Psalm 46, Israel believed there were two things to be anxious about, two things that were really dangerous: the sea and the nations. They believed that the earth was held up by mountains that went deep into the ocean, and that the water was trying to topple those mountains, threatening to destroy the world. But Israel also saw another terrible threat: the nations around them, nations that sought to spread their power, to enslave and loot and destroy other people and cities. Those were the things to be scared of most: those mountains giving way deep within the waters, and the powerful nations around them destroying their world with violence and war. And that's why, in this psalm about vulnerability, we read first about the mountains in the sea and then about the nations in their battles — the psalmist goes right for the things that really scare us, the things that we're so helpless against. And the word is, even then, "We will not fear."

We will not fear, though the mountains shake in the heart of the sea, says the beginning of Psalm 46. We will not fear, though the nations are pulling out bows and spears and hacking each other to pieces, says the end of Psalm 46. We will not fear, because the world does not finally rest on mountains in the ocean; it rests on the God of Jacob. And the world does not finally need nations to behave themselves, because the Lord makes wars cease and breaks their weapons in two.

This is vulnerability in Israel: when there's an earthquake or a flood or some army camped outside your walls — that's vulnerability. But even when that happens, the Lord of hosts is with us, and we will not fear. And the reason comes at the very center of the psalm. Between the descriptions of the sea quaking and the nations killing each other is the central moment of this psalm, and it is why we are not afraid: "There is a river whose streams make glad the city of God, the holy habitation of the Most High. God is in the midst of the city; it shall not be moved."

The picture is one in which everything outside is chaos, up for grabs, doomed — but right in the middle is the city of God, and the city of God is not moved. She is not threatened. She remains standing through it all. Therefore we will not fear, because the place we are in cannot be shaken; it cannot be threatened by earthquakes or wars or divorce or cancer. Even though the mountains shake in the heart of the sea, we will not fear, because the city of God will not be moved.

There's no claim here that praying enough will spare you pain, nothing here to say that, if you only have enough faith, everything is going to flow smoothly, with no tragic deaths, no heart-wrenching breakups, no disastrous accidents. What is here is a prayer, a psalm, a statement of faith that whatever happens to knock us down — whatever happens to take away our success or our power or our influence, to make us vulnerable — we remember, we know, that "the Lord of hosts is with us; the God of Jacob is our refuge," and so we will not fear, not like others do.

And I hope that idea, that reality, makes a monumental difference for each of us here today, makes a difference for us in all our vulnerability, all the weakness and the worry and the fear that we wouldn't dare speak of to another living soul. I hope that even in the really difficult times we can pray these words, we can sing this psalm, we can profess this faith, right in the middle of our vulnerability, and not fear, because the Lord of hosts is with us, the God of Jacob is our refuge. I hope that every one of us can say, However much I hurt, however vulnerable I am, there is one thing I know: where God is, there I have a place to hide, there I know I am safe, there I will live and nothing will put me at risk. I hope it's true that our faith carries us through those days, because, if it doesn't, if it only works on the pleasant ones, then it doesn't really work at all.

And that brings me to what else I hope, and this hope is specifically for this congregation, for our church, right now: I hope not only that we see that we have a strength that doesn't come from money or health or power or influence, but also that we realize that this time right now — this time of vulnerability, of fear, and even of death — this time is an opportunity for us. Remember in 2 Corinthians 12, when Paul talks about his thorn in the flesh? And he says, "Three times I appealed to the Lord about this, that it would leave me, but he said to me, 'My grace is sufficient for you, for my power is made perfect in weakness.'" *His power is made perfect in weakness.* Those words transformed Paul, transformed his attitude about weakness and strength, and made him see that in his weakness God may be glorified.

We have that same opportunity now. Undoubtedly, this year some things are not going to be done that we would like done. Undoubtedly we will lack some programs and some energy and some smooth operating that would normally be here. But let's not dwell on that; let's not concentrate on what we're missing or losing or lacking. Let's see what we have before us, and that is an opportunity for God to be glorified in our weakness, in our losses, in our vulnerability.

Paul's right. It is an amazing thing to say: we have a kind of strength that not only outlasts weakness; it shines in weakness. Because, then, when we remember who is our refuge, even then, God is glorified when we are weak. We have an opportunity right now as a congregation that doesn't come along often: to display something about the power of God amid the power of cancer. And I hope we take that opportunity.

Because, if we do, I am sure that, whatever details or events or sermons lose something because of these difficult battles, there will be far greater gains, far greater growth than could ever be measured with a human eye. Because of that power of God, Paul says, "Whenever I am weak, then I am strong." May the same be true of us, that God may be glorified and we grow closer to him. That is the amazing opportunity our vulnerability affords us today. We must not waste it.

I learned a lesson about the psalms that day ten years ago, and from it I learned something about God. I learned that when I am vulnerable — and not one of us in this world isn't, not really — I do not have to fear, because he is with me. And everything that I can lose, whether job or home or life, none of it threatens my place with my God. No matter how hard the earth shakes, the city of God stands eternal.

These are honest words, because the truth is that, just as other nations devastated Jerusalem the earthly city of God, so enemies like death and disease and sin pour into the church. It's not a *place* that protects us. It's a *God* who protects us, a God who was with Jacob, a God who was with Israel, a God-with-us. Jesus Christ knows what it's like to be vulnerable. And he's the one preparing a place for us, a place that will not rust or wither. He's the one who makes us strong even when we are weak. He's the one who is with us; and even if the earth itself turns on us, we need not fear, for in him the Lord of hosts is with us, in him the God of Jacob is our refuge.

Sharing a Mind

Text: Philippians 4:2-9

I urge Euodia and I urge Syntyche to be of the same mind in the Lord. Yes, and I ask you also, my loyal companion, help these women, for they have struggled beside me in the work of the gospel, together with Clement and the rest of my co-workers, whose names are in the book of life. Rejoice in the Lord always; again I will say, Rejoice. Let your gentleness be known to everyone. The Lord is near. Do not worry about anything, but in everything by prayer and supplication with thanksgiving let your request be made known to God. And the peace of God, which surpasses all understanding, will guard your hearts and your minds in Christ Jesus. Finally beloved, whatever is true, whatever is honorable, whatever is just, whatever is pure, whatever is pleasing, whatever is commendable, if there is any excellence and if there is anything worthy of praise, think about these things. Keep on doing the things that you have learned and received and heard and seen in me, and the God of peace will be with you.

Philippians 4:2-9

This is some chapter — actually it's only half a chapter. But it reads like *Greatest Quotations of the Apostle Paul.* "Rejoice in the Lord always; again I will say, Rejoice"; and "The peace of God, which surpasses all understanding, will guard your hearts and your minds in Christ Jesus"; and "whatever is true, whatever is honorable, whatever is just, whatever is pure, whatever is pleasing, whatever is commendable . . . think about these things."

These are famously powerful words for the Philippian church, powerful words to remind them of all that they have in Jesus Christ, powerful words to encourage them by. It's a great way to end a letter. So my question is, Why introduce them with something so small? Why does Paul begin this paragraph full of such grand Christian vision, why does he open this set of wonderful proclamations, with some problem between two of the church's leaders? How can he lead up to the joy of the Lord and the incomparable peace of God with, "I sure hope Euodia and Syntyche can patch things up"?

I mean, this is awfully personal, to begin with. To center on these people and their problem with each other when he's got such universal things to say, to pick out one relationship within the church that could be doing better when it's the Philippian congregation's relationship with the living God that's really on his mind — it seems like Paul has lost sight of the forest for the trees.

And, for another thing, singling these two out is awfully embarrassing. After all, his words aren't just read by the pastor and then highlighted in the bulletin. What Paul says here is heard by the whole congregation; everyone is going to be reminded — publicly — that Euodia and Syntyche don't get along. And is that really necessary? Should the congregational prayer name a couple of elders who don't see eye-to-eye or two committee chairs who don't work so well together? Don't leaders in the church deserve better than that?

This topic is just too small for this chapter. It's just not important enough to be lumped in with the great phrases of Paul's preaching. This is a lousy preamble to "Rejoice in the Lord always." This issue just doesn't matter that much. And I know that's true. I know that, whatever is going on between these two church leaders, it's not very big. And I know that because of the way Paul talks about it.

This thing between Syntyche and Euodia can't be very big because Paul doesn't pick sides, he doesn't get specific, he doesn't go into details. All he says is, "I urge Euodia and I urge Syntyche" to find a way, to do something about this. When Paul addresses a situation in which something is seriously wrong and somebody is responsible for it, he doesn't waste any time. He doesn't worry that someone will be angry, or that he'll make waves, or that he'll be misunderstood. In those serious situations Paul gets right to the point. He talks about the matter and then he gives orders: he tells the Ephesians to ignore certain teachers or he demands that somebody knock off what they're doing or he tells the Corinthians in no uncertain terms that they are abusing the Lord's Supper. When there's something going on that Paul thinks is big and clear and sinful, he does not hesitate to let the church know it.

But not here, not with this situation. There are no details, no orders, no pronouncements; only names. Paul uses names because these are his friends, his "co-workers." But he makes no judgments, because, whatever it is, whatever item of ministry or personality Euodia and Syntyche can't get together on, whatever is between them, it is not some denial of Jesus Christ, not some promotion of heresy, not some terrible behavior. What's going on between them isn't like that; it's something small, but it's also something that gets in the way of the things that really matter, the things that are big.

That's the answer to the question I posed. Why begin a section that includes such big things with something so personal and embarrassing and small? Because it's the small, personal, embarrassing things that get in the way of what really matters. Before we can rejoice in the Lord always, we must learn to come together in the Lord. Before Paul can tell the Philippians to realize how big and wide and deep and high is the grace of God, they must realize how small it is. We read this and we want to know, How can Paul's most beautiful section begin with Euodia and Syntyche's dispute over who ushers down the center aisle? And Paul shoots back, If you can't get past ushering assignments, then you can't move on to what really marks the life of the Christian. What's small can get in the way of what's big.

So before we move on to the famous lines of Philippians 4, we need to spend some time on the forgotten part of it, on this little request of Paul to his two trusted leaders. Because these words say something to every element of our life together and every little opinion that we don't share with each other, because it's not what Euodia and Syntyche think that is a concern to Paul, it's how they think it.

I'm very thankful for the Bible version we use this morning, which gives a more accurate translation of what Paul really says there in verse 2. Some translations paraphrase this; they say things like, "I urge Euodia and I urge Syntyche to *agree* with each other in the Lord." But that gives us the wrong idea about what Paul wants. He's not pleading with them to agree with each other. That's not what Paul says. What Paul says is "I urge Euodia and I urge Syntyche to be of the same mind." He's not looking for them to figure out who's right, to settle this thing, to have the same *opinion*. Paul wants more than that: he wants them to have the same *mind*. And having the same mind isn't about what you think; it's about how you see. Having the same mind is seeing the world in the same way: where it's going, whose it is, how it's saved. Paul wants Euodia and Syntyche to remember what they are about here, what the purpose of their lives is, what really matters. He wants them to be of the same mind. And the mind he wants them to have is that of Jesus Christ; he wants them to let him take them past what is small and onto and into a kingdom that encompasses the whole world.

And that's the word for us from this text: Put your focus on what really matters. The word of Philippians 4 says, before you can get to rejoicing in the Lord always, before you can get to the big ideas of verse 4 and verse 7, you must respond to verse 2. You must move yourself and your opinions out of the center of your mind and replace them with Jesus Christ. And you have to do that, says Paul, because the little things get in the way.

If we are going to be a mature body of Jesus Christ, if we are going to rejoice in the Lord always and have the peace of God guard our hearts and minds and concentrate on what is true and honorable and pleasing, then we must have the same mind. If we are going to possess those lovely things that Paul speaks of, if we are going to have that foundation beneath us which removes anxiety and provides peace, we must share the mind of our Lord. We must empty ourselves. That's how Paul sees that mind operating — it's a giving up of ourselves. When we have our own mind, says Paul, we're missing something. When the things that separate us from each other, the disagreements we have over our ministry or personality, when those are the theme in the church, we suffer. Needing our own way, harping on what's wrong, looking for what (or who) we don't like — these things matter. Pettiness gets between us and God. That's the reason for beginning the biggest chapter in his repertoire with the small matter of Euodia and Syntyche.

These words are for Paul's friends, people he cares about and is grateful for. May we hear them that way as well. And then may we decentralize our own minds, decentralize those little things which divide us, and be of the same mind in the Lord, be one body. May we be people whose children don't know whom we don't care for; people who do not count how many didn't call when we were sick; people who do not take offense easily; people whose mind comes from Jesus Christ. May we receive Paul's loving words to his friends in love ourselves and let our differences be superseded by this same mind that we share, in the knowledge that there's something so much bigger than us here. Let's hear verse 2 so we can arrive at the joy of verse 4.

Those are the alternatives. We can have our own mind that says, I come first, I was wronged, I didn't like that. Or we can have the same mind, and with it we will know that we are a work of God here, that he has created a community, a family, the beginnings of heaven already now. We can dwell on differences, or we can display the mind of Christ and practice extending grace to each other — practice peace and patience and kindness and gentleness. When we have the mind of Jesus Christ, we are a people at rest — with God, but also with each other — because we belong to a kingdom that is coming all the time; it's not far away. Paul says that in verse 5: "The Lord is near." That's the reason you can rejoice always, says Paul. That's why you don't have to worry about anything. That's how you can relax and let your minds drift to what is honorable and just and pure, because the Lord is near. And we know that.

In his book *The Shantung Compound* Langdon Gilkey describes his experience in China during World War II. The country was overrun by the army of Japan, and the Japanese immediately gathered up all of the citizens of their enemy nations living in China and put them in an internment camp. In that camp the internees were left to run their own community — they arranged their own government, sorted out their supplies, assigned their living quarters. In this environment, which lacked enough of everything, emotions ran high, and the internees selfishly battled over every last inch and crumb and job.

In the camp were teachers, missionaries, business people — all the different types of foreigners living in China at the time. But no group behaved any better than the others, says Gilkey — every kind of person, facing such fear and need, revealed a great ability to fend for themselves at the expense of others; every kind, that is, except one: the Catholic monks. The monks were different, writes Gilkey; they had long been disciplined to noncompetitive, unselfish cooperation. That was especially clear one tense afternoon.

The internees had a black market arrangement with the Chinese farmers outside the camp. They would exchange goods over the wall. When the Japanese discovered this, they shot two farmers and gathered up the internees. A Japanese officer proceeded to harangue them for several minutes, and he screamed that the next prisoner caught in such activity would be shot, too. Everyone listened in fear; no one moved a muscle.

The officer then took his speech to where the Catholic monks were gathered in order to intimidate them in the same way. But this time, as he carried on, some of the Belgian monks began moving slowly toward him; when the others noticed, they joined in, moving and laughing until the small, armed officer was enveloped by a crowd of big, bearded monks. They were moving closer and closer, getting louder and louder. When they were within inches of him, he pushed through them and ran off. The monks thought the whole thing delightful. They were from all over the globe, but they shared a Lord, and so they shared a life and a will and a mind. And they did not worry about anything.

Langdon Gilkey speaks with amazement about them. On our side, he says, it was every man for himself, and, if someone had taken a step toward that officer, the rest of us would have watched in curiosity to see what they would do to him; but there, with the monks, when one moved into danger, they all went with him. And so, he writes, the day these monks and priests were released was the saddest day in the camp, because the grace and peace of their lives had meant so much to all the rest.

If the Lord is near, if his Spirit is within us, we share much more than a building or a preacher or even bread and wine. If the Lord is near, we share a future; we share a joy; we share a peace from worry; we share a mind. And then this supper is so much more than three hundred cups and bits of bread; then it is, as we call it, a celebration. It is a celebration because we are one body, not competitive, not struggling for power, one body unlike the rest of the world; because we have been marked, changed, overwhelmed, by one piece of perfect knowledge: The Lord is near. Let us receive him. Amen.

LENT

Remembering the Way

Text: Deuteronomy 26:1-11

When the priest takes the basket from your hand and sets it down before the altar of the Lord your God, you shall make this response before the Lord your God: "A wandering Aramean was my ancestor; he went down into Egypt and lived there as an alien, few in number, and there he became a great nation, mighty and populous. When the Egyptians treated us harshly and afflicted us, by imposing hard labor on us, we cried to the Lord, the Lord God of our ancestors; the Lord heard our voice and saw our affliction, our toil, and our oppression. The Lord brought us out of Egypt with a mighty hand and an outstretched arm, with a terrifying display of power, and with signs and wonders; and he brought us into this place and gave us this land, a land flowing with milk and honey. So now I bring the first of the fruit of the ground that you, O Lord, have given me."

Deuteronomy 26:4-10

An event that took place one Sunday night in 1963, in Greenville, South Carolina, brought about, or at least sealed, or symbolized, the end of an empire that had lasted over sixteen centuries. On that Sunday night, in the little metropolis of Greenville, for the first time ever on the Lord's Day, the Fox Theater was open for business. And on that night, seven teenagers who were regular attenders of the Methodist Youth Fellowship at Buncombe Street Church made a pact to enter the front door of the church, be seen, and then quietly slip out the back and catch the show at the Fox Theater.

And with that, says William Willimon, the 1,630-year-old empire called Christendom came to an end. With that, the Christian advantage was over. The church-supporting societal structure began with the conversion of a Roman emperor named Constantine, who saw a cross in the sky before he won a battle. It ended right there in 1963 when the Fox Theater went head to head with the church over who would provide the worldview for the young. At least it ended in Greenville. It ended for that town planted in the heart of America's Bible belt, where the rush hour occurred weekly, at 9:45 on Sunday morning, where everyone was assumed to be a Christian. And, once Christendom collapsed in Greenville, there weren't too many places it would hold up. The Fox Theaters of the world would bow to the church no longer.

William Willimon grew up in Greenville, South Carolina; he was one of those seven teenagers from that Sunday evening. He's watched the world change; and today, as the minister to Duke University, what Willimon says about that change is this: After that, never again could young parents or college students or pastors or auto mechanics assume that people simply grew up Christian by living in places like Greenville. And that change, that new hostility from the forces around us, says Willimon, is the best thing that could have happened to the church of Jesus Christ.

Because of that change, we should no longer be tempted to believe that the culture and the church are on the same page. Now we should no longer be tempted to believe that what makes a good American makes a good Christian. Now we should know that we are a peculiar people, that we do not really belong, that, no matter what's closed on Sunday and no matter how friendly our environment is, we are strangers here, with our own story and our own identity. Now we should better resemble the people God has called us to be.

Because what makes the people of God is not a lifestyle, or a value system, or even a set of Sunday activities. What makes us the people God has called us to be is a story. And *that* never changes.

In Deuteronomy 26 Moses is giving instruction to the people of Israel before they enter their new land, the land they've been promised. And this is crucial instruction, life-and-death instruction, because if they forget who they are, says Moses, if they forget what brought them here, if they forget their story, they will perish; they will be destroyed like the nations that the Lord destroyed around them.

So, after you're there, says Moses, after you've built your houses and your schools, after you've established your roles and your families and your lives, after you've made that place home and you've taken in your first crop, there is something you must do, there is a way you must worship: You must take the first of that crop, and you must go to the tabernacle, to the priest, and acknowledge that you have come to the land the Lord promised to give you. And then you must declare, "My father was a wandering Aramean, and he went down into Egypt with a few people, and lived there and became a great nation, powerful and numerous. But the

Egyptians mistreated us and made us suffer, putting us to hard labor. Then we cried out to the Lord, the God of our fathers, and the Lord heard our voice and saw our misery. So the Lord brought us out of Egypt with a mighty hand and an outstretched arm, with great terror and with miraculous signs and wonders. He brought us to this place and gave us this land, a land flowing with milk and honey; and now I bring the firstfruits of the soil that you, O Lord, have given me."

That's what Moses commands, that each of them go into the presence of the Lord and, whether they feel like it or not, whether they witnessed it all or not, declare how this land came to be theirs. That's what makes them God's people. Moses doesn't tell them to talk about the Ten Commandments or their obedience to them, as important as they are; he doesn't tell them to speak of their priorities or their customs or their lifestyle. He says, Tell the story. Because the story is what makes them God's people, and, when they remember the story, when they live out the story, nothing on earth will change them into anything else.

And what a story that is. Nobody else has a story anything like it. Other nations may have similar ideas about how to structure a society or even how the world began or what worship looks like. But no one else can tell that story about who they are. Only God's people come from that wandering Aramean.

That was Jacob, of course. He had died five hundred years earlier, but they are to call him "father" in the tabernacle, and they are to say, "The Egyptians mistreated us," even though they weren't there themselves. The language speaks of *their* experience because it's *their* story, a story of how God kept a promise to give them a land, how God's constant presence brought them this good life. It's the story of this Jewish farmer, bringing his firstfruits to the tabernacle, remembering out loud that Jacob and Egypt and slavery and manna and, now, this land all belong to his story, making him who he is today, and that God is behind it. His God is the creator, not only of the world, but of him, and of his people, his history, his identity. And that cannot be forgotten. It is always the story that makes God's people, whether his people are Old Testament Israel or the New Testament church.

William Willimon is right: in the postmodern world in which we live, the church finds itself much less comfortable, without the old prerogatives and respect, without the free rides from movie theaters and politicians and school curricula. But it's also true, as Willimon says, that we are better off today. In the past, when we shared more with our environment, when *we* almost assumed we would grow up good Christians as long as we grew up good Americans, we were able to forget, or repress, or ignore the strangeness of being God's people. In the past, when the Christian values were more the norm for the culture, it was easy to believe that the culture's values were the norm for Christians. That's not the case anymore, though some make the same mistaken connection between some political party and the church.

We don't fit as well today, and that's just fine, because we never really did fit well. Our culture may have used our language; it may have put the name of God on our money and prayed to some generic divine being before congressional sessions; perhaps evolution wasn't emphasized in schools, and theaters were closed on Sunday — but all of those things, however much they're valued or believed by Christians, do not identify us. It's not three or four characteristics — however important they may be — that make us who we are; it's that we know the story, that we're *part* of the story.

"My father was a wandering Aramean." That's what makes us God's people. We, too, belong to that story. There's more to it now, of course, about seven times more. But it's still a story of God taking ordinary, often foolish, individuals and using them to bring us somewhere new, where *we* will flourish as Israel was meant to flourish, with the wilderness behind us. Ours is a story that centers on Jesus Christ, but it is *our* story, and that story is what makes us God's people. And, as long as we remember the story, as long as we live out the story, nothing on earth will change us into anything else.

Whether we like it or not, whether we want it to be true or not, no matter what language and customs and appearances we share with our environment, we remain different, as different as Israel was from the nations around her. We do not bow before some generic God; we are not some aggregate of do-gooders; we are not simply out to build community in a world of individuals. We are a people who know Truth itself; we have met him, and that's how we are bound together, and that's why we do not fit. Our story makes us not fit. It makes us strangers, often at odds with the things which those around us hold most dear and good. It gives us a whole different view of things.

If you doubt that, just read the Sermon on the Mount and ask yourself if what you read has *ever* been what the empires and nations and cultures of the world value, even at the height of Christendom. "Blessed are the poor . . . blessed are the meek . . . do good to those who hate you . . . love your enemies." That belongs to our story, because the Lord who brought us new life gave those words to his people.

On August 6, 1945, the first atomic bomb was dropped on a Japanese city. Turning to a group of sailors with him on the battle cruiser *Augusta,* President Harry Truman, who has been described as an outstanding Baptist layman, said, "This is the greatest thing in history."[1] Whatever else that bomb was, it was not that. We don't fit in such a world. It is a radical thing to follow Jesus Christ, and closing your theater on Sunday doesn't even put you in the right hemisphere.

In one of his novels, Frederick Buechner has a scene in which the narrator, a young man named Antonio Parr, has been away for some weeks and on his return finds that his small son and some other children have made a sign for him that reads WELCOME HONE with the last little leg of the *m* in *home* missing so that it turns into an *n*. "It seemed oddly fitting," Antonio Parr says when he first sees it. "It was good to get home, but it was home with something missing or out of whack about it. It wasn't much, to be sure, just some minor stroke or serif, but even a minor stroke can make a major difference." And then a little while later he thinks about it a second time and goes on to add, "WELCOME HONE, the sign said, and I can't help thinking again of Gideon and Barak, of Samson and David and all the rest of the crowd . . . who, because some small but crucial thing was missing, kept looking for it . . . wherever they went till their eyes were dim and their arches fallen."[2]

About that, Buechner says elsewhere, it's like the Letter to the Hebrews, in chapter 11, "where, after listing some of the great heroes and heroines of Biblical faith," the author of Hebrews writes that "all these people were still living by faith when they died. They did not receive the things promised; they only saw them and welcomed them from a distance. And they admitted that they were aliens and strangers on earth. People who say such things show that they are looking for a country of their own."[3]

In that same passage from Hebrews, the writer goes on to say, "If they had been thinking of the country they had left, they would have had opportunity to return. Instead they were longing for a better country — a heavenly one. Therefore God is not ashamed to be called their God, for he has prepared a city for them."

God's people, the ones living out his salvation, are always sojourners

1. Recounted in Stanley Hauerwas and William H. Willimon, *Resident Aliens: Life in the Christian Community* (Nashville: Abingdon Press, 1989), p. 26.

2. Frederick Buechner, *Treasure Hunt,* in *The Book of Bebb* (San Francisco: Harper & Row, 1990), p. 529.

3. Frederick Buechner, *The Longing for Home* (San Francisco: HarperSanFrancisco, 1996), pp. 17-18.

here, never really at home, never really able to find what they're looking for, because what they're looking for, what we're looking for, is a land where Jesus Christ is not crucified but is king, a land where "Love your enemies" and "Blessed are the meek" are the rules of the day, a land where the greatest among us is the servant of everyone.

We are journeying, because we know the Truth about the world; we know what's wrong and it makes us strangers, it makes us exiles, it makes us aliens. In Lent we're reminded of that; we're reminded of how much we don't fit; we're reminded that, in *this* world, the price for being God's people is always death. But we're also reminded that, as Moses knew, and as Jesus made possible for us, the way to life is through remembering our story, the way to life is through death itself. Because, in this strange place that cannot be our home, those who find their life will lose it, and those who lose their life for Christ's sake will find it. Amen.

A Gruesome Promise

Text: Genesis 15

After these things the word of the Lord came to Abram in a vision, "Do not be afraid, Abram, I am your shield; your reward shall be very great." But Abram said, "O Lord God, what will you give me, for I continue childless, and the heir of my house is Eliezer of Damascus?" And Abram said, "You have given me no offspring, and so a slave born in my house is to be my heir." But the word of the Lord came to him, "This man shall not be your heir; no one but your very own issue shall be your heir." He brought him outside and said, "Look toward heaven and count the stars, if you are able to count them." Then he said to him, "So shall your descendants be." And he believed the Lord; and the Lord reckoned it to him as righteousness.

Genesis 15:1-6

In Flannery O'Connor's story "Greenleaf," there is a character, Mrs. May, whose life is completely barren. Her husband died and left her a run-down farm from which to eke out a living. Her two sons are no help to her and show her little respect. Life for Mrs. May is one long complaint. Each day is a pathetic repeat of the one before.

But it's Mrs. May's spiritual life that I'm particularly interested in this morning, a "sort-of" spirituality that all of us should reflect upon, the kind of reflection that Lent is all about. Flannery O'Connor describes Mrs. May's "faith" this way: she "thought the word, Jesus, should be kept inside the church building like other words inside the bedroom. She was a good Christian woman with a large respect for religion, though she did not, of course, believe any of it was true."[4]

At first glance, when you come to Genesis 15, you may have the idea that Abram is the same way. And it is *Abram* here, not yet Abraham, because Abraham means "father of many," and Abram is the father of nobody. As a matter of fact not even Mrs. May is more barren than Abram in Genesis 15: he has an old wife, no children, and no place he can even call home. Abram had the same problem in Genesis 12, but he's even worse off now, because in Genesis 12 God came to Abram, out of the blue, no warning, no invitation, no reason, and made him a promise. It was Abram's fresh start. But now things aren't so fresh anymore. Now it's three chapters later, and Abram's wondering how much of a start it really was. Because for three chapters he's been wandering around the Middle East, doing what God says, counting on this new life, and nothing has happened — except that Sarah's gotten older, and God's promise is that much harder to believe.

And that's why, on first glance here, you may get the idea that Abram's faith is in the same ballpark as Mrs. May's. Because the way chapter 15 begins it doesn't sound like Abram believes much of it to be true: "Do not be afraid, Abram. I am your shield, your very great reward." But Abram said, "O Sovereign Lord, what can you give me, since I remain childless and the one who will inherit my estate is Eliezer of Damascus?" And Abram said, "You have given me no children; so a servant in my household will be my heir."

But then it becomes clear that Abram is not Mrs. May at all; he's actually the opposite of her. The Lord says to Abram, "This man will not be your heir, but a son coming from your own body will be your heir." And then the Lord shows Abram the stars in the sky and tells him, "Your offspring will be as difficult to count as these." *And Abram believed the Lord.*

---

4. Flannery O'Connor, "Greenleaf," in *Complete Stories* (New York: Farrar, Straus and Giroux, 1971), p. 316.

Abram is nothing like Mrs. May. Abram doesn't respect religion at all. God tells him not to be afraid, that everything is going to work out fine, and Abram speaks up. He talks back. He questions. Abram wants to know what kind of reward can replace the son that God hasn't given him. Abram is calling God onto the carpet. He doesn't respect religion at all. But he does believe that what God says is true.

And that's the tremendous difference between Abram and Mrs. May; it's the difference between having some sort of respect for religion and belonging to Jesus Christ; it's the difference between those who are sojourners on earth and looking toward a better place, a real home, and those who are settled in right here. "Abram believed the Lord, and the Lord credited it to him as righteousness."

But belief's not easy, and the Lord doesn't let up. He wants more than just faith in one element of his program. He wants more than Abram holding on to the idea that, yes, somehow, some way, he will have a son of his own. He wants Abram holding on to *him*, believing in him, putting his faith in him. So the Lord goes on from talking about children to talking about real estate. "I am the Lord," he says, "who brought you out of Ur of the Chaldeans to give you this land."

And, just like before, Abram's faith is being pushed, because he doesn't see any reason, any evidence, that this land will be his. So he speaks up again to the God he trusts: "O Sovereign Lord, how can I know that I will gain possession of it?" And that's when God responds with something Abram can see as well as hear. That's when God initiates this strange ceremony, this cutting up of the animals and creating a path with their corpses.

In seminary we learned that there are three significant covenant encounters between God and Abraham: the call of Abram in Genesis 12, this scene in Genesis 15, and the establishment of the rite of circumcision in Genesis 17. I remember, as I was considering these three events, that this one, this covenant ceremony in Genesis 15, was one I didn't appreciate, one I didn't care to think about. I could cherish the divine call of Abram in Genesis 12, that beautiful story of God's stepping into Abram's dead-end life, and I could appreciate the symbol of circumcision in chapter 17. But I saw nothing in the spreading of these carcasses in Genesis 15. It was just too primitive, too unnecessary, too gruesome.

And my estimation was exactly right: it *is* gruesome. It's not allegory or poetry going on here; it's Abram slaughtering five animals and cutting three of them in half, then making some sort of passageway with the remains. And, as if to remind us how real it all is, how bloody, how deadly serious Abram's faith and God's promises are, we're told that vultures swooped down upon the carcasses but Abram drove them away. There is blood on this relationship.

So then God lays it out for Abram in a way that he never has before. He tells him about his descendants, about their hard times in Egypt as slaves, about Abram's own life, and about the way one day his children, thousands upon thousands of them, will enter this land and have it for their very own. He tells Abram all of this with the blood still on the ground, the pieces still forming their gruesome corridor. And then a smoking firepot with a blazing torch passes between the pieces, and right there the Lord makes a covenant with Abram, an oath to do everything that he promised.

And that is the Lord's response to Abram's doubts, his wondering if any of what God has said is ever going to come true. This is what Abram receives from the Lord to help him along the way: God's Word and its seal, in a bloody covenant. This is what Abram receives to help him hold on to God, to help him trust that all these things will come about, no matter how unlikely and distant they seem right now. This is what Abram receives to help him journey as God's child in a strange land: the promise of God sealed in blood.

It is no easy thing to believe against odds and appearances. I hope I never sound like it is easy. Faith remains a work of God himself, an amazing thing to behold. It is difficult to journey as a peculiar people, a different people, as the people of God are in this world. It is difficult not to fit in and not to see always that better country we long for. But we are helped along the way, too, just like Abram. And we are helped in exactly the same fashion: we have the Word of God, the promise of God, sealed in blood.

If it's true that we are aliens here, strangers in a place that cannot be our home, not as it is, then it is also true that our business with God is just as serious as Abram's. And the way we are encouraged and sustained must also come from God himself. Last Sunday I mentioned William Willimon from Duke University. Along with Stanley Hauerwas, Willimon has written a book called *Resident Aliens*. Their thesis is that, since we don't fit in here, we are strangers here, with our own story, our own faith; and our role as the church is to live out that story, to carry on Abram's faith. To do that, only one thing may be our focus: what God has done, what God is doing, what God will do in the world. We must remember the gruesome promise. It must sustain us in our doubts, our questions, our fear.

It's easier to take our help from somewhere else. It's easier to try to sustain ourselves on the difficult journey by making ourselves feel better, by pretending that everything is fine, by trading in truth for niceness. We must resist that. We must resist the temptation to give up talking about faith and doubt and blood and replace it with sentiment. Willimon and Hauerwas say that sentimentality is the way our unbelief is lived out, the way we avoid facing the serious truths of God's Word. Sentimentality, that attitude of being always ready to understand but not to judge, corrupts the church. "Sentimentality is the subjecting of the church year to Mother's Day. . . . Sentimentality is the necessity of the church to side with the Sandinistas against the Contras. Sentimentality is 'the family that prays together stays together.' Without God, without the One whose death on the cross challenges all our 'good feelings,' who stands beyond and over and against our human anxieties, all we have left is sentiment."[5] They're right. We prefer covenants that don't kill and worship services that don't face the reality of God. We want to think that life with God is about feeling good and being nice, that it doesn't take anybody's dying. But it does. There is still blood on this relationship.

It's hard to do what Abram did; it's hard to give up the religion and speak of what we really believe and whether we really believe it. It's easier to carry ourselves along with cute things, with worship that celebrates people, or events, or our church, instead of proclaiming a promise that is often gruesome and demands a faith that makes us into something different from the world. But, if we are going to be children of Abraham, our worship, our faith must be that, it must speak the Word of God, even when it has blood on it.

And it still does. You know, this ceremony between the carcasses is a primitive way of making a covenant. It is as serious a bond as two parties could make. Because, as you walk through those dead animals, you are saying, "May this happen to me, if I do not keep my oath." The Lord God Almighty walked that path and made that promise to Abram, with the commitment to die himself if he does not keep his Word. Who would have thought that he would experience death *in order* to keep his Word?

But he did. So now, instead of the carcasses of animals, we have a font, a supper, a cross to remind us what's at stake; but they still have to do with blood to remind us how serious God is about the promises he makes. His love for his people is so great, his determination to bring them home is so intense, that he will face death rather than fail. It is up to us whether we want to be like Mrs. May, as so many around us are,

---

5. Hauerwas and Willimon, *Resident Aliens,* pp. 120-21.

thinking that religion deserves some attention but that's about it, so that life goes on barren of meaning and hope, or whether we want to be like Abram and believe the promise, be bound together with God in a life-and-death covenant, and let that covenant promise then determine every moment, every decision, every inch of our lives, until it brings us home, knowing that the one who calls us is faithful and he will do it. Amen.

If You Think

Text: 1 Corinthians 10:1-17

Therefore, my dear friends, flee from the worship of idols. I speak as to sensible people; judge for yourselves what I say. The cup of blessing that we bless, is it not a sharing in the blood of Christ? The bread that we break, is it not a sharing in the body of Christ? Because there is one bread, we who are many are one body, for we all partake of the one bread.

1 Corinthians 10:14-17

Last week I mentioned Flannery O'Connor's joyless "Mrs. May," who considered herself "a good Christian woman with a large respect for religion, though she did not, of course, believe any of it was true." I've thought about her more this week, and I've wondered how this happens, that religion and life, Christianity and faith can be pushed so far apart. But, then again, I don't think it's anything new.

The Corinthians seem to be suffering from the same delusion, the delusion that religion and not faith is what matters. To see that, we need to understand the circumstances behind what we read. In the first-century Greek world the spiritual and the commercial weren't so separated as they are here. In that world the temples of the pagan gods were almost like shopping malls, and, like the shopping mall, in the center of the temple was the place to eat, the food court. The temple was the place where people gathered to worship their idols, to make sacrifices to their gods, that's true; but more than that, the temple was a place for people to gather to eat and socialize and laugh together.

So your average Corinthian family, when they wanted to get together with friends, would probably go to the temple of some deity and have a drink. When they wanted to get a bite to eat, they'd wind up at the temple. When they wanted to celebrate a birthday or have a family reunion, the temple was the place to do it. Many aspects of their lives involved the temple of one or another Greek god.

And when these people became Christians, it was difficult for them to think of giving up going to the temples, because the temples were a regular part of their lives. And so, many of them didn't give it up. They kept on going to the temples for food and drink and conversation, even though a big part of what went on at the temples was worship and sacrifice and praise aimed at an idol.

Now the fact that idol worship was going on at their parties didn't worry the Corinthians, at least they said it didn't. It didn't worry them because, they figured, "We've been baptized into Jesus Christ, we've participated in the Lord's Supper. And, since we have baptism and the Lord's Supper, we don't have to worry about going into these temples and eating food sacrificed to some other god or hanging around while people worship him. We don't have to worry about that because our baptism will protect us. We have nothing to fear from these idol worship services because we have communion." That's what the Corinthians were doing and saying, and what we read is what the apostle Paul has to say about that.

But to understand Paul's response there's something else we have to know. We have to know that the Lord whose promise stands behind baptism and whose blood stands behind communion — the God who delivered the Corinthians from their bondage, their slavery to sin — is the same God who delivered Israel from her bondage, her slavery in Egypt, 1,500 years earlier. The Corinthians' God is the same God who was there in the Red Sea with the Israelites and who remembered them in the Passover.

So Paul's answer to the Corinthians is to remind them of the Israelites. The Israelites, says Paul to the Corinthians, were like you: they too went through baptism, a baptism into Moses, because Moses delivered them just as Christ delivered you. And not only were all of the Israelites baptized, but all of them also ate a spiritual food and drank a spiritual drink. They too were fed at God's table; and, just as Christ is really present in the Christian meal, so he was really present in the Israelites' meals in the wilderness. So Israel was baptized, Israel celebrated communion, Israel had the presence of Jesus Christ.

And all of those religious advantages of Israel — being part of a body that God had saved, having a deliverer who was sent by God, being baptized and fed at the Lord's table, being in the presence of Christ — all of those advantages still were not enough to bring the people of Israel into the promised land. That is Paul's word in 1 Corinthians 10.

Baptism. Communion. Jesus Christ. "Nevertheless, God was not pleased with most of them, and they were struck down in the wilderness." In spite of all their religious advantages, they didn't reach their goal, they didn't finish their journey, they perished in the desert, they died. And, with that, Paul turns to the Corinthians and says, "So if you think you are standing firm, be careful that you don't fall!"

That's how attitudes like Mrs. May's happen — we let Christianity become a set of behaviors instead of a life-changing experience, so we *think* we are standing firm when we're really not. We *think* that we can take care of the spiritual element by satisfying some requirements when it's not so. We *think* that we are saved by respecting religion when worrying about religion actually gets in the way of belonging to Jesus Christ.

But it's so easy to do, isn't it? It's so easy to have a healthy respect for religion and never really face the question of whether you believe it's true, and what difference it makes if you do. And here the church hasn't helped. Because the church and its preachers have often spoken as if salvation lies in this font or that table or so many of these prayers. But it's not so, and we need to know that.

The Corinthians, at least some of them, liked to think that baptism and the Lord's Supper provided some sort of spiritual rust-proofing that would keep their souls from corrupting. And the truth is, the church today, at least some of us, think exactly the same thing. We think that, if we put our time in here, if we have our children baptized, if we pay religion some respect, we'll be okay, we'll be standing firm, we will not fall. And we never really have to consider whether we believe any of it to be true.

The word of Paul, the word of *God*, is that it won't work. Israel had all the religion you could fit into one life: they ate with God, they were kept alive by God, they were led around by God — *our* God. Nevertheless, he was not pleased with most of them; they were struck down in the wilderness. It didn't work for them; it wouldn't work for the Corinthians; it won't work for us.

And we have to be honest about this; we cannot be afraid of speaking the truth. We cannot pretend — or go on pretending — that we ourselves don't fall into the Corinthian trap, that some of us aren't here Sunday after Sunday, coming to this table, believing that the ceremony will bring the salvation. And I'm not guessing here. I know that it's true; I've seen it. In my few years in ministry I've had far too many experiences of professions of faith and baptisms that included all the right words, that made all the right promises, that nodded along to all the statements of faith, and then, within a few weeks or months, it became clear that they weren't professing a faith or receiving a promise at all; they were just practicing religion. It makes me feel deceived, and, more than that, it makes me sad.

And our celebrations of the Lord's Supper can be the same way — some sort of protection from God, some magical dispensation from the church. But you know what the Lord's Supper is? It's not protection; it's participation — participation in the body of Jesus Christ, participation in the blood of Jesus Christ. And when you have union with Jesus Christ you do not receive protection; you receive new life.

But, when we have new life, when our citizenship is transferred to another kingdom, when we belong to Jesus Christ, we are no longer at home here, no longer at home in temples of other gods or a world with other masters. And that is the Corinthian problem: their home is here, and they think a little religion will give them a home with God as well. It doesn't work that way. Not with this God. We can no longer belong to the temples and idols and principles of this world, when we have participated in the body and blood of Christ — whether or not we practice our religion well.

In his book *The Longing for Home*, Frederick Buechner tells of one of his favorite preachers, George Buttrick. Buechner says that one year in mid-December Buttrick said something in a sermon that he never forgot. He said that the previous week he had overheard someone ask, "Are you going home for Christmas?" And, Buechner says, Buttrick peered out at his congregation and asked it again, "Are you going home for Christmas?" And he asked it in such a way that brought tears to the eyes, because the truth was so obvious: home is in Bethlehem, home is at the cross, home is where Christ is.[6] And, for Christ, we must never forget, home was not here, not like this. And for us who are his body, who share this loaf, it cannot be home, either. For us home is following Jesus, and Jesus rules over a kingdom that is not of this world.

The Lord's Supper is appropriate in Lent, because Lent is a time to consider anew, to hear again, that we, by the grace of God, participate in the body and blood of Jesus Christ. Lent is a time for us to consider what it means to be one body, one people, called out of the world, set apart from the world, different from the world. Lent is a time to consider

6. Buechner, *The Longing for Home*, pp. 23, 28.

whether we have communion with other gods and whether we truly are joined to Christ.

And that's how we have to hear the words of Paul this morning, not as the words of a man who is out to criticize the Corinthians or belittle them or hit them over the head with laws and rules, but as the words of a preacher who more than anything else wants these people to be joined to Jesus Christ, to participate in Jesus Christ, to have new life in Jesus Christ, life that is not tied to this failing world but to a kingdom that will never end. We must hear these words as words of love, and we must hear them today.

If you think Christianity is a religion to practice and not a faith to fill every inch of your life, then you are wrong. If you think that you can put an hour in or participate in a ceremony without joining the church, without becoming part of the loaf that is the body of Jesus Christ, you are fooling yourself. If you think that this supper is something you can take without becoming part of an alien people, without losing your life and finding it made over in Jesus Christ, then do not come to this table, because it will do you no good. If you think that salvation lies in what lands on your head or goes in your stomach, then read these words again. If you think salvation lies anywhere but in receiving the promise of God and being transformed by it, be careful that you do not fall.

Mrs. May grumbles and complains and resents her way through Flannery O'Connor's story until she dies uncomfortably, believing herself all along to be a good Christian woman, I suppose. And I guess, by some definition, she was one. But she was terribly stuck, stuck right here, without a vision of a kingdom that is so different, without the life that comes only from a faith that fills you and not a religion that you practice. Somehow she participated in Christianity but never participated in Jesus Christ. And that is a shame. Because God so loved the world that he gave himself up, just so Mrs. May and you and I would not fall but stand, would not die but live.

The Steadfast Face of God

Texts: Leviticus 17; Luke 9:46-62

If anyone of the house of Israel or of the aliens who reside among them eats any blood, I will set my face against that person who eats blood, and will cut that person off from the people. For the life of the flesh is in the blood; and I have given it to you for making atonement for your lives on the altar; for as life, it is the blood that makes atonement.

Leviticus 17:10-11

When the days drew near for him to be taken up, he set his face to go to Jerusalem. And he sent messengers ahead of him. On their way they entered a village of the Samaritans to make ready for him; but they did not receive him, because his face was set toward Jerusalem.

Luke 9:51-53

In one of Willa Cather's vivid novels, the main figure, Father Latour, has to pay an official visit on a crude and careless priest. Cather says this: "Father Latour disliked the priest's personality so much that he could scarcely look at him. His fat face was irritatingly stupid, and had the grey, oily look of soft cheeses."[7] Cather puts the worst face on her character to tell us who this man is, what he's like, how greasy and decadent he's become. It's all there in his face.

The truth is that faces tell us a lot. Faces tell us race, sex, health, and even thoughts — Shakespeare's Duncan is right to say, "There's no art to find the mind's construction in the face." That's why a great actress can sometimes bring off a dramatic scene without saying a word; she just moves some small muscles in her cheeks. Martin Luther once commented that a person's whole attitude toward God and humanity is written in his face — and that once past the age of 30 a person is therefore accountable for the shape of his face.

Maybe not. But we all know that faces speak: nervousness, embarrass-

7. Willa Cather, *Death Comes for the Archbishop* (New York: Alfred A. Knopf, 1927), p. 145.

This sermon is indebted to Neal Plantinga.

ment, delight, anger, wonder, sheepishness, guilt — all these inner things may be advertised to the world on our face. The concept of face is in fact so close to that of personality that one of the world's most famous cases of multiple personality — that rare neurosis where more than one person inhabits a human body — is called "The Three Faces of Eve." Centuries ago when the Greek fathers of the church wanted to speak of the persons in the Holy Trinity, one word they chose was the word for face. The three faces of God!

And there's something biblical about the idea: across the pages of Scripture the character of God is called his face. Is God gracious? Does he flood our lives with the warmth of his mercy? Yes. But the biblical way to speak of that is to say that God makes his face to shine upon us. Has God become so disgusted with his miserable creatures that he is ready to give up on them? At times, yes. And the Bible says then, God hides his face. And when people pray, when psalmists and prophets and widows lift up their cries to heaven, it is called "seeking his face." And once more God turns toward them and lifts up his face upon them and gives them his peace.

Our Old Testament lesson this morning from the book of Leviticus also speaks of the face of God. But Leviticus, of course, is not an easy book to read. It is, after all, a book of sacrifice and ritual, of blood and ceremony. It's difficult for us to read the book of Leviticus and see its place in the big picture, see its place in the gospel, see it in overarching themes of grace or hope. And, even with help from theologians and study Bibles to understand it all a bit better, Leviticus is not our first choice for daily devotions, because it's all such a long way from our world.

A few weeks ago we talked about the covenant of Genesis 15, and I mentioned my uncomfortable reaction to the ceremony between God and Abram. It was just too primitive for my taste. I think Leviticus is that way for all of us — it's just too primitive, there's just too much blood on everything. And there's too much sacrifice. We're troubled by that refrain: "an aroma pleasing to the Lord," as if God can be pacified and appeased by sinful creatures if they just offer up to him the right animal, the right amount of blood. And yet, in this difficult, troubling, gory book, there is the presence of God, the attention of God, the *face* of God.

Behind the ceremony and the ritual and the sacrifice in Leviticus is the idea that, for atonement to be made, for human beings to be made right with God, blood must be shed. This is God's way. He cannot simply forgive. He cannot just declare a general amnesty. He will not freely pardon. No, in God's way atonement must be costly for the one who provides it. And it must be provided in a particular way. The person who offers must bring his best. It calls for blood.

And that is where God's face enters Leviticus 17. Verse 10 reads, "If any Israelite or any alien living among them eats any blood, I will set my face against that person who eats blood and will cut that person off from the people." Blood is the life-fluid and must be devoutly respected. Life may not be casually consumed. But even more, shed blood is a ransom; it's a payment to God. The death of an animal yields blood, which is a ransom price for the life of sinners. Animal blood is a sacred ransom both provided by God and protected by God. So God is thoroughly angry with anyone who profanes the ransom. Such a person will be cut off; God is dead set against such persons. He *sets his face* against them.

Sin is so corrupting, so destructive to the relationship of God and human beings that there must be a ransom. When someone sins, someone must pay. As the author of Hebrews puts it, "Without the shedding of blood, there is no forgiveness of sins" (9:22). In Leviticus, for those sinners who penitently come to the tabernacle with their bleating sheep or trussed-up ox, the animal satisfies. In this strange and ancient exchange, blood is shed and manipulated as a ransom for the life of the believer. But for those who do not follow God's way there is no substitute: they themselves must pay. For when someone sins, someone must pay. And the wages of sin is death.

It is never explained. It is just so. At the center of the universe, in the halls of heaven's justice, according to the inscrutable will of God, when someone sins, someone pays. God cannot tolerate sin. God will not go soft on sin. God cannot overlook sin. Sin registers on the face of God. And so the axe must fall, sacrifice must be made, blood must be shed. The sinner or else a graciously given substitute — one or the other must die.

In the ninth chapter of his Gospel Luke writes, "When the days drew near for him to be taken up, Jesus set his face to go to Jerusalem." When we consider the face of Jesus, most of us picture those perfect placid heads that so often adorn Sunday school rooms and living rooms. But think of this face that Luke tells us about. "When the days drew near, he set his face." In a purposely solemn use of an old Hebrew expression, Luke tells us what ought to be in minds and hearts in Lent. That one phrase says it all. He set his face. His face, tense and determined, tells us that he is on his way to die and that he knows it. The only way for him to be taken up to God is by way of a Roman torture instrument.

His face tells us that in death there is a horror against which even the Son of God must grit his teeth. His face, set like flint, tells us the road ahead is mined. He will walk now without fanfare, but that steadfast look will be on his face. He will chat with the disciples and make little detours.

He will pause to talk with nameless people and reach God's mercy out to unimportant rascals. But there will always be Jerusalem in his eyes and Caiaphas and Roman politicians in his thoughts.

Jerusalem — the city for which every Jewish exile longed and ached, the very center and symbol of God's dwelling with his people — this city has now become a symbol of all that has gone wrong in our world. David's son is not welcome in David's city. The very Son of God is not safe in Jerusalem. He fits only a cross outside the city.

Yet now, as Luke tells it, Jesus the Christ deliberately turns and walks toward Jerusalem. Here he brings toward its climax what he has been sent to do; here he summons all his courage and determination and sets his face. All hell has broken loose in this sorry world of ours, and every crease, every line in that set face of our Lord tells us that all heaven has come to do battle.

But the look in Luke is not simply the anger of God against his disobedient people — not just that, not just what Leviticus tells us about. No, what we now read in his face is the sheer determination of God to defeat the evil that is dug in against him. The look on the flint-like face of Christ is the look of the infinite determination of God. It was God's determination to bridge the gap between himself and his people once and for all, to give sin its wage by making the atoning blood that would flow his own, or his Son's. Think of that: the blameless face of God set again — but not against the sinner, against sin.

So, through the rest of this Gospel — which has a long way to go yet — through Jesus' teaching and preaching and healing, every step he takes, everything he does, moves him closer to Jerusalem, closer to a cross, closer to paying the ransom with his own blood. In everything he does, there is the steadfast face of God, aimed at the cross, aimed at our sin. When someone sins, someone must pay. With every fiber of his being, with complete resoluteness, Jesus Christ has determined to pay. He set his face.

If it were different, if it weren't gory, if sin didn't require payment, then I guess the whole Christian faith would be more palatable. Then there would be no Leviticus, no talk of sacrifices and blood and the need for atonement. Then there would be no Jerusalem, not the way Jesus is going to experience it. Then Luke 9–19 would be nothing more than Jesus the teacher, Jesus the story-teller, Jesus the healer. But he's not that. He's not a good teacher or a moral example. Not just that, anyway. He's a sacrifice. Because that's what it takes: when someone sins, someone must pay.

And that makes the Christian faith difficult, politically incorrect. It never wavers on the idea that every one of us is polluted with sin. And it never wavers on the idea that sin must be paid for in blood, either a substitute's or our own. It would be easy if there were nothing for Jesus to set his face toward, if he could live out his days as a wise old carpenter and forget Jerusalem altogether, but it's not like that. When someone sins, someone must pay. And someone has. Knowing that, following Jesus wherever he goes, receiving him as our eternal substitute, makes us different — it changes our decisions, our careers, our families, our attitudes, our *faces*.

And so now in Lent, with bittersweet love for God, with a chastened spirit, with mixed humility and gratitude, let us watch Jesus Christ our Lord head toward the city, head into the Jerusalem of our lives. Here he comes, against the grain of all our failure and guilt and sadness. A fearful, powerful Son of God, determined to reach for every last one of us and to pull us *free* of all that threatens to undo us. For this he goes to die. For when someone sins, someone pays.

"When the days drew near for him to be taken up, he set his face to go to Jerusalem." None of us can explain this. We hardly dare to touch it. But perhaps our hearts can hold it and cling to it, and perhaps when we are tempted, or defiant, or humbled, we can see in our mind's eye the steadfast face of God, so that once more, with wondrous love, we come clean. Amen.

— FIFTH SUNDAY IN LENT —

A Question Ahead of Its Time

Text: John 18:38

Pilate asked him, "What is truth?" After he had said this, he went out to the Jews again and told them, "I find no case against him. . . ."

John 18:38

There is no better theologically interested writer in our day than Frederick Buechner. And Frederick Buechner knows Pontius Pilate. This is how Buechner describes him: On this day Pilate

makes his first major decision before he has even had his breakfast. While still in his pajamas he walks downstairs to the bar closet where he keeps his extra cigarettes, takes the two and a half cartons that he finds there and puts them out with the trash. . . .

It is a good start, and he feels better for it. Not even the morning paper upsets him, leafing through it in the back seat of the limousine as he is driven into the city. It contains the usual grim recital — poverty, crime, disease, corruption in high places, ignorance and superstition and indifference in low places and everywhere else — but he feels for the moment wonderfully insulated from it as the car rolls along and he glances out at the world from time to time through the tinted windows. Children are playing in the street, heavily armed policemen patrolling the seedier neighborhoods, sightseers feeding pigeons outside the temple gates. He is essentially a law-and-order man, and he is maintaining them as best he can. If the malcontents, the eggheads, and bleeding hearts, want to carry on about rottenness at the heart of things, that is their business. His concern is with rottenness in the streets, and his business is to keep the ship afloat from day to day. All in all he is not doing a bad job of it. There are no major complaints from Rome. The Jews are happy enough with their Jewish puppets. And he himself, if not exactly happy, is happy enough. . . .

The chief of the occupational forces is in a sweat because the high holidays are upon them and he expects trouble from the fanatics. The Jewish God, not knowing which side his matzoh is buttered on, wants Rome out, wants the peace that passeth all understanding for his people instead of the Pax Romana. Pilate starts to reach for a cigarette and then remembers. He picks up a pencil instead. He says that what passeth his understanding is the Jews themselves, who have never had it so good. He says that what passeth his understanding is how they can go on knocking themselves out for a God who runs history when it is precisely history that has run them over and left them with their ancient superstitions as much an anachronism as an Egyptian mummy or a stone ax. Besides, he says, Caesar is God. The chief of the occupational forces is a straight party-line man with an eye for promotion, and Pilate does not quite permit himself a wink as he says it. Caesar is God, he says, with only the faintest flicker of a smile. It is not returned, and he orders the guard doubled around the temple and the whole garrison put on alert until Passover passes over. . . .

There has been some kind of demonstration at one of the city gates with some up-country messiah at the center of it, and the question is how to handle it without making it worse. The Jews are playing it safe by passing the buck to Caesar. . . . "There is no God and Caesar is his name," Pilate permits himself to say this time but only to his secretary because she . . . won't get it anyway. He says he will see the man himself if that's what they want. If they want him to see their God, he will see him, too. The more the merrier.[8]

Of course we don't know if that's the real Pilate or not, if that's how this day began, if those were the things that went through his mind, if he really was cynical about Caesar and the Jews and life and faith and God; but if there's one hint that Buechner's picture of Pontius Pilate is nearly right, one hint that Pilate is indeed a modern person, it is our text for this morning. It is Pilate's question: "What is truth?"

He certainly does have a situation on his hands here. He's got the fate of a miracle-worker to decide, a man of the people, someone whose conviction could set off a riot. But he's also got the people's leaders to consider: they're the ones who have brought him in, who are behind this whole death-penalty campaign. And then there's his boss, Caesar, the emperor. Pilate can't be reported as pardoning royal impostors. That isn't a person standing in front of his desk; that's a landmine, and Pilate needs to tread carefully.

So he talks to the Jews, he talks to their leaders, and he talks to Jesus Christ. It turns out Jesus isn't the threat that he seemed: He's a king, but of another jurisdiction. He doesn't have an army, he has a sermon. He hasn't come to conquer Rome but to testify to truth.

And maybe Pilate is momentarily intrigued by this agenda, this terrorist who's not after terror but truth. Maybe that's why Pilate asks, or maybe he's just being sarcastic, or maybe he'd like to believe there's an answer but just can't. But for some reason Pilate does ask, "What is truth?" But he doesn't wait for the answer.

Old Pilate, the master politician, doesn't have time for truth. He's got to go back outside and work the crowd. Pilate can't wait for the answer to his question because he's got an image to work on, a career to advance, a nation to worry about. And, anyway, truth only gets you crucified; truth is old-fashioned; truth doesn't really exist. And that, most of all, is what makes Pilate a man for our time.

For almost all of history since Pontius Pilate asked his question and

---

8. Frederick Buechner, *Telling the Truth: The Gospel as Tragedy, Comedy, and Fairy Tale* (San Francisco: Harper & Row, 1977), pp. 8-11.

walked out the door, Western civilization has had an answer. For almost all of history we have had an answer for Pilate. What is truth? he wanted to know. We knew. We weren't always right about it, and sometimes we weren't consistent or loving, but we knew what it was. We knew how to live, how to speak, what to value. For century after century the answer to Pilate wasn't hard to find at all. In ethics, in art, in history, in politics, there was always truth. But not anymore. And so Pilate is a man ahead of his time.

David Wells, a theologian at Gordon-Conwell Seminary in Massachusetts, describes the change that has taken place:

> Western culture once valued the higher achievements of human nature — reasoned discourse, the good use of language, fair and impartial law, the importance of our collective memory, tradition, the core of moral axioms to which collective consent was given, those aesthetic achievements in the arts that represented the high-water marks of the human spirit. These are now all in retreat. Reasoned discourse has now largely disappeared; in a nation of plummeting literacy, language has been reduced to the lowest common denominator, to the vulgar catch phrases of the youth culture; the core of values has disintegrated; the arts are degraded; the law is politicized; politics is trivialized. In place of high culture, we have what is low. Unruly instinctual drives replace thought; the darker side of human nature destroys the nobler, leaving a trail of pornography, violence, and indifference.[9]

What is truth? We're not sure anymore. Watch a little daytime television and you'll see what I mean.

We're living in what philosophers call a postmodern world, a world in which there are no rules, a world in which there are no rights or wrongs, a world in which there are no absolutes. So parents leave their eight-year-olds to find their own moral way. Teachers are careful not to influence their students' values. Complete tolerance and unlimited freedom are hailed as the hallmarks of humanity. That is the modern world; and Pilate fits right in.

In the Roman empire and in American culture that may not be surprising. Perhaps it even works. Obviously, Pilate knows what he's doing; you don't get to where he is by being wrong a lot. Maybe that's how things

9. David F. Wells, *No Place for Truth, Or Whatever Happened to Evangelical Theology?* (Grand Rapids: Eerdmans, 1993), p. 169.

work in the world, at least right now. But it's not how they work in the church. It's never how they work in the church. In Lent we need to recall that.

In his book *No Place for Truth* David Wells complains that much of the church has become as modern as Pilate. Conservative Protestant Christians, says Wells, Christians like us, have gotten caught up in this new way of thinking, in shifting the focus from truth to image, to results, to success. "The biblical interest in righteousness," says Wells, "is replaced by a search for happiness, holiness by wholeness, truth by feeling, ethics by feeling good about one's self."[10]

In other words, the *church* has taken hold of the idea that the human being, the individual, the audience is the final judge of what is important and proper and worthwhile and true, the *church* has begun to believe that happiness is what we're about, the *church* has begun to place needs and desires over truth. So theology is considered a waste of time, because it doesn't make us feel good. Churches are shopped for, as people look for the one that offers the best product. Worship is punctuated by what amuses: skydivers dropping in during sermons, bodybuilders breaking boards at the pulpit, prayer groups outfitting themselves in combat fatigues.

Like Pilate, there are many inside the church with more important things to pursue than truth, things like results, image, success. There are many who believe that the truth is up to me, what matters before God is whether I'm having a good time, whether we're all getting along. That's frightening. David Wells writes, "The powerful vision of a humanity corrupted by sin being released to stand before God in all his glory and converse with him, gripped by the magnificent certainty of his truth, is now dying."[11] Some say the church is growing. But don't let growth alone convince you. Growth and death sometimes go together — it's called cancer. Some in the church are rushing out to deal with the crowds without pausing over what is the truth that comes by way of Jesus Christ. The problem is that there is no other way to follow him.

It's hard to fault Pilate, at least right at this moment. He asked a question he didn't think had an answer. And he asked it of a poor, beaten, wanna-be king who had lost every friend he ever had. Even if there were an answer, certainly this isn't the guy Pilate would expect it from. It's hard to blame Pilate for walking out the door and going back to business as usual.

---

10. Wells, *No Place for Truth*, p. 183.
11. Wells, *No Place for Truth*, p. 185.

It's too bad, though. It's too bad because, had he stopped, had he asked in faith instead of whatever it was he asked in, had he really wondered and waited, he might have realized that there was more truth in that room than anywhere else in the world at that moment. He would have learned that the answer to all of his worries and his addictions was standing before him. All he had to do was turn his back on his usual way of doing things. Pilate didn't know. But we do.

The temptation to let the world determine our priorities and our methods and our expectations is great. It's hard to fault Pilate for not recognizing the king before him, but what about the Jews? Why did they miss him? Because they were looking for a different kind of messiah, a kind that did business the way they wanted, the way that pleased them. But truth doesn't work that way. So they crucified him. They crucified the Truth that was sent from God.

Many amazing things are taking place in the church today — renewed interest in meaningful ministry, in relevant worship, in faithful evangelism — but thrown in among it all is a base worldliness that has no place in worship, no place in the church, no place in following Jesus Christ.

Every time we take a step away from thinking about what we're doing in worship, from reflecting on our faith, from poring over the Scriptures, from remembering that we stand before a holy God, we are taking a step away from Jesus Christ. We're following Pilate out the door.

Not too long ago Pope John Paul II was criticized by the *National Catholic Reporter* for a recent encyclical because "he wants us all to live in the world of truth." But life cannot be like that, said the editor. Christ was "anything but absolute, putting up instead an umbrella big enough for everyone." He's half right there. Everyone is welcome, but not like that, not as they are, not apart from truth.

To come to Jesus means coming on our knees. It means bowing and listening. It means learning and thinking. To come to Jesus means giving up being fulfilled in order to be redeemed. Otherwise, we're just walking by him, with better things to do.

An Alien King

Text: Mark 11:1-10; 15:25-30

Then they brought the colt to Jesus and threw their cloaks on it; and he sat on it. Many people spread their cloaks on the road, and others spread leafy branches that they had cut in the fields. Then those who went ahead and those who followed were shouting, "Hosanna! Blessed is the one who comes in the name of the Lord! Blessed is the coming kingdom of our ancestor David! Hosanna in the highest heaven!" . . . It was nine o'clock in the morning when they crucified him. The inscription of the charge against him read, "The King of the Jews."

Mark 11:7-10; 15:25-26

For five Sundays we've been thinking about what it means to live by faith in Jesus Christ, how that faith distinguishes us in a world that is marked by unbelief, how it leaves us strangers. An important book that's helped me to think about these things and that I've mentioned to you in these weeks is *Resident Aliens,* by Stanley Hauerwas and William Willimon. In their chapter about politics they say that Christians in America, on both ends of the spectrum, usually go about it as if their job is to underwrite democracy and to increase justice, as if their job as the church is to make things here a little bit better.

And that idea is almost right; it could almost work. But then you get to Palm Sunday, and Palm Sunday takes place in Lent. If only it were a week after Easter, if only this coronation of Jesus Christ didn't lead to a cross, if only being his disciple were about positive thinking or being nice, then we could sign on to the way of life around us, then our mission could be to make a pretty good place a better one, then we could underwrite the status quo. But we can't. And Palm Sunday reminds us why.

It's an amazing day, of course, one that warms our hearts and almost makes us believe that maybe now somebody's got the idea, now Jesus is finally being recognized for who he is. This is how it's supposed to be. "Hosanna!" they say. Save us! "Blessed is he who comes in the name of the Lord!" This is a truly triumphal entry into Jerusalem, with crowds lining the streets, throwing their coats on the road in front of the donkey on which Jesus rides. All of them shouting, "Hosanna in the highest!" How glorious! How fitting that Jesus Christ's entry into the capital city of God's people should be such a grand event. How fitting that our Messiah should be welcomed into Jerusalem in a first-century version of a ticker-tape parade.

But of course that's the problem, because it doesn't fit. It doesn't really fit at all. Because this is Lent we're in. For five weeks we've reflected upon the fact that we are a journeying people following in the footsteps of a suffering Savior. We've watched from a distance as he set his face to go to Jerusalem, and we knew that he was setting his face not to go to a parade of palms but to go to a cross. All along we've known that the cross is where he's been headed. And, now here we are, on the brink of beginning Holy Week, at the entrance into Jerusalem, just a few days before the agony of being betrayed and tried and whipped and mocked and killed, and what do we find? We find a coronation. We find a royal welcome for the man who has come to the capital city to suffer many things.

It doesn't fit because the king has come to die in Jerusalem, not reign there. It doesn't fit because the journey to suffering is still going on; his face is still set. It doesn't fit because the next time he's labeled king of the Jews it'll be part of some joke hanging over his bloody head. Maybe these Palm Sunday disciples haven't caught onto anything. "Hosanna in the highest!" — it just doesn't fit.

And so the timing here makes us a bit uncomfortable, doesn't it? It's a little strange singing "Hosanna, Loud Hosanna" when we remember that it's a tomb, not a palace, in which he'll spend the weekend. There's something wrong with making Palm Sunday a junior Easter celebration, honoring Christ the king, when we know that this coronation will be completed with a crown of thorns. And it's hard not to wonder — both about their worship and about our own — when we read the crowd's shouts of "Hosanna" and "Blessed is he who comes in the name of the Lord" and know that a crowd just like this one a few hours from now is going to be shouting with just as much passion, "Crucify him!"

So what are we to make of this? How are we to view this royal welcome? Is it simply an aberration, an unplanned part of the journey? Did Jesus Christ, on his way to the cross, happen to find himself among Jewish folk in the mood for an inauguration? Did he go along with it because he knew how bad things were going to get and being king for a day sounded like a nice change of pace? Was this triumphal entry part of his plan, or not?

Mark says it was. Jesus initiates the whole thing. He tells his disciples about the colt, he puts himself on it, he begins the parade. It's all carefully planned. The triumphal entry is part of his journey. Before he goes to the cross outside Jerusalem, he must be welcomed as a king in Jerusalem. Before he dies the death of an outlaw, he must be declared the king of God's people.

If Jesus Christ is an outlaw, then he dies alone, he dies for himself, and his death pays for his life. Not so, if he dies a king. If he dies a king, then he dies as a representative; he dies for his subjects, all of the ones who claim him as their head. The mystery of Palm Sunday is not that on Sunday Jesus is the popular choice to be king and on Friday he's one of Israel's Most Wanted. The mystery of Palm Sunday is that the king of God's people receives his coronation, on Sunday he accepts the declaration that he is the messiah, God's anointed one, and then as that king, as that messiah, he walks from the parade to the cross. He goes from the inauguration to his death, and he never stops being king.

Neither the crowd who honored Jesus Christ on Sunday nor the soldiers who nailed the charge above his head on Friday had much of an idea just how right they were. The crowd thought, "Maybe, finally, we have a deliverer, a king to drive out our enemies." When they shouted "Hosanna!" on Palm Sunday, when they shouted "Save us," it was the Roman corruption they had in mind, not their own. They were praising a messiah who was going to *kill* to save them; what they didn't realize is that they had so much more — they had a messiah who was going to *die* to save them.

Five days later the soldiers thought, "Here's just one more pretender for us to do away with, just like last week and the week before that — some clown who thought he could be the savior of the Jews. What a joke." And they nailed the joke on top of his cross: Jesus Christ, the King of the Jews. He'll be dead in three hours. They were sure that they had a king who was a fake because he ended up on a cross; what *they* didn't realize is that it was the King of kings they were nailing up there, and he had set his face toward that cross long before they got hold of him.

On Sunday and on Friday he is declared the King of the Jews, both in the triumphal entry and on the cross. And, even though both declarations are wrong, even though both of them miss just what kind of king he is, still the words of ignorant crowds and spiteful soldiers are absolutely right, because what he does on Palm Sunday, and on Maundy Thursday and on Good Friday, all of it he does as the king whom God has sent. He's the king riding into Jerusalem on that donkey, he's the king when he's spit on by Pilate's soldiers, he's the king when he's left to die a cursed death, and he is the king on Sunday morning when he's not in the tomb.

The mystery isn't, how does he go from being celebrated as a king to being damned as a criminal? The mystery is, what kind of king is inaugurated to die? What kind of king takes a parade to his crucifixion? What kind of king is Jesus Christ?

Palm Sunday is no contradiction. Jesus Christ is the king of God's people whether all of Jerusalem knows it or just a few stragglers waving at a donkey. He is the king of God's people whether he's the recipient of glory, laud, and honor or whether he's the target of mockery. And we may sing "Hosanna, Loud Hosanna" with joy, because we are acknowledging our king, and we are shouting to him "Hosanna, save us." We may sing, as long as we know that, five days after Palm Sunday, he did just that — he saved us. Five days later, with the colt and the palms a distant memory, he went on another kind of parade altogether, one in which he was bleeding and tired and carrying the instrument of his death. And there was shouting along that route, too. But this time no one was saying, "Blessed is he who comes in the name of the Lord."

That's the mystery of Palm Sunday, not how it doesn't fit into Holy Week, but how well it does. The mystery is that the king of glory could enter the city of his people and be put to death there. The mystery is that the same ones who yelled so loudly "Hosanna!" could a few days later yell more loudly "Crucify him" and not realize that they were yelling the same thing.

Filled with love for his people, he was willing to die in their place. He was so moved by the human cry, "Hosanna — save us," that he refused to "come down from the cross and save" himself. That's the kind of king he is — like no other, belonging to a different world, raising up a different kind of people.

And that brings us back to Willimon and Hauerwas and the church. Hauerwas and Willimon remember a time a few years ago when the National Council of Churches proclaimed one week in October "Peace with Justice Week." To help celebrate this week, the Council sent member congregations a "Peace with Justice" poster. The poster depicted a globe held aloft by a group of different-colored human hands. Willimon and Hauerwas hate that poster. It's a beautiful idea, an idea no one can object to, but it has nothing to do with Jesus Christ.

Hauerwas and Willimon say that words like "peace and justice" and "right to life" and almost all of the other favorite Christian slogans "are words awaiting content. The church doesn't really know what they mean apart from the life and death of Jesus of Nazareth. After all, Pilate permitted the killing of Jesus in order to secure both peace and justice (Roman style) in Judea. It is Jesus' story that gives content to our faith, and teaches us to be suspicious of any slogan that does not need God to make itself credible."[12]

If our king were like other kings and presidents and prime ministers, it might work. If Jesus Christ were a regular king, then "Peace with Justice Week" would work and being a Christian in this land would be as simple as voting Republican or Democrat. But he's not regular; *he* was inaugurated to die. *His* crown made him bleed. Palm Sunday is no contradiction, but it still doesn't fit because he's an alien king and we're an alien people.

So we praise this king with "Hosanna!" and "All glory!" but, when we do, we do it as he receives it — looking straight at the cross and knowing that that changes everything. The cross is a sign of what happens when you take God's account of reality more seriously than Caesar's. When you refuse to underwrite the status quo and instead proclaim, "Jesus is Lord!" then you believe that to find your life you must lose it. We are a community of the cross, strangers in a world that thinks only suckers end up on crosses. And being marked by a cross has a lot to do with dying, dying to the ways of the world, dying to other kingdoms, dying to accomplishment and success and status. But when Jesus Christ is your king, you don't stay dead for very long.

Blessed is the strange king who comes in the name of the Lord. And blessed are all those who belong to him.

12. Hauerwas and Willimon, *Resident Aliens,* p. 38.

EASTER

The First Word

Text: John 20:1-18

When she had said this, she turned around and saw Jesus standing there, but she did not know that it was Jesus. Jesus said to her, "Woman, why are you weeping? Whom are you looking for?" Supposing him to be the gardener, she said to him, "Sir, if you have carried him away, tell me where you have laid him, and I will take him away." Jesus said to her, "Mary!" She turned and said to him in Hebrew, "Rabbouni!" (which means Teacher). Jesus said to her, "Do not hold on to me, because I have not yet ascended to the Father. But go to my brothers and say to them, 'I am ascending to my Father and your Father, to my God and your God.'"

John 20:14-17

"Mary." It doesn't sound right. It's not the way you would expect someone who has been put to death and now come back to life to spread the news. And it's certainly not the way you would expect the Son of God to inaugurate his kingdom. You would expect, if you thought about it, an earthquake or a peal of thunder that stretches across every continent. And then, once he had everybody's attention, you would expect something majestic, something kingly, like a proclamation about who's running things now, or at least some lengthy prison terms for the scribes and Pharisees. You would expect some grand declaration of victory, some floating in the heavens where everybody could see him, some glorious return from the dead, something fantastic that would preempt all regular programming.

After all, just two days ago he said before the world — at least as much of the world as was still hanging around when he died — "It is finished," it's *over*, and he gave up his spirit. He was wrapped up in grave clothes and carried off to the cemetery and dropped in a tomb and sealed up there for eternity. He was dead — really dead, physically dead, a whole weekend's worth of dead. And, after all that, now he's back. He survived his own execution — and not by a last-minute pardon or some overturned conviction. He took the best shot his enemies could muster; he descended into hell.

But now, today, Sunday morning, the stone is rolled away, the tomb is open, the body's gone. We're so used to it that we can take for granted what actually happened here: an amazing, impossible, wondrous, world-changing event.

So, one really strange part of the story of the resurrection is that the whole thing happens as quietly as it does. Jesus doesn't burst the walls of the tomb with lightning bolts, while a voice out of heaven declares that Jesus is Lord. Instead, the resurrected Christ presents himself to the world by slipping in on an old friend who can't even make him out through the tears in her eyes.

"Mary," he says. And it doesn't sound right. Because, if he's going to do it this way, if he's going to show himself to the world one person at a time, it's the more famous disciples you'd expect him to begin with. And they're in this scene, too, of course. Peter and John, the disciple Jesus loved, have been with him from the beginning, were handpicked to follow him, and will soon be leaders of his church; they're at the tomb, too, and they're not like Mary Magdalene. They're not sitting off to the side weeping, sobbing, wondering what in the world to do next, because her whole world was crucified on Friday and stolen this morning. Peter and John are men of action. They run up to the entrance and see the clothes of a corpse, but no corpse. Peter runs inside and sees the head wrap but no head, and the cloth folded up, like somebody put it away, like it won't be needed anymore. And then at least one of them begins to put things together. One of them realizes the marvelous thing he's looking at and believes.

So, if Jesus is going to be making an entrance at all this morning, why doesn't he do it now, with his enthusiastic, believing disciples to welcome him? Why doesn't he show himself with them there, saying their names: "Peter," "John." Why does he wait until they leave to present himself? Why does he wait for Mary? It doesn't sound right.

But that's what he does. He chooses Mary to hear the message first; he chooses Mary to be the first witness of the resurrection; he chooses Mary to be the first one to lay eyes on the amazing thing God has done. He chooses her in spite of the fact that she's a woman and not a man, in spite of the fact that, in this culture, she's a vulnerable person, a second-class person, a person whose gender alone makes her unworthy of such attention. But gender never stands in Jesus' way. So he says it: "Mary."

And he chooses her in spite of the life that this Mary has lived and the rumors that fly around her. The word in the church about Mary Magdalene for the past nineteen centuries is that she was a prostitute. We don't know for sure about that, of course, because that's only rumor, that's only what people whispered behind her back. We know only that Mary Magdalene was possessed, driven by Satan, or at least some of his flunkies — seven of them, to be exact. Apparently, she's been in Jesus' following since the day he delivered her from those devils. But there are no two ways about it — Mary Magdalene is a woman with a past, a past that makes her unworthy to be the first one who sees him alive.

Yet, this is the person to whom the resurrected, triumphant Christ appears, a woman with tears streaming down her face, a woman so lost in her grief that she doesn't even seem to wonder about the two angels sitting in his tomb, a woman so caught up in sorrow that her only thought is that somebody has added insult to injury, has come along and taken the body, as if they didn't mock him enough when he was alive. Mary's thought is that her Rescuer, her teacher, her friend, who yesterday was just dead, is now dead and gone, and she has to get him back.

She never even considers that maybe something else has happened here. She doesn't consider that maybe the miracle of miracles has taken place, maybe he's alive. She doesn't have the faith of John, the disciple who looks into the same tomb she looks into and realizes that something is up, that good news is on the way, that Jesus doesn't need a tomb anymore. Mary doesn't look at it that way; she doesn't look at him that way. She doesn't believe. Not like that. In so many ways she is unworthy to hear him speak her name. But it doesn't matter: "Mary" is still the name he speaks.

And somehow that name is the beginning of everything. Until that moment he's only the gardener to her, somebody who might be able to help locate the body. Until that moment her tears are still flowing and her heart is still breaking. But then the resurrected Jesus speaks his first word: "Mary." And then she knows — her name on his lips again is all that it takes. She knows: her day of mourning is over, her meaning is restored, her Savior is alive. All it took was "Mary." With that word Jesus Christ announces himself as risen. With that word he presents himself to the world. "Mary": it doesn't sound right. It's not what we'd expect. But that's how we get the news: the stone is rolled away, death has been defeated, Jesus Christ is alive!

Mary has him back. "Rabbouni," she says. Just like old times. A new lease on life — for him *and* for her. And all Mary Magdalene can do is hold on to him, as if he's about to leave again, as if she might lose him again. But that's all wrong. That will happen in its own way later. But now isn't the time for good-byes. Now is the time for good news. Now is the time to let the others know what one word from him announced to Mary.

It still doesn't sound right. But there's no time to think about that now. Because, instead of talking and embracing and celebrating, there's a message that Mary has to take. And it's not just that he's alive, it's not just that her *Rabbouni* is back. The message that cannot wait, the message that Mary must take to Peter and John and all of the other disciples who haven't seen him yet, the message that Jesus trusts to Mary, is this: "I am ascending to my Father and your Father, to my God and your God." I died on a cross, I was sealed in a tomb, but now I'm alive. Celebrate that. But there's more than that to celebrate. Because now, Mary, now I'm not just *Rabbouni* to you. I'm not back — I'm going to my Father. And because of my cross, because of my death, because of my life, he's your Father, too. He's your God, too. Tell them that. Tell them the good news. Tell them, Mary.

Maybe the opening word of resurrection is "Mary" because it is all the unworthy ones like Mary that he died for in the first place. The opening word of resurrection is "Mary" because the message he gives her is a message first of all for her, a message that when he returns to his Father, it's not just his Father he's returning to. Maybe she doesn't have the same Jesus; maybe she doesn't have her *Rabbouni* anymore. But she has a living Lord and she has a Father, and both of them know her name.

I don't know what demons are rattling around in your past. I don't know what makes you unworthy of having your name spoken by Jesus Christ. I don't know what counts you out as Mary was counted out by her gender and her history and maybe even a shortness of her faith. But I know that no one who comes looking for the Savior is left at the tomb. I know that he knows your name. And in that one word lies your whole future, your whole world. But do you know who's saying it? Do you know that it's more than a teacher, more than a *Rabbouni*? Do you know that it is the Lord of all, who was dead and is now alive? Do you know that things are forever different, forever changed today? Now is the time for good news, for telling the others. If you don't know that, if you don't know what's changed, if you don't know that now the world is a new place, then this day has no meaning for you, because the resurrection of Jesus Christ has not become real for you.

He took off his grave clothes, he left his tomb, and he comes to Mary Magdalene in all of her tears, and he says her name, because he cares, because he lives for her as much as for any of the others, because he wants her to hope again. He wants *her* to live, too.

Short on faith, troubled by demons, the wrong kind of person — Mary, me, you. Mary is standing in for you outside the tomb. She's standing in for all of us. We just need to recognize who's calling. See through your tears. See Jesus, who was dead and now is alive. Then take your cue from Mary and do what he says, because you have seen the Lord. And your message from him is wondrous: the Father he returned to is his Father and *our* Father, the God receiving him to heaven will receive us. Take hope.

He knows the names of his disciples. None of their pasts sparkle; none of them is worthy. But it doesn't matter. Because his Father is our Father, and his God is our God. Because the kingdom of Jesus Christ doesn't begin with an announcement to the world of his Lordship; it doesn't begin with his appearing to the best or the brightest of his disciples. It begins when he says the name "Mary" and he makes Mary's tears go away. And it continues every time some follower of Jesus Christ is threatened again by hell or death, and there are more tears. Because then, even today, he speaks that disciple's name and receives her into his kingdom — the kingdom of his Father and her Father, his God and her God.

"Mary." It doesn't sound right. But it couldn't sound any better.

One Thing Left to Say

Text: Psalm 150

Praise the Lord!
Praise God in his sanctuary;
*   praise him in his mighty firmament!*
Praise him for his mighty deeds;
*   praise him according to his surpassing greatness!*
Praise him with trumpet sound;
*   praise him with lute and harp!*
Praise him with tambourine and dance;
*   praise him with strings and pipe!*
Praise him with clanging cymbals;
*   praise him with loud clashing cymbals!*

Let everything that breathes praise the Lord!
Praise the Lord!

Psalm 150

As I was thinking about this wonderful summons to praise the Lord that is our text for this morning, I happened to catch some footage of the aftermath of the bombing of the Alfred P. Murrah Federal Building in Oklahoma City, Oklahoma. I wasn't paying much attention but was thinking mostly on this sermon; the events in Oklahoma were only the backdrop then as I reflected on the words of Psalm 150: "Praise God in his sanctuary. . . . Praise him for his mighty deeds . . . praise him with lute and harp." Then I was thinking about that last verse, the summary verse of the psalm, the thrust of the psalm — "Let everything that breathes praise the Lord" — and for some reason right then I happened to glance back at the television screen, and I saw a woman being carried on a stretcher, away from the bombing. She was bloody and dirty and, most noticeably, she was breathing. Her breathing was most noticeable, I say, because her breaths were not the simple, subconscious actions we associate with the word *breathe*. These breaths were burdensome; they required the movement of most of her body if they were going to happen at all. Her entire torso nearly raised off the stretcher and then reclined into it with every single second, every single breath. This breathing was anything but subconscious or simple; it came hard, and it came painful.

And that is when I realized just how monumental, how radical is this simple psalm. That is when I understood what an extraordinary thing it is to say, "Let everything that breathes praise the Lord." Because everything that has breath also has wounds. Everything that has breath also has burdens. Everything that has breath also has grief, so that, sometimes, even the breathing is no small task. Yet there it is, the last word in the psalms: an unqualified, absolute, universal call for everything that breathes to praise God.

So it appears that the word of the Lord this morning is not only a call for us to praise him but also a summons for the residents of Kosovo to praise him. It appears that not only are those feeling especially good today to praise God but even those whose lives have been shattered this week by a bomb or an army or a diagnosis. *All* of us are to praise the Lord. After all, there are no caveats attached to Psalm 150 about grief or suffering, no exceptions listed for victims of mass violence, no conditions put in about when things are going especially well. All we have here is a call to get out the drums, strike up the band, and praise the Lord if there is still breath within you.

If this were the only psalm, it would make things even harder in Kosovo and Oklahoma City and the funeral home. Because if this were the only psalm, then the only way to speak of God, to think about God, to reflect upon God would be praise. If Psalm 150 were the entire book of Psalms, then "Praise the Lord" would be the response for every circumstance, for every occasion, for every experience, for every place. No matter what.

But, of course, Psalm 150 is not the only psalm. It's not the whole book of Psalms. It's only the last psalm. And we should never read just the last of anything. Psalm 150 is the last word in the prayer book of God's people. But before that have come a lot of other words. Before that in the psalms we read things like, "O Lord, how many are my foes! How many rise up against me! Answer me when I call to you, O my righteous God. Give me relief from my distress." Or, "O Lord, do not rebuke me in your anger or discipline me in your wrath." Other psalms say to God, "My God, my God, why have you forsaken me?" Or, "You have taken my companions and loved ones from me; the darkness is my closest friend." The psalms say all of that before they say, "Let everything that breathes praise the Lord."

You see, Psalm 150 comes from a people that knows what it means to suffer, to sin, to bleed, to mourn, and then to tell God about it. Psalm 150 is written by a people whose history is full of terrible problems: sinfulness and corruption, death and bloodshed, pain and rebellion, revenge and hatred. And those problems are a big part of the psalms that lead up to Psalm 150. So this call to praise the Lord is not spoken by somebody who doesn't know how bad things get, how bad they are. The psalmists know.

And the funny thing is that, by the end of the book, they're not any better off than they were earlier. It's not as if, by the time Psalm 150 was written, everything wrong in Judah had been cleaned up or set right or destroyed. Life isn't any happier at the last psalm than it is at the first one: their country is split in two; much of their land has been lost; many of them have been carried off into exile; and the future looks pretty bleak. The problems aren't gone by the time we get to the end of the book of Psalms. But the last word that's written is not a word about trouble or pain or guilt. It's a word about praise — praise to the Lord.

One thing that you have to understand about the psalms is that even the really grim ones, even the ones that sound as if God is part of the problem, every one of them is written while looking at God. No matter how low the psalmist gets, he does not take his eyes off God. And, if you keep your eyes on God long enough, you will get to Psalm 150. You will get to the point of praise. It doesn't necessarily happen overnight, it doesn't necessarily come easily, it doesn't necessarily mean that everything's right with your world. It means only that, if you keep your eyes on God, if you realize what he's about, if you recognize the wounds on his hands and the hole in his side, it will lead to praise. So, whatever else the psalmists have gone through, whatever else they have felt, whatever they have suffered and hated and ruined, in the end there is still one thing left to say: "Praise the Lord. Let everything that breathes praise the Lord."

So it makes sense that the lectionary assigns Psalm 150 to us on the Sunday after Easter. It's not because the arrival of Easter has changed everything, not because the arrival of Easter has removed the corruption and sin and suffering from our world so that there's nothing else to say but "Praise the Lord." The evening news and our own lives certainly show us that. The truth is that Easter Sunday doesn't make any difference that way. The problems that were here last week are all still here this morning, and in fact some of them have gotten worse, as we know. But that is not the point.

The point is that we who know Easter know God. We who know Easter know the great things he has done. We who know Easter know his power, not only the power of creation but the power of the cross. We who know Easter know that those scars on his hands and that hole in his side could only be the product of love. We know that the Lord of the universe is actually our Father. And when all is said and done, we who know him, we who know this God, must respond in praise. For us, in the end, there is one thing left to say: "Praise the Lord. Let everything that breathes praise the Lord."

So, in spite of the tragedy and suffering around us and within us, it is not shameful or artificial for us to be here today. It is not a shameful thing to sing "A Shout Rings Out, a Joyful Voice." It is not wrong for us here to praise the Lord on this Sunday after Easter in spite of what we have witnessed this week. As a matter of fact, maybe it is necessary. Because we who know this God know that, in spite of appearances, the real Lord of the universe is a Lord whose greatness is surpassing, whose love is unfailing, whose goodness never ends. And so we still can say, even now, even with wars and bombs and accidents on our minds, "Praise the Lord." We still can take Sunday morning to tell the Lord that he is God, that it is he who made us and we are his. We still can worship with some joy. And we should.

In one of his books, the Catholic churchman Richard John Neuhaus talks about an incident in Brooklyn, New York, a time when some of the inner-city pastors chose as their focus that year "liturgical renewal." They were out to make worship in the inner-city vital again. Well, an official from the diocese was terribly upset by the choice of worship as their year's focus. "Here you are surrounded by bombed-out housing, a school system that is a criminal exercise in dis-education, youth unemployment of forty percent, and children's lives devastated by drugs, and you're going to escape into 'liturgical renewal'?" he demanded. "Why don't you do something that makes a difference in the real world?"[1]

The "real world." He should have known better. The real world is not a world of poverty and war, drugs and bombs. Those things are intruders; they're trespassers; they don't belong here. The real world is the world in which the Lord is king. The real world is the one in which life has the final say. The real world is the one in which power and goodness work together to save lives, not take them. The real world is the world in which everything that breathes praises the Lord.

And so we are never more real than when we gather in worship. And we are never more accurate about the way the world really is than when we sing our hymns and offer our prayers and hear from God's Word as if he is the ruler of the universe. We are never more aware of what is really going on than when we move our problems and our fears and our pain out of the center of life and bring praise to the Lord. And we need to be here every week to remind ourselves of just what it is that is real. We need to gather like this to remember that, whatever else we have felt, whatever else we have suffered and hated and ruined, at the end of the day, there is still one thing left to say. "Praise the Lord. Let everything that has breath praise the Lord."

But what does this all mean for those whose breathing comes so hard, whose every inhale requires a full day's work? What do we say to that woman on my television screen? If I'm her friend or her nurse or her pastor, do I read Psalm 150 to her? Do I call her to praise the Lord, to say "Hallelujah" as she gasps for breath? No, of course not. And those who give advice like that in funeral homes and hospital rooms, those who claim that pain is the will of God, they don't know very well the God who has scars of his own. No, Psalm 150 is for another time. On days like that day in Oklahoma City, it is a time to weep.

But that weeping is not the last word; that time does not last forever. And those of us who act as though it does are focused too much on our-

1. Richard John Neuhaus, *Freedom for Ministry* (San Francisco: Harper & Row, 1979), p. 233.

selves and not enough on our God. Because, if we look upon him long enough, we will echo Psalm 150 and call all the world to join us in praising the Lord. And so one day, even someone whose breathing comes hard right now, even someone whose own prayer is stuck in a much darker psalm, one day I would hope even she would say, with you and with me:

> Hallelujah!
> Praise God in his holy house of worship,
>   praise him under the open skies;
> Praise him for his acts of power,
>   praise him for his magnificent greatness;
> Praise him with a blast on the trumpet,
>   praise him by strumming soft strings;
> Praise him with castanets and dance,
>   praise him with banjo and flute;
> Praise him with cymbals and a big bass drum,
>   praise him with fiddles and mandolin.
> Let every living, breathing creature praise Yahweh!
> Hallelujah!

Amen.

Resurrecting Peter

Text: John 21:15-25

When they had finished breakfast, Jesus said to Simon Peter, "Simon son of John, do you love me more than these?" He said to him, "Yes, Lord; you know that I love you." Jesus said to him, "Feed my lambs." A second time he said to him, "Simon son of John, do you love me?" He said to him, "Yes, Lord; you know that I love you." Jesus said, "Tend my sheep." He said to him the third time, "Simon son of John, do you love me?" Peter felt hurt because he said to him the third time, "Do you love me?" And he said to

*him, "Lord, you know everything; you know that I love you." Jesus said
to him, "Feed my sheep. Very truly, I tell you, when you were younger, you
used to fasten your own belt and go wherever you wished. But when you
grow old, you will stretch out your hands, and someone else will fasten a
belt around you and take you where you do not wish to go." (He said this
to indicate the kind of death by which he would glorify God.) After this he
said to him, "Follow me."*

John 21:15-19

In his book *Not the Way It's Supposed to Be,* Neal Plantinga at one point talks
about how we human beings prefer not to notice our sin.[2] We mask it from
the world's view; we deceive ourselves into believing that we've really done
nothing wrong; we explain our actions as necessary or "for the best." We
muster every conceivable excuse, we spend our entire defense budget on
this one enemy — just so we can avoid seeing ourselves for what we really
are. And that, to me, makes perfect sense.

Ian Bedloe is a normal young man in an especially cheery family in
Anne Tyler's novel *Saint Maybe.* His mind at seventeen years old is full of
hope and expectation concerning his college life, his career options, and
his girlfriend. Ian's brother, Danny, is in a very different position. He's recently married to a young woman named Lucy; he is blissfully happy, even
though he's just taken on the responsibility of Lucy's two children, and
there's one more on the way. The trouble is that Ian sees right through
Lucy. He sees that she's playing Danny for a fool, a chump who will work
long hours to pay the bills while she dallies behind his back.

Well, one evening after Ian has had to take care of the kids himself
and his own plans for the night have been ruined and his frustration with
Danny's ignorance of what's really going on here is at an all-time high, he
explodes at his brother. He tells him the whole sordid affair — about
Lucy's infidelity, about his being used, about the fool he is being played
for all the world to see. Danny — stunned, hurt, uncertain — leaves to go
home. At least that's what Ian thinks Danny is doing. A moment later he
hears Danny's car accelerating wildly toward the brick wall at the end of
their street. Another second, then the crash.

Ian is devastated by this turn of events. He learns that he was wrong
about Lucy, he learns that he misunderstood the situation. He knows that
he said those things to his brother because his own evening wasn't what

2. Cornelius Plantinga Jr., *Not the Way It's Supposed to Be: A Breviary of Sin* (Grand
Rapids: Eerdmans, 1995), pp. 105-12.

he had hoped. And so now Danny is dead. And Ian is left with the terrible knowledge of what brought it about. Ian is left with what he has done.

It makes perfect sense to hide our sin from ourselves as much as anyone else, because it is a devastating thing to be left with what we have done, to see sin in us unadorned by justifications, reasons, extenuating circumstances, or some tripe about what everybody else does. It is a devastating thing to know that we chose a selfish course, that we did what we did because it was easier or it was more fun, because we were more interested in our own pleasure or saving our skin than in anything or anybody else. It is a devastating thing to look in the mirror and see someone who has betrayed God. It is a devastating thing to be Ian Bedloe. And today it is a devastating thing to be the disciple Peter.

We don't hear much in John's Gospel about how Peter felt or what he did after his denial of Jesus. We don't read that he ran off and wept bitterly or that he felt great shame or that he tried to make up for it. All we read in John's Gospel is what happened around those denials: we read that, when disciples were abandoning him and Jesus asked the twelve if they would leave too, it was Peter who spoke up, "Lord, to whom can we go? You have the words of eternal life." And when Jesus was washing his disciples' feet, it was Peter who spoke up, first to resist such a service from Jesus, then to ask that his whole body be washed by him. When Jesus spoke of his going away the night before he died, when the other disciples were growing quiet, we read that it was Peter who proclaimed, "I will lay down my life for you." We read of Peter reaching out with his sword and Peter running into the tomb. We read of Peter in front of the faithful, showing the way.

Except outside of the high priest's office while Jesus was on trial. Just a few hours after he said he would die with Jesus, here he is, standing in the high priest's courtyard, saying, "I don't know the man. I'm not one of them. He's not my Lord." And — that fast — all of that faith, all of that loyalty, all of those good ideas and great intentions and courageous moments are voided by the wrong answer to a slave girl's question, voided by a lie to protect himself, voided by sin. Peter is no longer the faithful disciple, leading everybody else. Now he's just as lost and soiled and needy as the rest. And there's no way to mask it, no way to justify it, no way to pretend it's otherwise.

After Jesus' death we read that Peter runs past John right into the tomb to see what had happened. And, a few verses ago in chapter 21, we learn that Jesus motioned to the disciples in their boat while Jesus was on the shore, and immediately Peter leapt into the water. He's still out in front, still aching to serve, but now he's also a denier. Now his sin is before him, wherever he goes. Now there is something between Peter and Jesus.

The moment Jesus met this man, twenty chapters and three years ago, he said to him, "You are Simon, son of John. You will be called Peter." And, for twenty chapters and three years, when Jesus speaks to him, he calls him Peter — until this morning. Now it's Simon again: "Simon, son of John, do you love me more than these?" Now everything is in doubt. Now Peter is Simon, now the question to the disciple who has always been so quick to claim that he is loyal to Jesus, that he will die with him, even if no one else will, now the question to him is, "*Do* you love me more than these?"

But that's not the route Peter takes anymore. He used to talk about what he would do for Jesus as opposed to what others would do. He used to make big statements about how much he loved Jesus, but not anymore. Now Peter says, "Yes, Lord; *you* know that I love you." "Do you, Simon?" "Yes, Lord; you know that I love you." "Simon, do you love me?" Three times Jesus asks, and to hear him ask again hurts Peter, but once more he answers, "Lord, you know all things; you know that I love you."

And that's it: Simon is restored. Simon is Peter again. And Peter goes off to Pentecost. Peter goes off to feed Jesus' sheep. Jesus goes to be with his Father. The church will be built on a rock that crumbled before a slave girl. But it's a rock that belongs to Jesus.

And that's just it. The whole thing depends on Jesus. It's not about what Peter has done or how often he did it; it's not about whether Peter can live up to his boasts; it's not about whether Peter is worthy to feed Jesus' lambs. Peter's resurrection from denying his Lord depends only on Jesus; Peter's resurrection from dying in sin depends only on Jesus' resurrection; Peter's resurrection from his devastation depends only on whether he belongs to Jesus. "Do you love me?" Even that is up to Jesus: "Lord, you know all things; you know that I love you." And so he does. Jesus does know: "Feed my sheep, Peter." Jesus knows that Peter loves him, but loving Jesus isn't easy.

> "I tell you the truth, when you were younger you dressed yourself and went where you wanted; but when you are old you will stretch out your hands, and someone else will dress you and lead you where you do not want to go." Jesus said this to indicate the kind of death by which Peter would glorify God. Then he said to him, "Follow me!"

Loving Jesus means following a man with a cross. It means dying to what you used to be, what you'd like to be, what you're expected to be. It means taking the name Christ has given you. It means being Peter, not Simon. And that is hard. But there is no other way to resurrection. It all depends on whether you're with Jesus or not. Loving him means following him.

Ian Bedloe tries everything to be restored, to find peace of mind. He looks for a way out of his guilt for the words that ruined his brother and his family. Twice Ian thinks he finds his forgiveness in church, once in a Presbyterian service where the minister talks about the healing balm of God's mercy. Ian feels forgiven, but it doesn't last; it is just too simple, too easy, he thinks. A while later, he comes across a storefront church, the Church of the Second Chance. The minister there tells Ian that his forgiveness comes by making up for what he's done, by putting the wrong right, by making his own life a replacement for his brother's. Ian spends years doing just that. But he never believes he's done enough. He never believes God has finally forgiven him for the past, because he hasn't made up for the past.

And both times Ian is right. A declaration of pardon isn't enough to take the blood off his hands. But neither is a lifetime of scrubbing. What Ian is missing, in both cases, is Jesus. He's missing the question, Do you love me? And he's missing the life, and the death, that go with that love.

It is a devastating thing to see your sin with the pretense removed, with the make-up off. It is a devastating thing to face that what I did yesterday, or last week, or last year — or all three — can go by no other name, has no extenuating circumstances, is not justifiable. It is simply misery-producing, guilt-attaching, life-destroying, Christ-denying sin. But facing that devastation is necessary and recognizing our failure must happen; otherwise we remain in the world of self-deception, and we continue to believe that we're earning our way. Giving up our boasts and clinging to Jesus is the way to resurrection, *our* resurrection. By ourselves we'll always be Simon, son of John; he makes us Peter.

And so it's his resurrection that resurrects us. It's his resurrection that declares that Peter's career doesn't matter anymore. It's his resurrection that declares that it's not Peter's faithfulness that determines the future; it's Jesus'. It's his resurrection that takes Simon and turns him into Peter, the Rock upon whom a holy people will stand. By the power of the resurrection, Peter is forgiven. By the power of the resurrection, Peter has a future tending his Lord's sheep. By the power of the resurrection, Peter lives. It's all by the grace of God. It's all because Jesus gave him a new name, and he died so Peter could keep it.

So, by the grace of God, Peter goes on from here to lay the foundation of Jesus' church. The Rock upon which Jesus would build couldn't stand up to the challenge of a slave girl. He's a rock because Jesus makes him one. He's a rock by the grace of God.

That's hard for us to accept. We like to earn our way. We like to resurrect ourselves. We like to deserve our role in the kingdom. But then, when the cock crows and we see *our* denials — lies to improve our standing, lust to satisfy our libido, anger because we'd rather humiliate than forgive — then, when we see how *we* have failed, there is no place to turn, there is no way out — Simon can't name himself Peter.

But Jesus can. Jesus can resurrect a disciple who has failed miserably. He can use a rock that's crumbled. And that may be the most amazing part of all: now, after Peter blew his chance to stand behind all those big things he said — to be the one who would even *die* with Jesus — now, after he failed, his words will still come true. He will die for his Lord. He will be the Rock. And he will share in the resurrection. Through Jesus Christ, Amen.

— FOURTH SUNDAY OF EASTER —

Leaving before the Benediction

Texts: Matthew 5:21-24; Micah 6:6-8

"You have heard that it was said to those of ancient times, 'You shall not murder'; and 'whoever murders shall be liable to judgment.' But I say to you that if you are angry with a brother or sister, you will be liable to judgment; and if you insult a brother or sister, you will be liable to the council; and if you say, 'You fool,' you will be liable to the hell of fire. So when you are offering your gift at the altar, if you remember that your brother or sister has something against you, leave your gift there before the altar and go; first be reconciled to your brother or sister, and then come and offer your gift."

Matthew 5:21-24

"With what shall I come before the Lord,
  and bow myself before God on high?
Shall I come before him with burnt offerings,
  with calves a year old?
Will the Lord be pleased with thousands of rams,
  with ten thousands of rivers of oil?
Shall I give my firstborn for my transgression,
  the fruit of my body for the sin of my soul?"
He has told you, O mortal, what is good;
  and what does the Lord require of you
but to do justice, and to love kindness,
  and to walk humbly with your God?

Micah 6:6-8

I know someone with a disability. You can't see much wrong with her, but there's a frailty in her bones that makes it difficult for her to walk and to keep her balance and to hold on to things. And it only gets worse. I know her because she's been part of the same church community that I've been part of. She also belongs to a Christian Reformed Church; she attended the same large Christian school that I went to; in every way she was a very normal part of that community. Except, of course, for the disease in her bones. That made her different. That made her stand out sometimes. The time that I'm remembering today happened many years ago, when she was fourteen, or maybe fifteen, years old.

Every day this young woman would ride the bus to school, eight miles. And every day she would struggle to hold on to the seat in front of her as the school bus sped up and slowed down and made its turns, especially as it wound its way down an exit ramp leaving the freeway. And every day, or maybe it just seemed like every day, as the bus went through the curves of that ramp, the bus driver, a longtime member of that community himself, would yell toward the back of the bus, "Watch her fall, boys. Watch her fall." And when she did fall, as she almost always did, there would be laughter, and pain.

Neal Plantinga has said that, if a parent sees their child mocked just one time, they never forget it. In this situation, when an adult, a brother in Christ, whose role it was to protect children, actually pulled the trigger, leading the way in the ridicule, it's hard to imagine that parents could forgive, let alone forget; in this situation of such cruelty, it's hard to imagine that parents could ever let go of the anger toward a sadistic school bus driver. And I don't know that any of us would expect them to.

I don't think the people of Jesus' day would expect them to lose that anger either. In Jesus' day the popular theology had it that obedience to God meant obedience to the moral laws of the Hebrew Scriptures. So, especially if you were Jewish to begin with, you could be sure of your salvation, you could be spared the judgment of God, by doing God's commandments, especially the Ten Commandments, things like not taking the name of the Lord your God in vain, not stealing, not committing adultery, and, of course, not killing. Those are the lines that we are not to cross, they believed. Stay within those lines, and you will do well; you will avoid judgment, and you will live.

And that may just be the biggest problem between the Jews and Jesus: they think of religion as a behavior; Jesus thinks of religion as a relationship. So they say, "If I do these things, then God cannot touch me, then I will not be judged, then I am pure." Jesus says, "Unless your life is one of walking with God as Abraham walked with him, you cannot be pure; your behavior cannot save you; it will not be enough."

And, in this part of the Sermon on the Mount, Jesus shows them over and over that their behavior will never be enough. From adultery to divorce to oaths to murder, Jesus shows them that God wants more than their legal observance of his commandments; he wants their hearts. And if he doesn't have their hearts, then no amount of commandment-keeping is going to help them. "You have heard that it was said to those of ancient times, 'You shall not murder'; and 'whoever murders shall be liable to judgment.' But I say to you that if you are angry with a brother or sister, you will be liable to judgment."

Those are strange words to Jewish ears, at least to Jewish ears of the first century. They lived by their rules and regulations. They knew exactly how far you could travel on the Sabbath without breaking the commandment; they knew which behaviors brought judgment and which ones didn't; and there's no way someone whose religion is made up of behavior would expect parents whose daughter has been terrorized by one of their own to lose their anger, ever.

Erasmus wouldn't expect them to lose it, either. Those of you who remember your church history may recall Erasmus. He lived around the time of Martin Luther and was an important part of the Reformation, though he never actually left the Roman Catholic Church. One of Erasmus's most important contributions to Protestantism concerned the translation of the Bible. Erasmus insisted on going back to the Bible's original languages in order to translate them properly and understand what they're saying. And, of course, that's important work to do.

By looking closely at the Greek grammar of Matthew 5:22 we realize that, when Jesus says that anyone who is angry with his sister or brother will be subject to judgment, he doesn't mean that anyone who *gets* angry will be subject to judgment, he means that anyone who *stays* angry will be subject to judgment — anyone who carries their anger with them, who nurses it, who refuses to lay it down. So Jesus is talking about anyone who keeps on being angry. But that wasn't quite good enough for Erasmus.

Erasmus apparently thought Jesus was being a little bit too broad here, so in his edition of the New Testament he clarified Jesus a bit. He made Jesus' words a little bit easier to understand, a little bit easier to fit into our lives. In Erasmus' Bible there is one extra word in Matthew 5:22, a word which means "without a cause." So, according to Erasmus's version, the verse reads "Anyone who is angry with a brother or sister without a cause is subject to judgment." And that translation caught on so well that you can still find it in the King James Version today. So I think it's pretty unlikely that Erasmus would expect my friend's parents to let go of their anger.

But Jesus does. And we must be followers of Jesus and not Erasmus. We must define religion as Jesus did and not as an ordinary first-century Jewish person would have defined it. And so we must recognize that it's not our behavior God wants to own; it's our hearts. And when God owns the heart, we let go of the anger, even if we have a cause. We need to hear this today because there are a lot of behaviorists and a lot of Erasmians milling around the body of Christ, and the stakes are too high not to say something about them.

Not long ago a colleague of mine had a couple who were longtime members in his congregation turn on him. They attacked his character, they misreported his actions, they refused his hand; but they kept coming to church, so that they could remind him of what he had done to them. They heard words about reconciliation and forgiveness and all of that, but they weren't having any, because of the wrong they had endured. To them, the cause for their anger was so great that they were justified in bearing it for the rest of their lives and making sure there was hell to pay by others. According to Jesus, they had it all backwards.

Now, that's only one case; the sad thing is that there are so many like it. The sad thing is that I can report about so many other people, people that I'm not imagining or making up but people I know, who believe that, because their cause is good enough, they may guard their division; because they have a reason to be angry, they may nurse their grudge; because they are not at fault, they may refuse to come together. And to each one of them — and to each one of us who holds on to our anger toward a brother or sister for some holy reason — to all of us, Jesus says: Not good enough. If you are holding on to your anger, you are subject to judgment. As much cause as my friend and her parents have to take their grudge with them to the grave, Jesus Christ calls them not to do it, because they have a relationship with God. That's the point of these verses.

Here's the message for all of us who think that, if I just do the right things, God will save me, that it's okay to carry around a grudge if I just have enough reason for it. Here's the message of this entire passage: our relationships with each other affect our relationship with God. That's how Jesus can say, "So when you are offering your gift at the altar, if you remember that your brother or sister has something against you, leave your gift there before the altar and go; first be reconciled to your brother or sister, and then come and offer your gift."

Two things make those words striking. The first is that he doesn't say, If you're offering your gift and remember that *you* have something against your brother or sister. He says, If you remember that your brother or sister has something against you. The second thing that stands out here is the word he uses, *ti*. It's barely a syllable. It means something, anything, any little thing, any *ti*. In other words, it doesn't matter if it's my problem; it matters that there is a problem. And it doesn't matter if it's big; it matters if it's there. Our Lord is calling us, at the expense of our pride, at the expense of our rights, at the expense of our enjoying the anger, to make peace in his church. Otherwise we might as well not even bother to worship. Leave your gift at the altar, he says.

It's so human, for some reason, to believe that God can be bought. It's so natural to assume that he wants something *from* me, like a tender year-old calf or thousands of rams or my firstborn. But it's not behaviors, it's not sacrifices, it's not *things* that God wants. It's none of those, says Micah. God has showed us what he requires of us: to do justice, to love kindness, to walk humbly with him. What he wants is not behavior but relationship — relationship with others, relationship with him.

Jesus isn't saying that worship isn't important. When he says to leave your gift at the altar, he's not saying that worship doesn't matter, that all God wants from us is to treat each other well. What he means is much more ominous. What he means is, "Don't seek to speak to me if you're not willing to speak to your sister." "Don't come into my house thinking that your hymns or your prayers or your dollars will compensate for your attitude."

The custom in our denomination used to be that the Sunday before

Lord's Supper would be a time of preparation, and God's people would be called to examine themselves, to consider whether the gospel was really taking root in their lives. One thing right about that is the idea that, before we are united with our Lord in worship, before we come for communion with him, we must seek communion with each other. Before we take the sacrament, we should ask ourselves, Is my religion a series of behaviors like offering a few rams, or is it a humble walk with my God? Today, before we come to the Lord's table, let's ask questions like those. Not so that we'll leave before the benediction, but so that we'll set straight what's gotten pretty crooked. And, if you really think it doesn't matter or isn't important, read these words of Jesus one more time about the fire of hell and the judgment of God.

They don't get any stronger: *Don't speak to me, if you will not speak to your brother or sister.* According to Jesus, when we cut others off, God cuts us off. I think that's because people who hold on to anger, who savor a grudge, are people who don't know what it's like to walk with God. They know only about sacrificing rams. They know only about obeying laws and reading off commandments. They know only about getting what they deserve. So, says Jesus, that's exactly what they'll get.

Of course, when we hear these words from Matthew, if we're honest, few of us feel fit for worship because we fall so far short. We've held on to anger, we've sought revenge, we've had enemies. We still do. This is a message that can break our spirit and leave us mourning our weakness. But that is the joy of the gospel: our relationship with God, rather than our behavior, gives us a place. The God with whom we walk humbly is our Father, and he has made us stiff-necked people his children.

We *should* go to this supper humbled, sorrowful, mourning our divisions, looking for peace with each other, with everyone. And then we should remember that Jesus began this sermon with his benediction: "Blessed are the poor in spirit, for yours is the kingdom of heaven. Blessed are you who mourn, for you will be comforted. Blessed are the meek, for you will inherit the earth. . . . Blessed are you who seek peace, for you will be called children of God."

Yeast Changes Everything

Texts: Matthew 13:33; Micah 6:6-8

He told them another parable: "The kingdom of heaven is like yeast that a woman took and mixed in with three measures of flour until all of it was leavened."

Matthew 13:33

I thought the kingdom of heaven was like the Chicago Bulls — every once in a while there's a setback, a loss or two, but at the end of the year it's all the victories that stand out, all the success that's been had. That's what I thought about the kingdom. But then Arie Roodzant died.

Arie was a 61-year-old cattle farmer, a Dutch immigrant, who walked hunched over because of a disease in his legs. He didn't say much, and when he did speak he was so soft you could hardly hear him. He died one day on the edge of his farm while getting water for his animals. It was sudden and unexpected, but yet somehow fitting, because he died in the presence of his best friend, a three-year-old Scottish terrier named Rambo, and those he spent the most time with, his white Charolais cows. That was Arie's life. And that's why, at first, I didn't know what to say at his funeral.

Funerals, after all, are a time to talk about accomplishments. They're a time to look back upon all the progress that's been made, all the ways the kingdom of God has extended its reign through this person. But there wasn't much of that to talk about for Arie. There weren't any heroic acts or decades of service to a church that wouldn't have made it without him; he didn't convert friends or strangers to Jesus Christ; his family life was a struggle. So I didn't know what to say. Because the life that we were remembering that day was a quiet life and a painful life. It wasn't a spectacular life or a successful life. It wasn't like the Chicago Bulls.

Helmut Thielicke thought the kingdom of heaven was like a new world empire that would knock down and brush aside every pretender to its throne. Thielicke was one of the fine preachers of our century. He became a minister in Germany about the same time that Adolf Hitler rose to power.

Thielicke says that when he became a pastor he was full of energy and enthusiasm. He couldn't wait to get going and transform the world, certainly to transform Germany. He went into it with the determination to trust in Jesus' saying, "All authority in heaven and on earth has been given to me. Go therefore and make disciples of all nations. . . ." Thielicke says that he would recall those words of Jesus in order to assure himself that even Hitler "and his dreadful power machine were merely puppets hanging by strings in the hands of this mighty Lord."

So the new minister Helmut Thielicke arranged a Bible study. He found a place, he selected a topic, he invited everyone he could think of, he publicized what he was doing, and then he waited for that authority of Jesus Christ to do its stuff. And when the appointed time came, says Thielicke, "I was faced by two very old ladies and a still older organist. . . . So this was the extent of the accomplishment of this Lord, to whom all power in heaven and earth had been given, *supposedly* given. And outside marched the battalions of youth who were subject to altogether different lords. This was all he had to set before me on that evening." Three senior citizens who were too old and worn out for Adolf Hitler. The kingdom wasn't like an empire; it was like a nursing home. Helmut Thielicke was disappointed.

Thielicke goes on to say that those who followed Jesus probably felt the same way he did the night of his Bible study. After all, Jesus had come to them preaching, "Repent, for the kingdom of heaven is near." And when those people heard that, they knew exactly what to think. They thought that the kingdom of heaven was God sending a Messiah to them, someone who would put their enemies under their feet, who would restore glory to Israel, who would bring wealth and comfort and freedom to every family, every synagogue, every village, every life associated with the people of God. And every nation of the world would recognize the power of that kingdom and stream to Jerusalem.

But that, of course, did not happen. So there were people in Jesus' following who had given up everything — their employment, their families, their homes — in order to be part of the kingdom of heaven, to have the power, and then, a few weeks or months later, were wondering, "Where is the kingdom? Where is the power?" "Sure," they say, "there has been some impressive healing, and some interesting preaching, but we were expecting more, we were expecting glitz and glamour. We thought it would be so much bigger than this. We thought we would see results. We thought the kingdom of heaven was like the kingdom of David. Big. Bright. Glorious."

And how natural that thought is. How easy it is to identify the kingdom that Jesus brings with the kingdoms that we know. How easy it is to look at Superbowl champions and huge crowds and nuclear power and majestic royalty and believe that that's what the kingdom of heaven is like. But it's not. It's not like those big, impressive things at all. It's like *yeast*. "The kingdom of heaven is like yeast that a woman took and mixed in with three measures of flour until all of it was leavened." The kingdom of heaven is not like a mighty empire or a crushing tornado or a Superbowl champ. The kingdom of heaven is like yeast.

John Timmer says, "The kingdom of heaven is like a small amount of yeast that leavens a big lump of dough. At first nothing seems to happen. But then, slowly, the whole mass of dough begins to swell and bubble. Christians are like yeast. You and I are like yeast. Our role is not to grow big, but to leaven what is big. The Christian faith is not about big rallies, big churches, big audiences. It's not about public relations, image building, salesmanship and marketing techniques. It's about leavening. And in order to leaven, you don't have to be big."

And that message has to be told again and again, not only in Jesus' time but in Helmut Thielicke's time, and in our time, too. Because yeast never looks all that important. It never looks like it's doing anything. It never looks like it matters — until it's finished. We need to hear these words again and again, because we're prone to look for a kingdom that is big, that produces results.

And that is certainly true today. Today it is common to measure ministry by how big it is, especially the ministry of churches. There was a time when people would ask, "How's your church doing?" and mean by that "Is the worship meaningful? Is the preaching sound? Is there good fellowship and unity?" Today, more and more, when people ask, "How's your church doing?" they mean only one thing: "Is it growing? Can you count the victories? Are you becoming big?"

And that's a shame, because yeast doesn't have to be big. It has to be yeast. For over four hundred years we have said that there are three things that mark a church: the pure proclamation of the Word, the celebration of the sacraments, and the faithful exercise of discipline. For over four centuries we've said that, wherever there is a true body of Jesus Christ, there will also be these three things — preaching, sacraments, discipline. Often you hear that there should be something else, too — that there should be results; that wherever the true church is, there should be victory. But that's a mistake. Because, more often than not, the kingdom of God isn't something that can be seen, even while it's transforming the world.

And that's exactly what's going on here. It's not a little leavening that we're talking about. The *world* is being transformed, the whole world. As

Robert Farrar Capon says, "it may be stereotypically female work" this woman is pictured as doing, "but she does it with more than stereotypically male energy. This is no slip of a girl making two tiny loaves for her husband's pleasure. This is a *baker*, folks. Three measures is a bushel of flour, for crying out loud. That's 128 cups! That's 16 five-pound bags! And when you get done putting in the 42 or so cups of water you need to make it come together, you've got a little over 101 pounds of dough on your hands."[3] The kingdom of heaven is like yeast that a woman took and leavened a truckload of dough.

But you don't see it happening. You don't get results. Not yet. Literally this parable reads, The kingdom of heaven is like yeast that a woman took and *hid* in three measures of flour. It's hidden. You can't point it out. But what a difference it makes.

So let the message of the yeast make a difference for us, too. When we are tempted to see God's presence in the church programs we're a part of and to judge that presence by how well they go, how successful they are, let us remember that the beauty of being yeast is that it's working whether you see it or not. The beauty of being yeast is that not only in Sunday school and friendships do we usher in the kingdom of God, but also in Red Wings' games and staff lunches and Manhattan taxicabs we can — quietly, slowly, completely — change everything.

As John Timmer puts it, "So we must keep asking ourselves: Are we leaven or are we dough? Are we a small group of people in whom our Lord has instilled a vision, or are we a big lump of status quo dough?" That's the question this parable puts before us. Not "Are we big enough?" but "Are we willing to be little enough?"

Those famous words of Micah call for the same thing:

"With what shall I come before the Lord,
    and bow myself before God on high?
Shall I come before him with burnt offerings,
    with calves a year old?
Will the Lord be pleased with thousands of rams,
    with ten thousands of rivers of oil?
Shall I give my firstborn for my transgression,
    the fruit of my body for the sin of my soul?"

3. Robert Farrar Capon, *Kingdom, Grace, Judgment: Paradox, Outrage, and Vindication in the Parables of Jesus* (Grand Rapids: Eerdmans, 2002), p. 100.

No, says Micah, none of those *big* things are in order.

> He has told you, O mortal, what is good;
>   and what does the Lord require of you
> but to do justice, and to love kindness,
>   and to walk humbly with your God?

Somewhere in those things that are so hard to see lies the secret to being yeast that God will use. Those of us who think we can't make much of a difference in the kingdom of God ought to keep that in mind.

And so should young preachers. For a little while I wondered what to say about a man who was a model in walking humbly with his God because I couldn't find the scorecard that said he was important. The good news is that God doesn't use a scorecard; he uses us. He uses justice and kindness and faithfulness to change the whole world. He uses three people studying his Word in the midst of an evil reign, he uses a little girl who offers a prayer, he uses an immigrant farmer who was never really at home here, and he used a Savior who looked anything but a king.

Martin Luther said that one reason Satan didn't do better opposing Jesus is because he didn't recognize him. He didn't know who he was; he overlooked him, because Jesus conducted himself so humbly and associated with sinners and didn't seem all that important. According to Luther, the devil is farsighted: he looks only for what is big and high and attaches himself to that; he does not look at that which is low down and beneath himself.

It's an easy mistake to make, to think the little doesn't count, to look only for what is big. So Satan is forever missing the presence of God. Because he keeps looking for the big. He doesn't realize that God keeps coming and coming and coming small. Hidden. Quiet. In people who look for justice and love kindness and walk with him.

So God is not like Michael Jordan; he's not like the CEO of some *Fortune 500* company. He's like a woman who took some yeast and leavened everything in sight.

They Burn Offerings, Don't They?

Texts: Romans 12:1-21; Micah 6:1-8

I appeal to you therefore, brothers and sisters, by the mercies of God, to present your bodies as a living sacrifice, holy and acceptable to God, which is your spiritual worship. Do not be conformed to this world, but be transformed by the renewing of your minds, so that you may discern what is the will of God — what is good and acceptable and perfect. For by the grace given to me I say to everyone among you not to think of yourself more highly than you ought to think, but to think with sober judgment, each according to the measure of faith that God has assigned.

Romans 12:1-3

In his book *Lake Wobegon Days,* Garrison Keillor describes the very strict church in which he grew up. Sanctified Brethren, they were called — "A sect so tiny," says Keillor, "that nobody but us and God knew about it, so when kids asked what I was, I just said Protestant. It was too much to explain, like having six toes. You would rather keep your shoes on."

At one point the Lake Wobegon Sanctified Brethren merged with the congregation in St. Cloud, which meant that the Keillor family had to drive the thirty-two miles to St. Cloud each Sunday. One week, when they had to be back for prayer meeting in the afternoon and couldn't make the round trip in time, they decided to stay and have dinner in St. Cloud, at Phil's House of Good Food, a restaurant recommended by a friend. Keillor describes what happened:

The waitress came and stood by Dad. "Can I get you something from the bar?" she said. Dad blushed a deep red. The question seemed to imply that he looked like a drinker. "No," he whispered, as if she had offered to dance on the table.

"Ma'am? Something from the bar?" Mother looked at her in disbelief.

Suddenly the room changed for us. Our waitress looked hardened, rough, cheap — across the room, a woman laughed obscenely — the man with her lit a cigarette and blew a cloud of smoke — a swear word drifted out from the kitchen — even the soft lighting seemed suggestive, diabolical. To be seen in such a place on the Lord's Day — what had we done?

My mother rose from her chair. "We can't stay. I'm sorry," Dad told the waitress. We all got up and put on our coats. Everyone in the restaurant had a good look at us. A bald little man in a filthy white shirt emerged from the kitchen wiping his hands. "Folks? Something wrong?" he said. "We're in the wrong place," Mother told him. Mother always told the truth, or something close to it.

"This is *humiliating*," I said out on the sidewalk. "I feel like a *leper* or something. Why do we always have to make such a big production out of everything? Why can't we be like regular people?"

She put her hand on my shoulder. "Be not conformed to this world," she said. I knew the rest by heart: ". . . but be transformed by the renewing of your mind, that ye may prove what is that good and acceptable and perfect will of God."[4]

"The good and acceptable and perfect will of God." What is it? We don't think it's that we walk out of a restaurant that serves drinks anymore, though some of our parents or grandparents may have. But, if it's not that, if it's not walking out of restaurants and staying away from movie theaters and turning off our televisions on Sunday, what is it? What is God's will? What does God want from us?

Micah asked more or less the same question almost three thousand years ago: "With what shall I come before the Lord and bow down before God on high?" (6:6). What does the Lord want from me? What is his will for me?

Now a lot of people around Micah thought they had the answer to that question. They thought the answer was pretty simple: when you committed a sin or when you defiled yourself or when your city was at war or when somebody died — or whenever else you needed God — what you had to do was make a sacrifice. It was sort of a tradeoff: God's blessing and forgiveness and support in exchange for a burnt offering, a sacrificed animal.

But, as the prophets were always reminding the people of Israel, nothing like that could ever be enough to make things right between human beings and God. No offering could ever be enough to heal the relationship with God that was torn apart by sin. And that was Micah's problem:

4. Garrison Keillor, *Lake Wobegon Days* (New York: Viking Penguin, 1985), p. 110.

"Shall I come before him with burnt offerings,
   with calves a year old?
Will the Lord be pleased with thousands of rams,
   with ten thousands of rivers of oil?
Shall I give my firstborn for my transgression,
   the fruit of my body for the sin of my soul?"

No, Micah knows, none of it is enough, no burnt offering will ever make up for the damage sin has done. Thousands of rams won't do it, nor ten thousand rivers of oil, nor a firstborn child.

God isn't after the spectacular things, like the thousands of rams or ten thousand rivers of oil, or all the things that we can point to and say, Look at what I've done for the kingdom, look at how much I've produced for God. God is after the little things, the subtle things, like doing justice and loving mercy and walking humbly with your God. Well, here's today's message: compared to the little things, the spectacular is easy. It's the little things that are the challenge of discipleship.

It's easier to display your religion than it is to practice justice. It's easier to develop a program than it is to love mercy. It's easier to do the big stuff, because the big stuff doesn't have to touch your heart, it doesn't have to change who you are. But God wants to change who we are. He wants to change us from his enemies into his children. And the only way that could happen is if he provided the sacrifice himself.

So instead of asking for Micah's son, he gave us his own Son. The Lord required someone whose obedience would be perfect, whose mercy would not end, whose walk would never stumble; someone who would not simply *offer* sacrifices but someone who would *be* a sacrifice. The answer to Micah's question is Jesus Christ. "With what shall I come before the Lord and bow myself before God on high?" Shall I come with offerings? My wealth? My children? No, say the Scriptures, because God offered his firstborn for our transgression, he offered his Son for our sin.

What does God want from us? What will make us right with him? The answer is nothing. He wants nothing. We must do nothing. We are right with him. He made us right with him. With what shall I come before the Lord? Come before him with Jesus Christ. Come before him not with what *you* have done but with what *he* has done. Come before him speaking not of your goodness but of his mercy. That is the way to God; that is what he wants from you. His Son has done what God requires.

Paul's been telling that to the Romans for the better part of eleven chapters already. He's been explaining to them in as many ways as he knows how that all of us deserve judgment and death apart from Jesus Christ. But if you believe in Jesus Christ and cling to his promises, says Paul, God will let his righteousness be your righteousness. His obedience will be your obedience, and his life will be your life.

Then in chapters 9–11, in the section right before our Scripture passage, Paul goes on to talk about the Jews. He says to the gentile Christians of Rome, You may think that the Jews are God's enemies because they're rebelling right now. And you may think that rebellion cancels out God's promises to them. You may think that they are no longer his people because they oppose the gospel. But that's not true, Paul says. Because if he can cancel his promises to them, that would mean that he can cancel his promises to us. But that is not our God. Our God doesn't depend on our offerings.

The Jews have become disobedient so that they may receive mercy, Paul says, just as you gentiles have received mercy. "For God has imprisoned all in disobedience so that he may be merciful to all" (11:32). And then Paul offers a doxology on how mysterious and unsearchable and deep are the ways of this God, who seeks to pour his mercy on every human being.

And now, having said all of this, Paul speaks to the lives of the Roman Christians: "I appeal to you, therefore, brothers and sisters, by the mercies of God, to present your bodies as a living sacrifice, holy and acceptable to God." Offerings don't burn anymore, says Paul. Offerings aren't even a part of your lives, because nothing stands between you and God anymore. Because you have received his mercy, you know Jesus Christ. So now that you have experienced his unfathomable goodness, now that salvation is yours, don't spend any time worrying about burnt offerings; make your *life* an offering instead. Become a *living* sacrifice. Paul is convinced that anyone who has experienced the mercy of God and the sacrifice of Jesus Christ for their salvation will sacrifice themselves in response, will give up their lives for Christ as he gave up his for us. And when you do that, you no longer have to go around asking, What does the Lord want from me? What am I supposed to do? Then you will be able to discern what is the will of God — what is good and acceptable and perfect.

Paul uses most of the rest of the book of Romans to give examples of what it means to be living sacrifices, but that's made most clear in the rest of chapter 12. You know what he says there? Look for your gifts and use them well; practice your faith in the little things of life that come up every day. Listen to the paraphrase of some of these verses by Eugene Peterson:

So here's what I want you to do, God helping you: Take your every-day, ordinary life — your sleeping, eating, going-to-work and walking-around life — and place it before God as an offering. . . . The only accurate way to understand ourselves is by what God is and by what he does for us, not by what we are and what we do for him.

In this way we are like the various parts of a human body. Each part gets its meaning from the body as a whole, not the other way around. . . . So . . . let's just go ahead and be what we were made to be, without enviously or pridefully comparing ourselves with each other, or trying to be something we aren't.

If you preach, just preach God's message, nothing else; if you help, just help, don't take over; if you teach, stick to your teaching; if you give encouraging guidance, be careful that you don't get bossy; if you're put in charge, don't manipulate; if you're called to give aid to people in distress, keep your eyes open and be quick to respond; if you work with the disadvantaged, don't let yourself get irritated with them or depressed by them. Keep a smile on your face.

Love from the center of who you are; don't fake it. Run for dear life from evil; hold on for dear life to good. Be good friends who love deeply; practice playing second fiddle. . . .

Bless your enemies; no cursing under your breath. Laugh with your happy friends when they're happy; share tears when they're down. Get along with each other; don't be stuck up. Make friends with nobodies; don't be the great somebody.

Don't hit back; discover beauty in everyone. . . . Don't let evil get the best of you; get the best of evil by doing good.[5]

Being conformed to this world means using the world's standards. It means honoring what the world honors, glorifying the big and the beautiful and the spectacular. It means assuming that that's what God honors, too. But that's the opposite of what Paul's talking about when he tells the Roman Christians to be living sacrifices.

God doesn't want a set of behaviors. He doesn't want a burnt offering. He wants you. We're being called to turn our lives over to him, to use the gifts that we have in his service, to respond to his mercy by letting every

5. Eugene H. Peterson, *The Message: The Bible in Contemporary Language* (Colorado Springs: NavPress, 2002), pp. 2054-55.

day belong to the Lord. That's how we celebrate the salvation we have in Jesus Christ, by doing the non-spectacular little things that few people see and fewer applaud, by doing the non-spectacular little things that really show whether we belong to this world or whether we've been transformed by our Savior — not by pretending to be something we're not but by being the people God made us to be and by using our opportunities, our interests, and our abilities to present a living sacrifice to him.

Remember that the requirements of Micah 6 were filled long ago by God's own Son. But also remember that in order for his life to become ours, our lives must be sacrificed. And remember that in the typical events of a typical day we show ourselves to be people who conform to the pattern of this world or people who are being transformed by the power of Jesus Christ. And also remember that each of us has the opportunity to do justice and to love mercy and, in our own humble way, even to walk with our God. In his merciful name, Amen.

Waiting

Texts: Psalm 130; Acts 1:3-11

Out of the depths I cry to you, O Lord.
   Lord, hear my voice!
Let your ear be attentive
   to the voice of my supplications!
If you, O Lord, should mark iniquities,
   Lord, who could stand?
But there is forgiveness with you,
   so that you may be revered.

Psalm 130:1-4

While he was going and they were gazing up toward heaven, suddenly two men in white robes stood by them. They said, "Men of Galilee, why do you stand looking up toward heaven? This Jesus, who has been taken up from you into heaven, will come in the same way as you saw him go into heaven."

Acts 1:10-11

A while back, a journal that I receive noted a bumper sticker that read, "Jesus is coming! Look busy." Look busy. We smile, but it's so easy to think that way. It's so easy to await the return of Jesus with fear that we might not have been busy enough while he was gone. It's so easy to take the words of the angel as a threat: "Men of Galilee, why do you stand looking up toward heaven? This Jesus . . . will come in the same way you saw him go." . . . So get to work! It's so easy to think of Jesus' return like it's something we have to get through.

And that's too bad, because when we think that way, we miss most of the meaning of this day. We miss the importance of the ascension. The ascension of Jesus Christ to the right hand of the Father isn't about us being left alone; it's not about having just so much time to get things right before he comes back; it's not about a risk or a fear or a threat.

As our catechism says so well, it's about a guarantee. And the guarantee is that *we* will follow in his footsteps. The guarantee is that there's somebody at the right hand of God who knows our names and understands our lives. The guarantee is that we will not be left to work it out by ourselves. And that's why the ascension is something to celebrate — not because everything has been made right, but because we have the guarantee that everything will be right; not because now it is all so easy, but because there is one in heaven who knows how hard it gets.

There's a heresy going around — it turns up among television preachers with some frequency — that if only you believe, if only you cling to Jesus, then you will ascend to heaven, too. Well, that's not quite how it's put. It's put like this: If you want money, turn to Jesus. Send this much in, and Jesus will send you this much more. If you have health struggles or family problems and you're depressed, cast yourself on Jesus — today, right now — and it will all be gone. Trust Jesus, and you will be happy and healthy; you will prosper.

When we buy that line, we forget who it is that ascended to heaven and who it is that remains here. When we believe such health-and-wealth gospels, we forget where we are, we forget what life is like, we forget what faith is about. Because faith does not solve all our problems; faith does not sanitize our lives; faith does not bring us out of the depths. And that is exactly the glory of the ascension.

In spite of what anyone may tell us or how strong our faith may be or how much we pray, we spend our days edging around the depths, in danger of the slings and arrows of a world marked by death and violence and sin and sadness. We can talk about our comfort in Christ. We can say, God is with us. We can sing, "Happiness is to know the Savior." But we know that there is still plenty of pain to go around. We know that the depths are always within reach.

So we know, especially those of us who are older, the place of the one who prays, "Out of the depths I cry to you, O Lord. Lord, hear my voice!" It would be nice if it weren't so. It would be nice if things were simpler, if God's people were spared the pitfalls. Then the time right now, the time between Jesus' ascension and his return, would be about being busy. Instead, it's about waiting. Waiting for the Lord. Waiting in the depths. But that, too, is the glory of the ascension.

The angels said, "Men of Galilee, why do you stand looking up toward heaven? This Jesus, who has been taken from you into heaven, will come in the same way as you saw him go into heaven." That's not a threat. That's a promise. This friend of yours, this master of yours, this Savior of yours, he is going to come back to you in the same way that he left. The one who will bring history to a close is somebody you know. Don't worry. You don't need to stare up after him. He's coming back.

That's the glory of the ascension. We know the one who will be the judge. We know the one who rules the earth. He has bones like our bones and flesh like our flesh. He knows what it is to be human; he knows what it is to be in the depths.

"If you, O Lord, should mark iniquities, Lord, who could stand? But there is forgiveness with you, so that you may be revered." The God who will descend to us is one who's not marking our iniquities or keeping a record of sin; he's one who is fond of saying, "I do not condemn you; go in peace." The God who will descend to take the world to himself is a God who brings forgiveness in his hands. If it were any other way, we wouldn't have a prayer. If it were some other type of god coming, no amount of busyness would be enough. If it were someone other than Jesus Christ serving as judge, we'd be dead for sure, because then there would be a record of sin; then we would have to pay our own debt.

But that is the glory of the ascension. The one who is returning has scars on his hands. With this God there is forgiveness. So it is not *busyness* that gives us hope; it is not all that we accomplish that gives us hope; it is not what we do or what we are or what we say that gives us hope. It is *God* who gives us hope, the God with whom there is forgiveness, the one who ascended into heaven and will come back the same way.

The glory of the ascension is that we know who it is that will bring history to a close. We know his name, we know his methods, we know his heart. So even from the depths, *especially* from the depths, we can cry to this Lord and know that he will hear. We can cry to this Lord, because he's not looking for our sin; he's looking for our salvation.

And that's why we can say, even from the depths,

> I wait for the Lord, my soul waits,
>   and in his word I hope;
> my soul waits for the Lord,
>   more than those who watch for the morning,
>   more than those who watch for the morning.
>
> (Ps. 130:6)

Some of you know what it is to wait for the Lord, to strain to see a sign of his coming, as a watchman strains his eyes toward the horizon to see the first glimmer of the new day. You know what it is like to wait for the Lord, because you know the depths. Perhaps, until your wait is over, you always will.

For some of you the depths are not a momentary setback or an illness from which you will recover or saying good-bye as a first child leaves home. For you the depths are a more permanent state. They are the emptiness from the loss of a life-long companion. They are a sin you committed that, even now, years later, lies heavy on your heart. For you the depths are a marriage or a career or a life that you would love to have over but you can't. And so you endure; you play it out; and you cry to the Lord.

Nicholas Wolterstorff was already a renowned professor of philosophy when his twenty-five-year-old son Eric died in a mountain-climbing accident. In the year that followed he kept a diary of his thoughts, which he later published under the title *Lament for a Son*. There Wolterstorff writes, "Sometimes I think that happiness is over for me. I look at photos of the past and immediately comes the thought: that's when we were still happy. But I can still laugh, so I guess that isn't quite it. Perhaps what's over is happiness as the fundamental tone of my existence. Now sorrow is that. Sorrow is no longer the islands but the sea."[6]

Some of you are waiting for the Lord, more than watchmen wait for the morning. And so Psalm 130 is your psalm, because only when the one you know comes back, only then will you really be lifted from the depths and made whole. In some sense, of course, that makes Psalm 130 *our*

---

6. Nicholas Wolterstorff, *Lament for a Son* (Grand Rapids: Eerdmans, 1987), p. 47.

psalm, because we're all waiting for that. Amid all of the regrets of a soiled past, all of the hurt that seems to have picked us out of a crowd, all of the pain of a relationship that isn't right or a body that isn't working, amid all that makes us ashamed to stand before the Lord, we wait for the Lord, because he doesn't mark our iniquities, because with him there is forgiveness, because in his word we may hope. So we all wait.

But waiting here is not wondering. Waiting is not wallowing. And waiting is not lying around. Eugene Peterson says, "waiting does not mean doing nothing. It is not fatalistic resignation. It means going about our assigned tasks, confident that God will provide the meaning and the conclusions."

How easy it is to give up when you're in the depths. But that's not waiting. You see, waiting for the Lord is about hope, because you know who's coming. Waiting for the Lord is anticipation of a day when there will be no more death or mourning, no more sin or sacrifice, when every tear will be wiped away. And when we're doing that, when we're looking ahead, when we know the Lord, then, even as we hurt, even as we long for another day, we go about our assignments. We worship. We serve. We remember what Jesus gave us to do, and we can do it, because the future has already been taken care of. Because we know this God.

That's how we can say out of the depths, "O Israel, hope in the Lord! For with the Lord there is steadfast love, and with him is great power to redeem" (v. 7). There is no witness to the presence of God like the one that says those words while in the depths. When you say them then, when you believe them then, his kingdom is being built. So say them, display them; call the rest of us to believe them, too; call your world to believe them — even while you wait for the Lord with the longing of a watchman waiting for the morning.

Ascension Day is always a difficult day to preach. It tempts you to call upon helium balloons and jet packs. But that's not the main event here. This day isn't about space travel; it's about earth travel. The ascension of Jesus Christ means something for us right now. It means our future is secure. It means the Son of Man is on the throne of God. It means all we have to do is wait.

I've never cared for theology that fits on a bumper sticker. It seems to undervalue my seminary degree. But I like "Jesus is coming. Look busy!" It reminds us how foolish our ways can be, and how useless it is to rest on what *we* do. So go about the work of the Lord — not frightened or threatened or unsure, but as someone who's waiting for a person you've already met. A person who's coming to lift you up and take you with him.

Jesus is coming. Be at peace.

Religion in the Way

Text: Mark 9:30-41

*Then they came to Capernaum; and when he was in the house he asked
them, "What were you arguing about on the way?" But they were silent,
for on the way they had argued with one another who was the greatest. He
sat down, called the twelve, and said to them, "Whoever wants to be first
must be last of all and servant of all."*

Mark 9:33-35

Antonio Salieri is a religious man, a man serious about his faith. Salieri is
the protagonist in Peter Shaffer's novel and the film made from it,
Amadeus. From his childhood, Salieri wanted to be a world-class composer; he wanted, he says, to make music and bring glory to his God. So,
while a young boy, Salieri offers the boldest prayer he can imagine: "Lord,"
he says, "make me a great composer. Let me celebrate your glory through
music, and be celebrated myself. Make me famous through the world,
dear God. Make me immortal. After I die, let people speak my name forever with love for what I wrote. In return, I will give you my chastity, my industry, my deepest humility, every hour of my life. Amen." Such was the
devotion of Antonio Salieri.

And over the years, in various events — in the death of his father,
which forces a family move to Vienna, the city of musicians; in many opportunities afforded to him there; and in his appointment as the court
composer for Joseph, the music-loving emperor of Austria — in all of these
things Salieri is convinced that he is witnessing the answer to his old
prayer, and so his faith in God is great. He is witnessing the work of the
Lord. God has accepted his offer. His faith is verified by his success. So
each time he takes one more step toward the fame and glory he craves,
Salieri turns his face to a small crucifix on the wall near his piano and says
to Jesus upon that tiny cross, *Grazie, Signore.* Thank you, Sir.

But then God defaults on the loan. Salieri's star stops rising, and,
worse than that, the everlasting glory — *Salieri's* glory — will go to a boor-

ish, arrogant, vulgar genius who shows up in Vienna: Wolfgang Amadeus Mozart. Salieri soon realizes that his gift is mediocre next to Mozart's, and so all that he desired from life will go to another, to a man who has not dedicated himself to anything but pleasure, to a man not worthy of such wondrous talent.

So now Salieri prays again, but a far different prayer: "From now on we are enemies: you and I," he prays. "Because you choose for your instrument a boastful, lustful, smutty, infantile boy, and give me for reward only the ability to recognize the incarnation. Because you are unjust, unkind, I will block you. I swear it." The crucifix goes into the fireplace; the life of dedication to industry and chastity and humility becomes one dedicated to destroying a brighter light. Salieri spends his days cursing and opposing the God who failed to proceed according to his plan, the God who deigned to bless Amadeus.

Antonio Salieri is a religious man, and it shows. His religion shows in church, in prayer, in the crucifix over his piano. But it is exactly that religion — that *Christian* religion — that gets in the way of Antonio Salieri, because within all of his gussied-up, good-looking, pious religion is the drive to raise himself, to glorify himself, to celebrate himself. But you can't see it, because of all the religion.

When we read some of the stories of the disciples it can be easy for us to criticize, to take a sort of "Those dummies, I would have caught on so much faster" approach. Especially when we're reading the Gospel of Mark, because the picture of the disciples in Mark is the least flattering one that we have. In Mark these friends of Jesus are a little denser, a little slower, a little more self-absorbed. So we should be careful, then, that ours is not a holier-than-Peter attitude. Because the disciples are certainly not lacking in enthusiasm. They're certainly not lacking in devotion — they're certainly religious enough. But religion itself — even the religion of Jesus Christ — can get in the way. And in Mark 9, it does.

Not long before this scene, Mark tells us that Jesus "began to teach them that the Son of Man must undergo great suffering, and be rejected by the elders, chief priests, and the scribes, and be killed, and after three days rise again. He said all this quite openly," Mark says, and then Peter took him aside and rebuked him (8:31-32). Peter would hear no such thing from Jesus. In chapter 9 we may get an idea why.

In chapter 9, verses 31-32, Jesus picks up the subject of his suffering and death once more: the Son of Man is going to be betrayed into human hands, he says. They will kill him, and after three days he will rise again. This time there's no scolding from the disciples, only the comment that they did not understand what he was saying and were afraid to ask him about it.

Well, that awkward moment having passed, the group moves on to other things. Jesus wants to know, "What were you arguing about on the road?" The disciples don't know how to answer, because their argument concerned which of them was the greatest. Jesus gathers them around and tries to get through to them again: "Whoever wants to be first," he says, "must be last of all and servant of all." Welcoming me, he says, is like welcoming a little child; it has to do with forgetting your position and your prestige. But once more, no luck, because next we read that the disciples have been checking out the churches in the area, and — what do you know? — they found a man driving out demons in Jesus' name. We tried to stop him, they report, because he wasn't one of *us*. So once more Jesus tries to reset their thinking: whoever's not against us is for us, he says. If it's done in my name, then the doer *is* one of us.

Now during none of this does the disciples' interest in Jesus decline. During none of these events does the disciples' adoration of Jesus lessen. During none of these moments does the disciples' devotion to Jesus wane. They are no less religious today — in Mark 9 — than they were a few weeks ago in Mark 6 or 7. And that is just the problem, because it's their religion that keeps them from understanding the words of Jesus; it's their religion that keeps them from the kingdom of God; it's their religion that gets in the way.

You see, their religion is going to bring them greatness. They believe in Jesus. They know him to be the Messiah; and they know that Messiahs have great things in store for them and their followers. This man is going to be the conqueror of the Romans, the ruler of the Jews, the anointed of God, and his coattails are going to take them right to the top. There's no room in their religion for a Messiah who dies, or greatness that comes from being a servant, or some Johnny-come-lately signing on board. In their religion there's no place for Lent, or for a Messiah who's a servant, or for a Savior who's betrayed and rejected and killed. It's an idea they just can't get; it's an idea that doesn't fit into the magnificence and glory they see coming.

So Jesus can talk about the cross he's destined for, and he can talk about the leader in *his* kingdom being a servant, and he can talk about becoming like a little child and praising God for those who speak his Word — he can talk about these things, but it's not going to get through, not until they look outside their religion. The Jewish thinker Martin Buber said that "religion can hide from us the face of God as nothing else can."

Here the disciples are proving him right: the face of God is before them, but their religion is in the way.

It is religion facing the wrong direction that has the disciples thinking *palace* when Jesus is talking *cross*. It is religion facing the wrong direction that makes Antonio Salieri end his life against God rather than with him. It is religion facing the wrong direction that we must confront and correct before we can really celebrate Easter.

That's actually what Merold Westphal says in his book *Suspicion and Faith*.[7] Westphal says that, at least during Lent, and probably a lot more often than that, we must examine not only our lives and our career goals, our priorities and our choices; we must look at our religion, too. We must consider not only our commitment to what we believe but also why we believe it, what we want out of it, what we *get* out of it. During Lent we must ask, Are we bowing before God, or are we seeking things from God? Are we letting him mold us into his image, or have we molded him into ours? Many centuries ago the Greek historian Herodotus noticed that the gods of the Persians always looked a lot like Persians. In recent centuries some critics have made the same comment about Christians.

Three of these critics are Sigmund Freud, Karl Marx, and Friedrich Nietzsche. All of them were atheists. All of them had little use for Christianity. All of them declared that religion is something by which people use God to gain their own little kingdom. Freud said that human beings create God to be the parent they always wanted, someone to satisfy their needs and justify their desires. Karl Marx said that the rich use God to keep everybody else in their place, to make them believe that it is God's will that they accept life as it is without questioning or resistance. Friedrich Nietzsche said that actions, even those that are laced with nobility and morality, are never what they seem, and that people are actually always seeking power or control or fame. All three of these famous atheists believed the same thing about religion, especially the Christian religion. They believed that it's just a means to an end, a giant rationalization for people to do and have and be what they want, a way to justify injustice or greed or hate. Freud, Marx, and Nietzsche were the declared enemies of Christianity.

And the church has responded in kind. To each of these men Christians have risen up to declare that the world doesn't work the way they say it does. In each case we've said, The Christian religion is true. The God of

7. Merold Westphal, *Suspicion and Faith: The Religious Uses of Modern Atheism* (Grand Rapids: Eerdmans, 1993).

the Bible is real. And in each case, especially concerning Freud and Marx, we've been relieved and overjoyed to watch their theories collapse and be discarded by most of the world.

But before we do that, says Merold Westphal, before we attack them and argue with them and conquer them, let's say something else about these opponents and their ideas. Let's say that they're right.

Let's say that the things Freud and Nietzsche and Marx have claimed about Christianity are often true. Ours *is* a religion that has been used. It's been used to maintain class divisions, to justify personal desire, to hold on to power. It's been used to defend slavery, to sanctify aggression, to demean other human beings. And these uses of it have been accompanied by Bible-thumping, Scripture-quoting, and pious-looking activity. And for all of it repentance must be offered, a cleansing must take place. Even our religion itself, our devotion itself, our Christianity itself must pass through Lent.

Persian gods look like Persians. Salieri's god must bestow talent upon him. The disciples' messiah will not die but will produce them a kingdom. And all of it seems right. All of it is good-looking, noble-sounding religion, and within it are motives far more self-concerned, far less godly. But it's hard to see, because of all the religion.

As we live after Easter, let us take care not to deny the cross. Let us take care to listen to our God as well as talk about him. Let us choose to let him shape us instead of the more satisfying course by which we shape him. At a time when so many are so quick to speak of God's will on everything from weapons bans to illegal immigration, we *must* pause to ask, Whose agenda are we really pursuing? Whose interests do we really have in mind?

How much do our politics, our prayers, our pronouncements have to do more with self-righteousness than with righteousness, more with economics than with justice, more with our will than with our Lord's? "'The Son of Man is to be betrayed into human hands, and they will kill him, and three days after being killed he will rise again.' But they did not understand what he was saying." They didn't understand him, because they were so sure how it was all going to go; they thought they knew exactly what God was up to.

The great theologian Karl Barth said that we get it all wrong when we think that the world crucified Jesus Christ; it wasn't the world, says Barth, it was the church that did it. It was the ones who knew him, who worshiped him, who were waiting for him. The world wanted to let him off with a fine; the *church* demanded his death — because he wasn't the kind of God that fit their religion, and their religion wasn't about to budge.

There's a nineteenth-century hymn titled "Not for Our Sins Alone." It goes like this:

Not for our sins alone thy mercy, Lord, we sue;
let fall thy pitying glance on our devotions too,
what we have done for thee, and what we think to do.
The holiest hours we spend in prayer upon our knees,
the times when most we deem our songs of praise will please,
thou searcher of all hearts, forgiveness pour on these.

Even those things we do in the name of God must be examined; even they must go through Lent. But even they were nailed to the cross, and even amid them, we disciples may find life — because the Son of Man was betrayed into human hands, and we killed him, and three days after being killed, he rose again — for us and for our salvation. Amen.

PENTECOST

Home Is Where the Spirit Is

Text: Romans 8:12-17

So then, brothers and sisters, we are debtors, not to the flesh, to live accord-
ing to the flesh — for if you live according to the flesh, you will die; but if
by the Spirit you put to death the deeds of the body, you will live. For all
who are led by the Spirit of God are children of God. For you did not re-
ceive a spirit of slavery to fall back into fear, but you have received a spirit
of adoption. When we cry, "Abba! Father!" it is that very Spirit bearing
witness with our spirit that we are children of God, and if children, then
heirs, heirs of God and joint heirs with Christ — if, in fact, we suffer with
him so that we may also be glorified with him.

Romans 8:12-17

We have a confession to make. And, if you're like me, you're somewhat embarrassed about it, because it's a confession that we're out of step with a
good portion of contemporary Christianity. The confession is this: we af-
firm the doctrine of the Trinity wholeheartedly, and yet, in all honesty,
we're a little uncomfortable when it comes to celebrating the gifts of the
Holy Spirit. The truth is, we Reformed folk do fine with events like Lent
and Easter and Labor Day, but we get a little queasy on Pentecost. On Pentecost it can feel like we're a visiting team, like we're playing in somebody
else's ballpark. At least that's the way it can feel today, when possessing
the Holy Spirit is so often identified with possessing special powers or insight or losing control of our actions or speech. Most of *us* don't know the
Spirit that way; most of us are embarrassingly calm. So we read Acts 2, we
state our faith in the Holy Trinity, we celebrate Pentecost, but it doesn't
always feel like a good fit for us, because it seems we have so little to show
for it. And sometimes we wonder, and we are right to wonder: if possessing the Holy Spirit doesn't have to mean speaking in tongues or healing
someone or having some ecstatic vision, then what *does* it mean? What
kind of Spirit *is* it that we have received?

Which brings us right to where Paul is in Romans 8:14-17. Paul is out to answer the question, What difference does Pentecost make? What kind of Spirit is it that we have received? And what Paul says first about that Spirit is what it is not: it is *not* a spirit of slavery. When Paul describes the kind of Spirit we have received he begins by saying, "For you did not receive a spirit of slavery. . . ." When I read that, it really struck me. I never really thought about slavery as having a spirit before Paul said it here. And then I considered what a spirit like that might look like, what difference a spirit of slavery might make.

And that's when I remembered Toni Morrison's novel *Beloved. Beloved* is about a black woman whose past as a slave affects every day of her life and every experience she has, even though she escaped many years ago and now is living in Ohio in the days after the Civil War. So *Beloved* is not so much about slavery as it is about the spirit of slavery, because the slavery's been done with for a while. In some ways *Beloved* is a parable about the work of an unholy spirit.

One of Morrison's paragraphs captures the fruit of that spirit well. It's a description of a slave named Baby Suggs. Morrison writes,

> In all of Baby's life . . . men and women were moved around like checkers. Anybody Baby Suggs knew, let alone loved, who hadn't run off or been hanged, got rented out, loaned out, bought up, brought back, stored up, mortgaged, won, stolen, or seized. So Baby's eight children had six fathers. What she called the nastiness of life was the shock she received upon learning that nobody stopped playing checkers just because the pieces included her children.[1]

I don't know everything that this kind of spirit does and I don't know everything that Paul has in mind here in Romans 8, but I know this: the spirit of slavery takes human beings and turns them into checkers.

And whether you're an actual slave or not doesn't really matter. You can become a checker; you can lose freedom and dignity and humanity and home. You see, checkers never have a home. They wouldn't be checkers if they did. Wherever people turn into checkers, there is a spirit of slavery, and that spirit is the antithesis of the Spirit poured out at Pentecost, the antithesis of the Spirit that we have received.

And the difference between those two spirits is at the heart of Jesus' problem with the Pharisees. The Pharisees treat people like they're check-

1. Toni Morrison, *Beloved* (Harmondsworth: Penguin, 1987), p. 23.

ers; they treat people like they should always be afraid. You may travel this far on the Sabbath, they say, but no farther. You must sacrifice this and this and that, they say, but you may keep the rest. You must do this, this, and this to fulfill the law, they say, but if you slip up, you will die. They're playing checkers — they're moving people around, telling them the rules, running their lives — and they're forgetting that those pieces are somebody's children.

Do you remember the story in Luke 7 when Jesus is eating at the house of Simon the Pharisee, and a sinful woman comes in? This woman has found something in Jesus that has changed her life, and she has come to this Pharisee's house — uninvited, unwelcome, unliked — to thank Jesus by anointing him with an expensive jar of perfume. But she's a sinner — a prostitute or something, someone who's fallen short of the rules by a long way. So Simon is indignant as he watches this take place — this sinful stranger in his house, contaminating his guest — and he mutters to himself, If Jesus really were a prophet, he'd know what kind of person is hanging all over him right now, and he'd put a stop to it.

Jesus knows what he's thinking, and he knows who she is and *what* she is. He knows the terrible failure in her life, and he knows what Simon expects from her, what Simon *demands* from her. But Jesus doesn't talk about any of those things. He doesn't talk to her about her past and he doesn't talk to Simon about his law. Instead he tells Simon the Pharisee, You know, people who are forgiven of a lot sure know how to be thankful. And he tells her, "Your sins are forgiven. Your faith has saved you. Go in peace." She was a slave to the world; Simon thought she should be a slave to the law. Jesus didn't want her to be either one. So he says, "You're forgiven. Go in peace. And never stop being thankful." The other options made her less of a person and more like a checker; Jesus made her more of a person than she ever was before. He set her free. *That's* the work of the Spirit you have received.

Paul writes these words in Romans to people who know the spirit of slavery — some of them because they actually are slaves, but others because they're so wrapped up in the world around them, they're so worldly, that they have no control. They're driven by what people think or by how prosperous they can be or by some life of sin they don't see any way out of. There are others in Paul's audience who are caught up in Judaism, who are busy saving themselves by airtight obedience to the law. They're doing a lot of right things, but they're doing them because they think they earn something through doing them. They're jot-and-tittle people. And in all of these people it's the same spirit of slavery, because, any way you look at it, they're just checkers getting moved around by some other spirit that always tells them what to do next.

And that's a frightening way to live. Checkers always live in fear, because at any time they can lose everything, at any time they can mess up a command, at any time they can be shipped off far from home. A spirit of slavery is a spirit of fear, because you can never predict what the master wants next, because slave-owners don't think twice about moving you around. But, says Paul, you didn't receive that kind of spirit: "you did not receive a spirit of slavery to fall back into fear, but you have received a spirit of adoption."

Do you want to know what the Holy Spirit does, what difference he makes? He's the one who tells you the same thing Jesus told that sinful woman: you're not a slave anymore. You're forgiven. Go in peace. Don't ever stop being as thankful as you are today. The Heidelberg Catechism says the same thing: the Holy Spirit makes me "share in Christ," he "comforts me and will abide with me forever." Go in peace. Your sins are forgiven. You've been adopted. *That's* the Spirit that we've received. And that Spirit doesn't produce any fear at all; that Spirit produces only peace, because by that Spirit we know to say "Abba! Father!" to the God of the universe, the judge of every human being. We don't come in fear; we come as family. We say, "Abba."

It would be nice if we knew enough Aramaic to understand that word, *Abba.* A lot of good work has been done to figure it out, to understand exactly what this word means about our relationship with God. One of my professors told us once that he never really appreciated this word until one day when he was standing in a crowded airport in some Arab country. Near him was a small child who had momentarily lost sight of his father. And the boy was saying, "Abba! Abba!" He was calling to the one he knew loved him, the one he knew would be there for him, the one who would bring him home.

Paul says that we can call on God the same way, because we did not receive a spirit of slavery but a spirit of adoption. So now you're not filled with fear, you're filled with peace; you say, "Abba! Father!" By the presence of the Holy Spirit, you know yourself as a daughter of God, a son of God. By the presence of the Holy Spirit, you know yourself as an heir of God and a joint heir with Christ.

In a lot of ways it's easier to be a slave. It's easier to let the world determine your course and your priorities. And it's easier to have rules determine how you're saved. After all, checkers get all their decisions made for them; they don't have to think too hard. But they don't have a life, either. Slavery never works, for anybody. But we're not slaves; we're not checkers. We're children. In this world being children of the heavenly Father is not easy, and it always brings some suffering with it, the suffering of Jesus Christ. But every day as we share in his suffering we also share in his life, and by his Spirit we hear him say, "Your sins are forgiven. Go in peace. Never stop being thankful."

We needn't be embarrassed on Pentecost. We're still plenty trinitarian. We do fine by the Holy Spirit. Even if his presence for us doesn't usually have to do with something sensational, there's still plenty to say, there's still plenty to celebrate, because we haven't received a spirit of slavery that leads to fear, a spirit that turns you into a checker. The Spirit we've received is a spirit of adoption: a spirit that gives you a home, a spirit that makes you a child of God, a spirit that sets you free. And, believe me, for that we must never stop giving thanks. After all, the Lord of heaven and earth, from his glorious throne, has sent out his Spirit to our hearts, to say, "*You* are my child. *Your* sins are forgiven. Go in peace." Amen.

— TRINITY SUNDAY —

As They Are One

Text: John 17:20-26

> *"I ask not only on behalf of these, but also on behalf of those who will believe in me through their word, that they may all be one. As you, Father, are in me and I am in you, may they also be in us, so that the world may believe that you have sent me. The glory that you have given me I have given them, so that they may be one, as we are one, I in them and you in me, that they may become completely one, so that the world may know that you have sent me and have loved them even as you have loved me. Father, I desire that those also, whom you have given me, may be with me where I am, to see my glory, which you have given me because you loved me before the foundation of the world."*
>
> John 17:20-24

This week begins the Christian Reformed Synod, which is the annual general assembly of the Christian Reformed Church in North America. *Synod* isn't a word you run into a lot anymore, but we still use it for our denominational meeting and our collective voice as a church. But the word *synod* didn't start out meaning "denominational meeting" or "church authority." It started as a Greek word meaning a "journey" or a "group of travelers"; a *synodos* was a fellow traveler. So the idea of going to synod has within it the idea of meeting with fellow travelers, with people headed in the same direction, pointed at the same goal. And, when you go to synod, that's a lot of what you see. You realize that all of the money we send off to our denomination makes a difference that is easy for us to forget back home. You see how our contributions bring relief to devastated areas around our world, and provide education, and support scholarship. You see how much ministry, real *ministry,* we do together. And you are thankful, and you feel like we are indeed fellow travelers.

But those shared ministries and accomplishments are not what most of us think of when we think of synod these days. Because, while our history and our money and our theology may have us traveling together, our differences still tear us apart. And, often in the last decade or so, we've been as torn apart as we have been together. We are a divided church. In some important matters we disagree about the course we should take. So there are certain camps, certain mindsets, certain types, and some of the division between them runs pretty deep. And that divisive part, that part that grabs most of the headlines, doesn't make you feel so good when you go to synod.

These differences cover a lot more than the role of women as elders and ministers. But that of course is the first issue that comes to mind when we think about division in the Christian Reformed Church today. We see it at synod, we see it in our regional classis, we see it in this congregation. And division is a terrible thing to see, because division causes pain and it strains relationships and it creates walls. So when I speak of the division in the church, believe me, I do not speak of it lightly. Division brings with it things like anger and even hatred toward those on the other side. It is a cancer in the body of Christ. It is no small matter. But this morning I want to say that division also brings with it something else. On this morning, this Trinity Sunday, as we consider the words of Jesus Christ, I want to say to you that division also brings with it an opportunity, a wonderful divine opportunity. And that is the opportunity to be an answer to Jesus' prayer, to answer the prayer of our Lord himself.

In John 17 Jesus is praying for the last time. Chapter 18 begins by telling us that, when he had finished praying, he went to an olive grove, and that's where Judas met him with the soldiers who arrested him. So this is

Jesus' final recorded time of prayer with his Father. It's a long prayer in John 17: he prays for himself, and then he prays for his disciples, and then he prays for you and me: "I ask . . . also on behalf of those who will believe in me," he says, "that they may all be one. . . . The glory that you have given me I have given them, so that they may be one, as we are one." And right here, in these words our Lord prays, the doctrine of the Trinity and the Christian Reformed Synod meet, the doctrine of the Trinity and our congregational life meet, the doctrine of the Trinity and our divisions meet. "I ask also on behalf of those who will believe in me . . . , that they may be one as we are one." The one time Jesus bowed in prayer about us — you and me, those who *will* believe in him — he prayed that we would be one as the Father and the Son and the Holy Spirit themselves are one.

Now that sounds impossible to me — at least it did. The way I understood the Trinity, Jesus' hope could be fulfilled only if all of us were identical: if we all agreed on everything, if we all voted for the same people, if we all understood the Bible to say the exact same thing. As I understood the Trinity, the Father, the Son, and the Holy Spirit were all pretty much the same person. We gave them different names for the different things they did. Sometimes we called God the Father and sometimes we called him the Christ and sometimes we called him the Spirit, but in effect, in point of fact, there was just one of them. After all, how else could we refer to these three as one God, unless they're really all the same?

My problem was that I thought the mystery of the Trinity was a mathematical mystery. I thought the mystery of the Trinity was one of numbers: one plus one plus one must somehow equal one; somehow three must add up to one. That's the mistake the Roman side of the church, the Western side, our side, has made for a long time: the idea that the three of the Trinity isn't a real three; that the three isn't really meaning three different persons, three different individuals, but just three different names for the same thing. You can call him Father, you can call him Son, you can call him Spirit, and all three times you're really talking about the same thing. The church has a name for thinking like that about God; it's called modalism, and modalism is heresy.

You see, the mystery of the Trinity is not a mathematical mystery. The mystery is not how one person can also be three persons. The mystery of our God is not how we can call one three; the mystery is how we can refer to three separate individuals in the singular, as one. The mystery is how the Father and the Son and the Holy Spirit can be so united, so much part of the same mission, so much in fellowship together, that we call them one God. That's the mystery.

And it has to be that way, because, if there is one thing that is biblically obvious, it is that the Father and the Son and the Holy Spirit are not the same person. The Son became human, not the Spirit, not the Father. The Spirit was poured out at Pentecost, not the Son, not the Father. And now it is the Father hearing the prayer of the Son, and the Son looking toward heaven saying, "Father, I pray for those who will come after me." Whatever it means that they are one, it does not mean that they are the same. Not at all.

That's why the church has been so careful with its language about the Trinity. "Three persons but still one God," we say. "One God but made up of three distinct, separate persons," we say. So the mystery is that these three distinct persons, each of whom has his own will, his own emotion, his own personality, can so share one purpose, one goal, one love for the others, can so submit to the others' well-being, that, even though they are three, we call them one. And we refer to all of them together as "he." One God.

Jesus Christ, in his last private moment on earth, prayed that we would be the same way. His prayer for us is that, in spite of all that divides us, in spite of the different personalities and interests and backgrounds, in spite of the different ideas and beliefs and convictions, in spite of the fact that we are distinct persons with our own centers of will and emotion and thought, we would reenact the divine mystery and be one, as he and the Father and the Spirit are one. That is the opportunity that our divisions present to us — the opportunity to answer Jesus' prayer and be united, be one, in spite of our differences. But that is not easy, certainly not today.

A few years ago I attended a conference in which the main speaker was Philip Yancey. Yancey writes a column that appears in every other issue of *Christianity Today;* he shares the space with Chuck Colson. Some years ago Yancey wrote an article in his column about a breakfast he had with President Clinton. He mentioned it to us because one thing about that article surprised and troubled him, and that was the hate mail it generated. *Christianity Today* received about five hundred letters, almost none of them friendly or kind, many of them describing his breakfast as an alliance with Hitler or stained by the blood of fetuses.

Yancey went on to tell us about others who have been attacked for what they've written: Madeleine L'Engle and Richard Foster and Eugene Peterson. All of them have been called New Age or demonic for what they've said, yet all of them are careful Christians. After the incident with the Clinton article, Yancey received a letter from Chuck Colson. Colson told him, "I know what you're going through, because you should read my mail. I got together with some Catholics and signed a document about a lot of things we agree on," said Colson. "I thought they were good things. But the firestorm I have endured makes what I experienced after Watergate look small."

Disagreement and division bring the opportunity to look like God, to be a living image of the divine being that is Father, Son, and Holy Spirit. They bring the opportunity to answer the prayer of Jesus Christ, to give him what he most wanted for us: that we would be one as God himself is one. "The firestorm I have endured makes what I experienced after Watergate look small." Those are sad words in the church of Jesus Christ.

But division doesn't have to do that to us. It often does, but it doesn't have to. We can barrel through the walls between us by placing before us the doctrine of the Trinity, by remembering that the Father and the Son and the Spirit are so bound up together, so able to love each other, so willing to submit to the others, that they are three persons but only one God. That is the pattern we must follow; that is the prayer of Jesus Christ for us.

And it must begin right here, because there is disagreement in every church, and this one is certainly not immune from it. We have our differences about ministry and our differences about issues and our differences because sometimes we don't like each other. It's all division, it's all very common, and it all brings a certain measure of pain and sometimes much worse things. But it also brings an opportunity, an opportunity to be like the God who is three in one, an opportunity to answer Jesus' prayer, an opportunity to show the world Jesus Christ.

And that last part is true, too. We have an opportunity to show the world Jesus Christ. Missions are on our minds a lot today — how we do them, how we preach the gospel in this world. Let me give you the first way: by being one with each other. "May they become completely one," prayed Jesus, "so that the world may know that you have sent me and have loved them even as you have loved me." That's what's at stake: when we overcome our differences, when we love and respect and support each other in spite of what divides us, just by watching us, the world will know that God the Father sent God the Son to be their Savior.

We still have a lot of issues to be settled, by Synod and by us. The issues aren't going to stop, the things to disagree on aren't going to go away. And maybe that's just what we should want — opportunities to show the world that God loves them, opportunities to remember that we are fellow travelers, opportunities to be one as God the Father, God the Son, and God the Holy Spirit are one, to be one as they are one.

You may be in the church, but you'll never be part of it, you'll never belong to it, as long as you can't disagree without anger, without condemnation, without hatred, because then we are nothing like the holy Trinity at all. Then we're just interested in getting our way. The church may actually be a better place when nobody gets their way, when we stop talking about what I want and what I think and instead submit to each other, to sacrifice something of ourselves in order to be traveling together.

I suppose then nobody would be satisfied. Nobody would really have what they want — except perhaps Jesus Christ. What he wants for us, what he prays for you and for me, is not that we always get it right, not that we're always consistent, but that we are one, as they are one — the mystery of the Trinity present in the mystery of our communion. It is an amazing, humbling, divine opportunity — for us, right now. In the name of the Father and the Son and the Holy Spirit, Amen.

Labels

Text: John 7:53–8:11

The scribes and the Pharisees brought a woman who had been caught in adultery; and making her stand before all of them, they said to him, "Teacher, this woman was caught in the very act of committing adultery. Now in the law Moses commanded us to stone such women. Now what do you say?" They said this to test him, so that they might have some charge to bring against him. Jesus bent down and wrote with his finger on the ground. When they kept on questioning him, he straightened up and said to them, "Let anyone among you who is without sin be the first to throw a stone at her." And once again he bent down and wrote on the ground. When they heard it, they went away, one by one, beginning with the elders; and Jesus was left alone with the woman standing before him. Jesus straightened up and said to her, "Woman, where are they? Has no one condemned you?" She said, "No one, sir." And Jesus said, "Neither do I condemn you. Go your way, and from now on do not sin again."

John 8:3-11

If you really want to get things done, you have to identify, you have to organize. The instruction manual to my date book says just that. To manage your
time, it says, you should make a to-do list, then you should go through it and
put the items into groups according to importance and urgency and type.
Label everything; that's what you have to do. Identify, prioritize, classify,
LABEL everything. That's the foundation of good time management, the
key to personal success. According to the experts at Day-Timer — who don't
come cheap by the way — there's a place for everything, and, if we want to get
things done, to be efficient, we should see to it that everything is in its place.

Well, let me tell you, the scribes and the Pharisees are efficient.
They're the best time managers you've ever seen. The scribes and the Pharisees have a place for everything you can imagine. They have a place for
prayer and a place for worship and a place for foreigners and a place for
women and a place for oxen and a place for lepers — and a place for sinners. And in John 8 they put some anonymous woman, some sinner, in
her place. "The scribes and the Pharisees brought a woman who had been
caught in adultery," and, before turning to Jesus with their question, they
make her stand before all of them. Efficiency at work — that's what's happening here. They put her in her place.

These religious day-timers do to her what they do best. They've identified what she is, determined their response, and labeled her urgent.
They've paged through their catalogue of sin, found the retail price for
adultery, taped the bill to her forehead, taken her outside, put her in the
middle of a mob, and now are going to make her pay. And they want Jesus
to ring it up on the register.

And, by the way, you can't argue with their paperwork. That's the
thing about scribes and Pharisees: they're expert paper shufflers. They
never make an accounting error. Their checkbooks always balance. They
do their writing in stone. And they do it with stones. And now all they
want Jesus to do is validate their arithmetic. "Now in the law Moses commanded us to stone such women. Now what do you say?"

And it looks like they've got him this time; it looks like Jesus is going
to have to do things their way. There's no denying that the woman has
been tagged correctly — she's been caught red-handed; she's as guilty as
sin. And there's no denying that Moses said what the scribes and Pharisees are claiming — they don't make mistakes like that. So it looks like
this time Jesus is left doodling in the dirt. It looks like this time the
scribes and the Pharisees are right. And it looks like the woman with that
awful label "adulteress" is just a stone's throw away from her death. So
what do you say, Jesus, huh? They want an answer.

And then the tables turn. Jesus hasn't seemed too interested so far. He isn't the time manager the scribes and the Pharisees are. He's been bent over writing in the dirt all this time, oblivious to the excitement around him. But then Jesus straightens up and, with one statement, one response to their demands for his approval, his acquiescence in their death penalty, he compels them to drop their rocks and walk away. His one-line answer makes them put down their books, forget about their label, and go home.

"Let anyone among you who is without sin be the first to throw a stone at her."

Back to doodling.

You're right, says Jesus. You do know how to add. You've tagged her correctly. You've got the right label — she's an adulteress; she's a sinner. And you've looked up the right punishment for somebody with this blot on their record: death. She's guilty and she deserves to die. Everything you claim is correct. Now one of you who doesn't share her guilt, go ahead, get things started; throw your rock at her. One of you who is without sin, go on — let's get this execution rolling. Someone here who *doesn't* deserve death, you're up first — let her have it.

Now that's an answer those old bookkeepers, the scribes and the Pharisees, aren't expecting. Your system is just fine, says Jesus. It's just that none of you is innocent enough to operate it. Executioners aren't on death row themselves. You may not carry around the label of adulterer, but you're guilty, too. There's just some other word stuck to your forehead, some word like "liar" or "hypocrite" or "thief" or "hater" or "idolater" or "self-righteous snob." You belong in the middle with her, not on the outside winding up with a stone.

And surprisingly enough, the scribes and the Pharisees and everyone else who has gathered around Jesus, so ready just a moment or two ago to trap him and to kill her, agree; they see it, too. "When they heard it, they went away, one by one, beginning with the elders." The ones who have lived a while are the first to lose the thrill, to drop their rocks, to wander off. The ones who have lived the longest, the ones with the most to remember, are the first ones who no longer have the stomach for murdering sinners this afternoon. Jesus' answer hits too close to home. Eventually, every person there walks off, before the labels they deserve put them in their place, put them in her place. It's hard to focus on somebody else's adultery when you've got your own past to live with.

"Let anyone among you who is without sin be the first to throw a stone at her." It's pretty difficult to hear those words and a few seconds later crush some sinner's skull with a rock. It's pretty difficult to look in the mirror and see yourself as innocent enough to serve as an executioner of others. Yet that can be easy to forget.

You do get more things done when you've got neat categories and easy-to-use labels. But that's just the problem: the system that's neat, that puts everything in its place, that condemns those who deserve it, is a system that promises nothing, only death, only slavery, only a label you can never lose. Jesus offers something else, something very different. It's something that's probably not really all that efficient, but in it is freedom and a new beginning and life. And that's what we regular church-goers, who can practice our religion so efficiently, need to remember.

I think it's always tempting to label others, to pick out the sins that don't belong to us and say, "Aha, there, those are the people who should die — that adulterer, that thief, that homosexual, he should die. Right, Jesus? That's what they deserve." It's so easy to pick out the sins we love to hate, the sins we are pretty sure we'll never have to worry about committing, and say, "Those are the ones, those are the really evil ones, the unforgivable ones, those are the deadly ones."

That's still going on — too much, too easily. There are too many people holding Bibles and seeking to condemn others who fail, who sin, as if the rest of us could make it on our own righteousness. That's what Jesus rejects again and again and again — the idea that those other people really deserve to die but *we're* okay. He's not excusing this woman. He's not making excuses for her or minimizing her sin. He doesn't even question that she's worthy of death. What he questions, what he denies, is not that she is guilty but that the mob ready to kill her is innocent. What he denies is that *any* of them may condemn her. What he denies is that any of them is without sin.

We need to proclaim that Jesus Christ is the light of the world and that living in his light means living lives of faithfulness and kindness and goodness and patience and peace and self-control. We're looking to be disciples, and we're looking to make disciples. But we're not looking to convict sinners, are we? We're not looking to label people, I hope. We're not looking to condemn. And if we are, we need to see that we're condemning ourselves. Our gospel must not come with labels that send some people to eternal death and us to eternal life. Our gospel must come with the recognition that all of us are a stone's throw away from that death, and all of us, guilty as we are, are capable of being made free from sin.

When we approach those around us as bookkeepers of morality or insiders on God's will rather than as proclaimers of good news, when we put them in their place rather than Jesus in ours, when we hold out a stone of damnation rather than a word of grace, then we've got it all wrong. We're doing things like Jesus' enemies rather than like Jesus himself. We're pretending that we are somehow without sin and so we can cast the first stone.

The ironic thing about this story is, of course, that one person there could have thrown the stone and begun that woman's death. One person there did fit the bill — he was without sin, he was guilt-free. But that person came not to judge the world but to save it (John 12:47); he came to call not the righteous, but sinners (Mark 2:17). And rather than pick up a stone and label her for all time as an adulteress, he left her with this: "If no one else condemns you, then neither do I. Go and sin no more."

In Jesus' words to that woman lies not only her hope for life but ours, too. If he picks up that stone and puts her to death, then he must do the same for every worshiper, every minister, every Christian, because none of us is without sin. But he let the stones lie. Instead, he spoke those amazing words of grace: "Neither do I condemn you."

It's easier when you have labels. Then you can take care of all the adulterers, all the ones who have had an abortion, all the alcoholics, all the drug-users, all the sinners. They can all go to hell where they belong. And those without sin can be saved. But the system that puts people in their place, that gives them what they deserve, that responds to sin efficiently — that system will stone us, too.

You know, counting up sins, making sure the accounts of justice are balanced, labeling human beings — that's not our job. That's what Satan does. He accuses us before God; he labels us as "sinners" and then calls for the law to be followed. Satan requests of God the same thing that the scribes and the Pharisees request of Jesus: that he go by the book, that he follow the rules, that he give the sinners what they deserve. It's the dark side of us that wants sacrifice rather than mercy, that wants others to die rather than be forgiven; it's the sinful part of us that looks at other human beings and demands that God go by the book.

So let's respond to these words as we ought — with praise. Praise God that he changed the labels, that he took the one Satan planted on our foreheads and attached it to his own Son instead, that he became sin for us. Praise God that the one person standing before that woman with the right to throw a stone, the only one without sin, did not condemn her. Praise him that, when Jesus Christ knew that death was the only way to pay for that woman's adultery, he chose not her death but his own. Praise him that, when Jesus Christ knew that death was the only way to pay for our betrayals, our disobedience, our pride, he chose not our deaths but his own. And he turned from the faces of adulterers and prostitutes and idolaters and quick-tempered and greedy human beings like you and me, and he set his face toward the cross. And he died, wearing all those labels, in order to say, "Neither do I condemn you."

Let's praise God for this table, where we remember that his blood was shed for people labeled "sinner," where we over and over again trade in the labels that we earn for the label that he gives, where we remind ourselves that Satan catches us in our sin and demands that we die, but God, who prefers mercy to sacrifice and life to death, refuses to go by the book. Instead, his Son died, and we're left alone with him to hear the words, "Neither do I condemn you. Leave your life of sin."

Losses That Count

Texts: Psalm 88; John 11:1-44

Martha said to Jesus, "Lord, if you had been here, my brother would not have died. But even now I know that God will give you whatever you ask of him." Jesus said to her, "Your brother will rise again." Martha said to him, "I know that he will rise again in the resurrection on the last day." Jesus said to her, "I am the resurrection and the life. Those who believe in me, even though they die, will live, and everyone who lives and believes in me will never die. Do you believe this?" She said to him, "Yes, Lord, I believe that you are the Messiah, the Son of God, the one coming into the world."

John 11:21-27

Some heresies never go away. Some false teachings about God or salvation or Jesus Christ linger through the centuries, even after they have been struck down by the Scriptures, even after they have been declared wrong by the church. One of the most persistent of these heresies is called docetism. Docetism is from the Greek word that means "to seem." Docetists believe that Jesus Christ was not a real human being; he only *seemed* human. The second person of the divine Trinity did not *become* a human being; he just sort of lived in one for a while. He wasn't born from a woman's womb, he didn't die on a cross, and he himself — God himself — didn't experience real human life.

I suppose that the idea of God becoming one of us is so strange, so foreign, that the docetists make pretty good sense. It's hard to picture Jesus Christ experiencing life as we experience it; it's easier to think of him as the baby in "Away in a Manger": no crying he makes. But one thing the Gospel writers make clear about the Savior is that, as strange and illogical as it may seem, he is a living, breathing, complete human being. He had scratches and hobbies and hopes and relatives and fears; and, at least in one family, he had friends. Lazarus and Martha and Mary, says John, were Jesus' friends.

And so on that day in Bethany, when Jesus walks in on the death of his friend, we see his humanity up close, because before he calls on the power of God he weeps the tears of a human being. The one who is the resurrection and the life, the one to whom all authority and power have been given, the one who will in just a moment call Lazarus out of his tomb, even *he* can't look death in the eye without flinching. Jesus wept — don't ever doubt his humanity again.

Some of the residue of docetism in the church today claims that since we know God, since we know Jesus Christ, since we have memorized Romans 8:28 ("we know that all things work together for good . . ."), then we may not mourn, we may not grieve the losses in our lives, we may only smile and say that God's will has been done. Part of the docetism of today says that we must only *seem* like human beings. But docetism is heresy; the Scriptures teach something else. The Scriptures teach that there is a time to mourn as well as a time to dance. The Scriptures teach that facing life's slings and arrows is no easy task, and weeping over them is not out of line.

And those who doubt that, those who believe that someone of Christian faith should not grieve or mourn, should pick up their Bibles. They should turn to this story of the Messiah who wept outside a tomb. They should turn to the Sermon on the Mount. They should turn to the Psalms, the prayer book of God's people. Hear the words of Psalm 88 in the New International Version:

O Lord, the God who saves me,
    day and night I cry out before you.

May my prayer come before you;
　　turn your ear to my cry. . . .
You have put me in the lowest pit,
　　in the darkest depths.
Your wrath lies heavily upon me;
　　you have overwhelmed me with all your waves.
You have taken from me my closest friends
　　and have made me repulsive to them.
I am confined and cannot escape;
　　my eyes are dim with grief. . . .
But I cry to you for help, O Lord;
　　in the morning my prayer comes before you.
Why, O Lord, do you reject me
　　and hide your face from me?
From my youth I have been afflicted and close to death;
　　I have suffered your terrors and am in despair.
Your wrath has swept over me;
　　your terrors have destroyed me.
All day long they surround me like a flood;
　　they have completely engulfed me.
You have taken my companions and loved ones from me;
　　the darkness is my closest friend.

Amen. That's the prayer. The whole psalm is like that. The psalmist is grieving.

Thoughtful Christians know that loneliness and pain, disease and divorce — these are terrible things to bear. And none of them more so than that final enemy, death. And that is as true for us as it is for anyone else. I've learned that, mostly through the experience of others, through courageous people of faith who quietly speak of their loss, through writers like C. S. Lewis and Nick Wolterstorff. After Wolterstorff's twenty-five-year-old son died in a mountain-climbing accident, he wrote an amazing book called *Lament for a Son*. And that is just what it is. A lament. And that is not wrong.

This morning I want to say first that the deaths of those we love, especially when they are sudden or early or tragic, are losses that count. Tears are not wrong; they are not ungodly. Death remains a weapon of the enemy.

And, because of that, going on can be so hard to face. It is hard to face those people who don't know what to say when it happens, who are embarrassed by your loss. And it is even harder to face those others who think they know what to say but they only utter miserable heresies like "It's the Lord's will" or "It's not really so bad" or, like modern friends of Job, suggest "If only you had prayed more, or sinned less."

It's hard to face that the world doesn't stop along with you. When I was seventeen my oldest sister died. I don't remember that whole experience as well as I would expect to, but one sensation I will never forget: when I went back to school the next day everything was the same — the people, the noise, the jokes — but in the same old familiar territory, I was completely out of place.

It's so hard to face the holidays. It's hard to go back to work. It's hard to concentrate on something else. It's hard even to get out of bed. In so many personal and private ways, grief makes life hard.

And part of what's hard is that at the top of our belief system is a God to whom we ascribe the direction of the universe, a God who, we are told, has counted all the hairs of our head. And where is he now? "Why, O Lord, do you reject me and hide your face from me?" Neither the psalmist nor we receive an answer.

I don't think there is one, not one that we can handle, not one that fits within the confines of our world or minds. We do not know exactly why our perfectly good and perfectly powerful God must sometimes allow those we love dearly to be taken from us. All of that is beyond us. All those demands for justice, all the demands to know why — it can't be worked out like that; we can't know such things. But we can know, we do know that a young child's death or a husband's cancer or a mother's stroke is never what God desires. And we know that because we know him; we know that because we know Jesus Christ.

Those around Jesus thought he was weeping because he loved Lazarus, and I believe that. Lazarus was someone Jesus visited with, someone, Frederick Buechner says, who wasn't first a disciple or a student but a friend. He was someone Jesus could talk to and be himself with and confide in; and when Jesus stands outside his friend's grave, even though it will soon be opened, he weeps.

But he weeps not just for Lazarus and not just for himself. Jesus is grieving the grief of those around him, too. He's grieving because they don't know how to grieve. You see, Jesus' tears are different from theirs; John doesn't even use the same word. Jesus weeps at the power of sin and the sting of death, but he weeps as one who knows that this is not the last word, not on Lazarus, not on any who know him.

I can't imagine what it's like to lose a husband in a car accident one

Saturday afternoon, or to bury a ten-year-old daughter, or to see a best friend die of cancer. I'm not going to stand here this morning and say that I know what you go through in those situations, because I don't. And I'm not going to say that it's all right, because it's not. And I'm not going to tell you that it's the Lord's will, because I don't believe that, not as it is said.

What I will say is what Jesus said: He is the resurrection and the life. Anyone who believes in him will live, even though they die. That's what he said to Martha: I am life, even now, even today, even when Lazarus is in the tomb. I am life, and if you attach yourself to me, Martha, death can never be the same again.

I guess it's a wonderful thing that he raises Lazarus and gives him a few more years, but more important than the miracle, there is the sign. Jesus is the source of life, and those who know him never, never have to weep the same tears as the others. When he asks Martha, "Do you believe this?" that's what he's asking: Do you believe me? Do you trust me? The *resurrection* is still coming, but the *life* we have right now. And it makes a difference.

So it is with the writer of Psalm 88. Even though he has no idea why God has allowed such pain to come his way, even though he declares, "my eyes are dim with grief" and "the darkness is my closest friend," still he remembers who it is he is addressing. His prayer begins, "O Lord, the God who saves me." Even when we don't know why, we do know that: he is the God who saves us.

And so it is with Nicholas Wolterstorff, who had the courage to share with the world the experience of grieving his son, and we are better for having read his words. After pages of mourning, after carefully describing that this grief is real, after offering his own lament to God, it is Easter he remembers: "To believe in Christ's rising from the grave is to accept it as a sign of our own rising from our graves. If for each of us it was our destiny to be obliterated . . . then not Christ's rising but my dear son's early dying would be the logo of our fate. . . . So goodbye Eric, goodbye . . . until we see."[2] It is trusting Jesus that tells him there is still much to see.

And that's the difference here, that's why Jesus' tears are not the same, why they cannot be. A friend of mine who knows tells me that there is nothing so distinctively Christian as the response to death, nothing that so displays how set apart we are. "Do you believe this? Do you trust

2. Nicholas Wolterstorff, *Lament for a Son* (Grand Rapids: Eerdmans, 1987), pp. 92, 102.

me?" Jesus asked Martha, and everything in her life, every reaction to her brother's death, was hanging in the balance, determined by her answer.

We live in a culture that likes to pretend we're all really the same, whatever the faith, whatever the worldview. But that's all wrong. Christian faith changes everything; it makes us as different from the rest as Lazarus before and after Jesus shouted for him. And that reality is never put to the test like it is at a grave, because then we face Jesus' question for ourselves: "Even now I am the resurrection and the life. Do you believe this?" When you stand in the presence of those who do, it is like being in the presence of Jesus.

The funny thing about this story is that, by going back to Bethany, Jesus is walking into his own death. He not only weeps human tears but also sheds human blood — both times for us, for the ones he loves, just so light could shine on a people walking in thick darkness, just so Paul could be right to declare that we already have been raised with him. Easter is not only future, it is not only past, it is Today; it is life we possess right now. When we must look death in the eye, when we weep, may our tears be the tears of Jesus. May every one of us share Martha's trust in this person who loves us. May we remember Easter. When we are weak, we can be strong, by grieving as those who have hope. If that is not so, if the God who saves is not our God in these times, if in grief we do not better know our suffering Lord, then, as Nick Wolterstorff says, death has won, then death can be proud. Don't let death be proud. Don't let *Easter* be lost.

— FOURTH SUNDAY AFTER PENTECOST —

Filling Up on Grace

Text: 2 Corinthians 6:1-13

As we work together with him, we urge you also not to accept the grace of God in vain. . . . We have spoken frankly to you Corinthians; our heart is wide open to you. There is no restriction in our affections, but only in yours. In return — I speak as to children — open wide your hearts also.

2 Corinthians 6:1, 11-13

In one of his essays Walter Wangerin talks about the early years of his marriage. When his wife, Thanne, and he were first married, says Walter Wangerin, "we used to fight." Actually it was a one-sided fight, he says, because the talking was all his, the crying all hers. He would beg her to speak, to explain to him what grievous wrong he had committed that had so wounded her, so driven them apart. He would cajole her and stomp around the house and sigh loudly, and finally, says Wangerin, she would cease her tears and open her mouth. And then, he says, "then poured forth such an ocean of wrongs, such a delineation of sins in such numbered and dated detail that I would stand shocked before the passion in" her. And then he would be speechless.

And her attack would be so successful that it forced him to his final weapon: he would leave. He would leave in anger, in self-righteousness, in effrontery. "Without another word," says Wangerin, "I'd jam my arms into my overcoat, bolt down the stairs of our little apartment, and pitch myself into the cold St. Louis night, there to roam the sidewalks three hours at a stretch, wondering whether our marriage would survive, but confident that I had dealt guilt to Thanne's solar plexus. . . . *Take that.*"

That's how it would go in those early days. "But then it happened," he says, "that the Lord intervened, and one night there should have been a different ending to the battle." On that night, which happened to be his birthday, they followed their fighting script perfectly — talking, tears, silence, stomping, sighing, accusations. In fact, "all went well," says Walter, "right up to the jamming of my arms into the overcoat, the running downstairs, and the dramatic leap into the night." But then God had to step in:

When I slammed the front door, I caught my coat in it.

Mad and madder, I rifled my pockets for the key, to unlock the . . . door, to complete this most crucial tactic against Thanne's peace of mind. Take —

But there was no key. My tail was truly in the door, and the door was made of oak.

I had two alternatives. Either I could shed the coat and pace the night unhoused, unprotected. There was real drama in that, a tremendous statement of my heart's hurt — except that Thanne wouldn't know it, and the temperature was below freezing.

Or else I could ring the doorbell.

Ten minutes of blue shivering convinced me which was the more expedient measure. I rang the doorbell.

So then, my wife came down the steps. So then, my wife peeped out. So then, my wife unlocked the door — and what was she doing? Laughing! Oh, she laughed so hard the tears streamed down her face and she had to put her hand on my shoulder, to hold her up.

And I could have smiled a bit, too. I could have chuckled a tiny chuckle; for this was the gift of God, arranging armistice, staging reconciliation between a wife and her husband, a gift more sweet than all the rains of heaven. Laughter: extraordinary forgiveness!

But what did the dummy do? Well, he batted her hand away, cried "Hmpf!" and bolted to stalk the night more grimly than ever before.[3]

He refused the laughter. He refused to open wide his heart. So look at him, says Walter Wangerin, behold him — the stiff-necked, hard-hearted dummy!

This sermon would be easier to preach if I could just laugh at that story, laugh at the dummy, laugh at the fool who would rather stomp off angry than swallow his pride, or his righteousness, or himself. This sermon would be easier to preach if I could just say, Look at that dummy Wangerin, look at those dummies in Corinth, look at them — letting *little* things, letting *past* things, letting *petty* things get in the way of forgiveness and celebration. Look at those dummies, I want to say, as if I have never been a dummy myself.

But when I hear Paul's words, "We urge you not to accept the grace of God in vain," I know all too well what he's talking about. Probably the Corinthians do, too. Way off there in Greece, they have heard the news about this Jewish Savior, this gift of God not only to the Jews but also to *them*, to the Corinthians. They have accepted the grace of God, the love of God, which all by itself gives them life — they know the story, they know Paul, they have received the grace — but they run the risk that it won't show, that it won't make a difference, that it won't lead anywhere. That's what accepting the grace of God in vain means. It means the grace coming to you, being poured out on you, claiming you, but not changing you. It means God's love for his world, for you, falling down upon you and then not showing anywhere. It's grace without an end, without a purpose. It's grace that's empty. It doesn't fill you, it doesn't overflow into your life, it doesn't seep out. As strange as it sounds, you can accept the grace of God,

3. Walter Wangerin Jr., "Fights Unfought, Forgiveness Forgone," in *Ragman and Other Cries of Faith* (San Francisco: Harper & Row, 1984), pp. 126-27.

the astounding love of God, which is freely given to you without your doing anything to earn it, you can learn of your eternal life in the kingdom of God — you can accept all that without anything changing. It doesn't do anything; it doesn't lead anywhere. And that is a strange thing to say about the grace of God.

But the Corinthians may be proving that strange possibility. The Corinthians are having trouble reconciling; they're slamming the door and stomping off instead of coming together. And a good part of their trouble actually has to do with Paul the apostle; in truth, the Corinthians are not all that crazy about Paul. It seems that the ministry of Paul to First Church Corinth hasn't gone as smoothly as everybody planned. For some reason there are some folks — some false teachers — who like to point out things Paul does wrong, things to make him look bad, whether they're true or not. So when he said he would come for two short visits to them but instead made it one long one, these people talked about how Paul couldn't be trusted. And they said he wasn't a real apostle and that he was pocketing the budget envelopes as well.

So that's why Paul has that long paragraph about his ministry here, how he has commended himself in every way, how he has suffered all kinds of beatings and riots and hunger and jails, but that he's remained patient and kind and loving and that through him the power of God has been at work. So his point to the Corinthians is, Don't let those rumors about me make you different. Don't let problems with me shut up your hearts. Don't let yourselves focus on little things, selfish things, or you will have accepted the grace of God in vain.

It is such a strange idea, that you can receive the grace of God and not have it touch something, not have it change you, not have it fill you up with grace of your own. You can be a congregation whose preacher is the apostle Paul himself, you can be a thoughtful minister and writer like Walter Wangerin, you can be a life-long churchgoer and student of the Bible, and it's still possible that you will accept the grace of God in vain — like the Corinthians, at least at this time in their existence; and Walter Wangerin, at least on that cold night in St. Louis; and you and me, whenever we stomp off, whenever we grumble, whenever we try to get what we can and close up our hurts.

It's a strange thing to consider that you can actually accept the grace of God in vain, but it's also pretty easy to do. When you face a broken relationship or a lost job or a sadder life than you ever envisioned, it's easy to focus on the hard things and let them determine what comes next, how you act, who you are. But that's the Corinthian way. That's the way that has the grace of God at a dead end. But there's another way. There's Paul's way — the way that goes through calamities and beatings and sleepless nights and still focuses on something else, still lets something else say what comes next and how you will act and who you are. That's where patience and kindness and holiness come from — the grace of God filling you up.

It is a sad thing when the grace of God comes up empty. It is sad to see Christians at the funeral of a gay man celebrating his brutal beating. It is sad to encounter Christians who are more interested in some political victory than in loving their enemies or telling the truth. It is sad to see people in worship whose main thought is how it should be done differently. It is sad to hear from older, life-long Christians, approaching the end of their lives, who are hardly able to say a kind word about anybody or anything. It is sad, and it is discouraging. But it makes me so thankful for all those of that generation who are so full of kindness and peace and selflessness, who are so much wiser than I am and who teach me so much without trying to teach me at all. We need you older people to do that for us. And we also need to do it for each other.

It's easy to think that, if we're going to accomplish anything, we'd better get in and fight, we'd better run attack ads and spend a lot of money and crush our enemies and be successful — successful politicians, successful lawyers, successful churches. After all, we need to change the world, and that's how the world works. And that's exactly wrong. You know what makes a real difference in the world? It's not slogans or campaigns or money — those things are commonplace. What makes a real difference is forgiveness, peace, patience, kindness, opening wide your heart, filling up on the grace of God.

I've been a dummy like Walter Wangerin that night more times than I care to recall, but once or twice, through realizing the boundless grace of God that I've received, I have granted grace to someone else, someone who wronged me, someone who could be helped by me, someone who made a big mistake but didn't need to hear about it. And those few times when I have given grace, the results have amazed me because of the tremendous difference one gracious moment can make.

Philip Yancey talks about that in his book *What's So Amazing about Grace?* One of his many examples of the power of grace is a story from Ernest Hemingway. In the story, "a Spanish father decides to reconcile with his son who had run away to Madrid. Now remorseful, the father takes out this ad in the *El Liberal* newspaper: 'Paco meet me at Hotel Montana noon Tuesday All is forgiven Papa.' Paco is a common name in Spain, and when the father goes to the square he finds eight hundred young men named Paco waiting for their fathers."[4] Grace is what will change the world; it already has, in Christ. Don't receive it in vain.

"We urge you not to accept the grace of God in vain." Far more than I've extended grace, I've received it and witnessed it. I've had people pardon my foolishness, my shame, my anger — and I am changed because of them. I've watched a friend quietly share his wealth — without a tax advantage, without any present reward — and in doing so give a second chance at life to someone else who needed one. I know people who seek only to build up, people who, when they have a criticism, express it in a way that always reminds you that their love does not depend on your response. I know people who have lost a son or a wife — or both — and still greet each day with gentle spirits and kind hearts. People like these have accepted the grace of God, not in vain, but in all its fullness; and, more than they will ever know, they have changed me, and, more than the world will ever know, they have changed it.

There is something divine about putting aside your rights and your complaints and your offenses and your well-being and your comfort and opening wide your heart. That's how Paul could be such a miserable failure in the eyes of the world around him — with his shipwrecks and jail terms and beatings and execution — and still claim for himself the power of God, "poor but making many rich," as he put it.

I read Walter Wangerin's story and I smile, because our pride and stubbornness are indeed ridiculous. But I also read it and realize that when stomping off and shouting down and hating enemies and holding back forgiveness are our habits, it's not funny at all. When these are our habits, the grace of God has somehow misfired. And we're missing the day of salvation. And we're missing any real chance to make a difference. And we're missing any real chance to know our God.

So consider the meaning of these sacraments, hear the assurance that as far as the east is from the west, so far has the Lord cast our sin from us; sing the hymn that Christ is the world's true light. Learn the language of grace, and speak it in every way you can. Because then you will know the grace of God that is in you, and your world will, too. That's what Paul wants. That's what God wants. And that's how we can make a difference every day.

---

4. Philip Yancey, *What's So Amazing about Grace?* (Grand Rapids: Zondervan, 1997), pp. 37-38.

ORDINARY TIME

Master Copies

Text: Ephesians 4:17–5:20

Let no evil talk come out of your mouths, but only what is useful for building up, as there is need, so that your words may give grace to those who hear. And do not grieve the Holy Spirit of God, with which you were marked with a seal for the day of redemption. Put away from you all bitterness and wrath and anger and wrangling and slander, together with all malice, and be kind to one another, tender hearted, forgiving one another, as God in Christ has forgiven you. Therefore be imitators of God, as beloved children, and live in love, as Christ loved us and gave himself up for us, a fragrant offering and sacrifice to God.

Ephesians 4:29–5:2

It's August 20, 1911, a Sunday afternoon in Paris. Dozens of people are casually strolling through the Louvre, taking in the treasures of the renowned art museum. In the crowd is Vincenzo Perugia and a couple of friends. These guys, however, have more on their minds than art appreciation. At an opportune time, they sneak off into a storage closet, where they spend the night. On Monday morning, the day the museum is closed for maintenance, they emerge in work clothes. They then proceed, as professionally and nonchalantly as they possibly can, to remove from the wall the Louvre's most famous possession, the *Mona Lisa*. Perugia wraps a cloth around the frame and walks out a side door.

But that's only half the plan. Shoplifting the world's most renowned painting is only one step in a scheme that's been in the works for months. You see, Vincenzo Perugia is only an amateur art thief; his real job is art forgery. Several months earlier, Perugia had quietly let it be known that the *Mona Lisa* was going to be taken and available. He found six unethical American art collectors who were interested; he sold it to each of them for three hundred thousand dollars. He then arranged for six forgeries to be made and smuggled to the United States, all *before* the Monday in August when he walked out of the Louvre with the real thing. A couple of days after the theft was announced to the world, the fakes were delivered and paid for. Vincenzo Perugia came away with 1.8 million dollars, and he still had the real *Mona Lisa*. That's what's he really is — less a thief than a forger.

And there are many like him. DaVinci isn't the only one whose works have obeyed God's command to be fruitful and multiply. From Van Gogh to Picasso to Chagall, art forgery is big business — still today. It's even an actual occupation. And that's a problem for the art world, because some who can't make it on their own talent are making it nonetheless. Instead of studying the masters, they just copy them.

And that brings us to the apostle Paul and our Scripture lesson this morning, for the command Paul gives to the Ephesians in the first verse of chapter 5 is a command to forge, a command to reproduce the work of a master. Be imitators of God! he says. Copy the Lord! What an outlandish way to begin a chapter.

Be imitators of God? Is that what faith is all about? Impersonating God? Producing living, breathing copies of the Lord? What's this guy thinking?

Talking about imitation isn't so strange. We're used to that in the Scriptures, like when Moses tells the Israelites in Deuteronomy 18:9, "You must not learn to imitate the peoples around you," or when 2 Kings 17 says that the Israelites went into exile because they imitated those people.

We can understand the writer of Hebrews telling us to imitate the saints who have given up their lives for the church and Paul saying to imitate the churches that set an example in service and giving. We even understand Paul's urging us to imitate him, because he, after all, is a human being like us, with our limitations and our foibles and our sin. Nations and churches and people we can handle — no problem. But imitate God? Here Paul seems to be getting a little carried away.

How can we, in any sense, be imitators of Almighty God? Can we lift up our voice to the clouds or send out the lightning? Does our wisdom make the hawk soar or the eagle build its nest on high? Will the world rest in our hands and thrive under our lordship? Of course not, and God himself tells us that. "To whom then will you compare me, or who is my equal?" he asks in Isaiah 40:25. "To whom will you liken God, or what likeness compare with him?" (v. 18). And the answer of course is no one. Nothing. We cannot be imitators of God.

After all, this is the God we describe in words that are the opposite of us: *im*mortal, *in*visible, *super*natural, *omni*present, *all*-powerful. God is everything that we are not, says our theology. We die; he doesn't. We're stuck in one place; he's not. We're weak; he can do anything. Everything about him says that a human being can never go around masquerading himself or herself as God; there's just too much distance to cover.

So how can Paul expect the Ephesians to cross that gulf between us and God? How can the man who makes it so clear that we are nothing apart from God invigorating us, that each one of us has earned only death as the wage of our sin, that all flesh is indeed grass — how can he go on to command the church to be imitators of God?! It's not possible. It's an idea doomed to fail. Imitate God! Reach for the heavens! It can't be done.

And if we try to follow this advice literally, that's right, it won't be done. It will fail. And Paul knows that. And we need to know that, too. You see, Paul's words to the Ephesians aren't telling them to reach for the heavens. Instead, Paul is reminding them that the heavens have come down to Ephesus. To really understand that first line of chapter 5 we have to read the last line of chapter 4.

In the last line of chapter 4 Paul is talking about our need to be kind to each other and to forgive each other, and he closes it with the reminder ". . . as God in Christ has forgiven you. Therefore be imitators of God, as beloved children. . . ." Paul can't imagine being imitators of God apart from what Jesus Christ did for us with God. So, when Paul tells us to imitate God, he's not telling us to reach for the heavens; he's telling us that heaven has come down, that God has forgiven us, that he has infused us with his very life, that his Spirit resides within us, that *we* have been made sons and daughters of the Holy Almighty God himself — all by the blood and love and life and death of Jesus Christ.

As Paul writes these words, he knows that the gulf between human beings and God is as grand a canyon as ever, but he also knows that Jesus Christ has brought us together. Jesus Christ — fully divine, fully human — has destroyed the wall between us, has done away with the misery of our sin, which now makes it possible for Paul the apostle to say to the churches, "In Christ God forgave you. In Christ God made things right with you. So now, with the distance between you gone, with Jesus Christ as the source of your strength, be imitators of God!"

But what exactly does that mean? What would it look like? With the power and presence of Jesus Christ with us and for us, now, says Paul, we may even imitate God. But how?

There's something strange about this section of Ephesians, something that makes it not seem to fit together so well. The big thought here, after all, right in the center of things, is "Be imitators of God!" And this is the only place in all of his letters that Paul ever tells anyone to imitate

God. So we would think that such a big idea would be explained and elaborated on and surrounded by a bunch of big examples. We would expect Paul to say, "Be imitators of God, and here's what that means: Act like God everywhere. Build up the church. Defeat evil. Possess power. Stop war." That's what we would expect this section to deal with — the *big* things that human beings must accomplish if they're truly going to be imitators of God. But, if you go through all these thirty-six verses, that's not what you find. That's not what Paul talks about. Paul doesn't discuss wars ending and evil falling and victory being won and churches taking over. Paul doesn't talk about the bigness of imitating God at all.

What Paul does talk about is telling the truth to each other, not letting anger get the best of us. What Paul does say is that no one in the body of Jesus Christ should steal anything, that we all should put in a good day's work. What Paul is concerned about is unwholesome talk and bitterness and being unkind to each other. Everything around this huge command to be imitators of God deals with things that are part of life's routine, things that every one of us can practice every day. Nearly everything Paul has to say here about imitating God has to do with what kind of jokes we tell, how our conversations go, whether getting drunk is something we laugh at, whether we sing praise to God and mean it. Those everyday little things are what the apostle Paul ties to being imitators of God. Those everyday little things, says Paul, are pretty good indicators of whether we're imitating God or something more worldly, whether we know the love and forgiveness of Jesus Christ or not.

Being imitators of God doesn't, of course, have to do with impersonating him. It has to do with following him, with knowing him, with living out of his life, and love, and grace. "Once you were darkness, but now in the Lord you are light. Live as children of light" (Eph. 5:8). That's how we become imitators of God, by living as his children, knowing him as Father, reflecting his light. That's all it takes.

The real *Mona Lisa* was recovered two years later, when Vincenzo Perugia was arrested, and he still had it with him. Actually, most forgers are found out in the end. Nowadays they take an x-ray machine to the canvas so they can see under the paint, because a forgery is only skin deep, only one layer — it doesn't show all the change and the revision and the work that go into the original. An original always goes well beneath the surface. Imitations never have the depth of the master.

And the same is true of us, of course. The Master we're imitating just can't be copied. We always fall way short. We're lousy forgeries. Anyone who pays any real attention at all can see that we're nothing like the real thing. But that's not the point here, is it? The goal of these words isn't that we pretend to be God; we're not trying to fool anyone or take over for him. The goal is that, in the conversations and transactions and emotions of our lives — in a father's real forgiving of his teenager's recklessness, in two friends patiently talking into the night because they don't want their disagreement to go into a new day, in the way a boss treats her young intern, in a man's willingness to walk away rather than join in laughter at a degrading joke, in a college student's demeanor during a pick-up basketball game, in a couple's offering their daughter for baptism, in the hymns of a small congregation, in the faithfulness of a husband for four decades, in a mom's turning to her child and saying, "I'm sorry" — the goal is that, in those things and all things like them, whenever we live like children of our heavenly Father, the world around us will get a glimpse of God. The goal is that our faith and love and kindness and obedience will make us transparent, so people will see right through us to the living Lord. And then, in those ways, it can properly be said that we are his imitators.

The Importance of Old Sermons

Text: Hebrews 13:7-8

Remember your leaders, those who spoke the word of God to you; consider the outcome of their way of life, and imitate their faith. Jesus Christ is the same yesterday and today and forever.

Hebrews 13:7-8

A few years ago, during baseball's spring training, *Sports Illustrated* polled a number of major league players to determine their knowledge of baseball. But the poll wasn't about rules or who would win the pennant; it was about the game's past. The magazine was wondering, Just how much do major league ballplayers know about the first hundred years of their sport? The answer was pretty clear: not much. When asked about the two most famous New York Yankees of all time, the team's star first baseman admitted that, before he'd joined the Yankees, he had never heard of the one and thought the other was a cartoon character. With a couple of notable exceptions, the other players didn't do any better; their knowledge of the men who had gone before them and paved their way was almost nonexistent. The manager of the Montreal Expos summed things up pretty well: "I think," he said, "most guys know the *names* 'Babe Ruth' and 'Hank Aaron.'" Now, this is not to say that these ballplayers are dumb. Not at all. They know a lot of things, like the name of the man who created their labor union and the batting average of the guy they're pitching against and their agent's pager number. They know those things. It's the retired guys they have trouble with, the guys from the past. *Sports Illustrated*'s assessment of all this is that the answers to their poll would be highly entertaining, would make for a great laugh, if they weren't just a little bit depressing. For some reason, they figure, it matters when we forget about what's brought us to today, when our vision goes no further than the edge of our own lives. So they describe the current situation as "depressing."

And of course in that way we're talking about more than baseball. We live in a postmodern society, a society that more than ever before stresses change and progress and independence and the future at the expense of the past. Not long ago there was an advertisement for a Midwestern school of computers or technology that depicted two young men about the same age, one pictured slavishly studying for an exam on the Spanish-American War or some such event, the other already out of school and making terrific money and having a ball doing it. The ad ends with this comment by the money man, "While he's studying the past, I'm building the future. ITT Tech." Judging from the number of times the commercial ran, I'd say ITT Tech thought it was working.

This wasn't always the case. There was a time when a liberal arts education was a valued possession, when reflecting on history or studying literature or listening to the music of another time was considered anything but a waste of time or a hindrance to progress. But that's not really so anymore. We're moving forward into the future too fast to worry about the accomplishments or the people or the importance of the past. And, as *Sports Illustrated* has said, it might be fun if it weren't just a little bit sad.

And it's especially sad when that attitude moves from baseball players and college choices and the culture at large into the church. It's especially sad when it happens in the church because in the church's case it's not just the memory of a person that we're losing — as important as that is — but a vital part, a component of our faith, as well. That's what lies behind those New Testament commands to guard the deposit you have received, stand firm and hold on to the teachings that were passed on to you, and, as the author of Hebrews writes, "Remember your leaders, those who spoke the word of God to you."

The author of Hebrews thinks highly of the leaders in the church. In chapter 13 he talks about obeying them and greeting them. But here, in verse 7, he says something else, something different: He says, Remember them. "Remember your leaders, those who spoke the word of God to you." Not "listen as they speak" but "remember them who spoke." Past tense. You see, these leaders aren't speaking the word of God anymore. Their careers are over. It seems that their lives may be over. But the importance remains: "Remember them who spoke the word of God to you."

Now, the people who receive this letter don't have to think too hard when they hear these words. They don't have to check any books out of the library or take a class in Reformed theology to obey this command, because their church is only a few decades old, maybe just a few years old. They know how these people lived and who they were and what they did and how they died. They know how they acted and what they said and how they sounded. But that's not really the point. The point isn't: remember them and act like them, copy their mannerisms and their temper, and things like that. This command isn't about imitating *them;* it's about imitating their *faith.* It's not about remembering the way they spoke; it's about remembering that they spoke the word of God.

The issue here is maintaining the purity of the Christian faith or seeking ever to purify it; in Paul's words to Timothy, it's about guarding the deposit we have received (1 Tim. 6:20; 2 Tim. 1:14). That's what's on this writer's mind. We can see that in verse 9, where he says, "Do not be carried away by all kinds of strange teachings." That's what he's worried about. He wants their faith to remain pure, their doctrine to be true, their knowledge of God to be right and grounded in something. And much of the way the church does that, he says, is by remembering those who spoke the word of God to us. Because "Jesus Christ is the same yesterday and today and forever."

The world can change, styles can change, culture and language can change, but Jesus Christ is the same. His career will always be the center of history. His death will always be *the* important event in the life of every human being. So those who spoke his word faithfully at one time continue to speak his word faithfully now. Even a generation later, even five centuries later. And we are called to remember them, to guard the deposit we've been given, to stand firm and hold on to the teachings that have been passed on to us; we're called to do that because these men and women spoke of Jesus Christ.

Whether we like it or not, whether it's fashionable or not, we cannot forget that we have a past. We have a history that tells us who we are. It's not always pretty, it's certainly not perfect, but through it God has guided us. And he has taught us. He has taken nineteen and a half centuries to bring us to this point. We have to respect that, to remember our leaders who spoke the word of God to us; and, when it was the word of God they spoke, we have to let them continue to speak, because what they spoke still matters today.

Our tradition helps us understand that God created this world good, and so when our scientists explore it and our poets proclaim it and our judges uphold it, they are doing the will of God. Our history emphasizes that God is immensely sovereign, almighty, a God whom nothing can stand against. But that sovereignty isn't a threat; it's a comfort, because that sovereignty, that power, guarantees the covenant he has with us, a covenant that will not fail, because he will not fail. The centuries-old tradition in which we stand has considered how to read the Scriptures, how to respect them and understand them faithfully; and if we remember that tradition now we will never flounder around in all kinds of strange teachings, getting all excited because some Hebrew word sounds like "Saddam Hussein." We have a way to come to the Bible. Our spiritual ancestors gave their lives to determine and proclaim that it is not money that is our heavenly comfort; it is not penance, or good deeds, or confession, or even a declaration from the church that gives us comfort and the hope of salvation. It is grace; it is the act of God. That is the Reformation. We're constantly tempted to believe that salvation rests on something we do, something we earn, some baptism we have or church membership we keep, but those are dead ends. And we remember that better when we remember those who spoke the word of God to us.

They weren't perfect people, of course, not at all. And it's hardly a perfect tradition. And I'm the last person who would say that we should repeat things the same way year after year, week after week. I'm scared of that kind of thinking, I'm scared of traditionalism: spitting out the Apostles' Creed just because this is the place we always spit out the Apostles' Creed. That's not tradition; that is traditionalism. The noted historian Jaroslav Pelikan once said, "Tradition is the living faith of the dead; traditionalism is the dead faith of the living." Reformed people cannot be traditionalists, ever, by definition. But that living faith cannot be rediscovered every twenty years; we must remember it, and we must pass it on, as it has been passed on to us.

There was a time in baseball when the players were fans, mostly. They knew the game; they loved the game; they remembered the game. And there was a time in the church, certainly in the Christian Reformed Church in its early days, like many denominations, when people sitting in the pews, some with no more than a fourth-grade education, could correct a preacher's theology, because they knew who they were, they knew their catechism, they guarded the deposit, they remembered those who had come before them. It's not really like that now. And in the words of *Sports Illustrated,* that might be something to smile at, if it weren't just a bit depressing.

That's why we shouldn't leave the remembering to Reformation Day. Part of being the people of God is remembering our leaders who spoke his word to us. And, for all their foibles, for all the things we may understand a little better today, for all the things we must sort through, one thing we must declare: those reformers spoke the word of God. They did it in Geneva and Heidelberg, and they still do it in Modesto and Boston. At least they can. But first we must remember them; first we must let them.

This may not be politically correct in this age of generic Christianity, but I have to say, I'm proud of our tradition. I'm glad it's there. I cherish the chance to study it, first in seminary and now in ministry. It's funny how in this day of encouraging people to remember our Japanese heritage or our Dutch heritage or our Irish heritage, it's not encouraged to remember our theological heritage. But that's the one we should concentrate on the most, because, before we're Japanese or Dutch or Irish, we're Christian, we're part of the people of God. That's the history we need to value.

I'm grateful for those of you who work at remembering, who insist that the faith of those who have gone before us live in us still. I'm grateful for you because you are of immense value to young preachers who are tempted to ignore the past and go their own way. I'm grateful for confessions that are still important enough to us to be in our hymnals, for Reformation Day services that insist that Jesus Christ is the same yesterday and today and forever, for adult education classes that study the doctrines of the church.

I know that this topic is not very popular in the church today. I know that people don't want to hear about doctrine now, that there's a movement to accentuate the emotional aspects of the faith and to downplay the theological ones, to make sure that worship gives us a good time, regardless of how ridiculous or wrong the words we sing or the things we do. I know there's something romantic about flipping open your Bible and letting it speak to you without giving any thought to how the church has treated these things or what the principles of interpretation are. I know that in some places there's such a desire to make churches grow that church leaders figure, "If the culture's not interested in the past, then neither are we. If the culture doesn't want to deal with theology, then we'll leave theology out." I know all that's there; I just think it's a big step in the wrong direction. Because, like it or not, faith is not based on feeling but on fact. It's a mistake to try to go from the first century to the twentieth as if nothing came in between. The deposit we are to guard today has been transmitted from Paul to Timothy to Augustine to Calvin to Abraham Kuyper to you and me. There are a lot of leaders who have spoken the word of God to us, a lot of old sermons to remember. In a day when we're taught to think that life begins and ends with me and my good time, how important it is to know that the church begins and ends with Jesus Christ, that his disciples have been doing this work of serving him for thousands of years, and that they can teach us about serving him today. They must.

When I was growing up in the western suburbs of Chicago, there was a new church in the area that everyone was talking about. It was established by a former Christian Reformed minister named Arthur DeKruyter. By the time I was in high school thousands of people were attending this church and listening to DeKruyter preach. I hadn't thought about him for some years when I came across a letter he wrote to *The Banner*, our denominational magazine, a few years ago. Here's what he says:

> Since I left the Christian Reformed Church, I have followed with interest the struggles of the CRC to find its identity and achieve its goals of growth and significance. In meeting with CRC leaders and reading certain articles [in *The Banner*], I note an assumption that the CRC is no longer relevant because of its liturgy and tradition. After forty years of ministry and the blessing of leading a church from five families to five thousand members, I am convinced that innovation and change are neither the guarantee of success nor the necessary elements of relevancy. The CRC is losing enthusiasm for its heritage, commitment to its distinctiveness, and communication of biblical truth according to Reformed standards. But trading liturgy for religious programming, denominational loyalty for independence, and Reformed preaching for faddish how-to solutions is not the answer. I plead with you to trust each other, pray for vision, and get back to your wonderful heritage, which, when given spiritual freedom, speaks so adequately to contemporary needs.

Instead of making decisions by staring into the future, with all its sociological trends and new inventions and emphasis on entertainment, maybe we would better prepare ourselves for what's next by looking back, considering this precious gift of Christian tradition we possess, remembering those who spoke the word of God to us, and then living out what we learn every way that we can. It will make a difference.

It's interesting that chapter 13 of Hebrews isn't a doctrinal chapter; it's not the teaching part of the letter. It's mostly the part in which the writer says good-bye and makes a few personal comments to these Christians. This is where he gives the church practical advice, things that matter to this church right now, immediately. And how interesting it is that in that advice, along with "Pray for us" and "Love each other" and "Keep your lives free from the love of money," is this word: "Remember your leaders, those who spoke the word of God to you." Whether we honor that word, whether we remember who we are and the leaders who spoke the word of God to us, will make a difference, and, when we forget, it's more than just a little bit depressing.

SERMONS FROM THE MINOR PROPHETS

— FOURTEENTH SUNDAY IN ORDINARY TIME —

God Pacing

Text: Hosea 4:16-18; 11:1-11

When Israel was a child, I loved him,
*   and out of Egypt I called my son.*
The more I called them,
*   the more they went from me;*
they kept sacrificing to the Baals,
*   and offering incense to idols.*
Yet it was I who taught Ephraim to walk,

I took them up in my arms;
  but they did not know that I healed them.
I led them with cords of human kindness,
  with bands of love.
I was to them like those
  who lift infants to their cheeks.
  I bent down to them and fed them.
They shall return to the land of Egypt,
  and Assyria shall be their king,
  because they have refused to return to me.

Hosea 11:1-5

Macon Leary is Anne Tyler's "accidental tourist," a put-upon guidebook writer who's perennially uncomfortable, always striving to avoid change. At this point in the story Macon and his wife are separated, as they independently try to put their lives back together after the murder of their adolescent son a year or so ago. Macon has befriended a young woman and, just now, begun to mentor her young son, Alexander.

At first Macon didn't care much for Alexander; he certainly felt no bond with him, no special hope for him. But now — as he has shopped with this little boy for his first pair of jeans, as he has taught him to fix a leaky faucet, as he has talked to him about his day at school — without Macon's planning it or even knowing it, Alexander has begun to matter to him. It all becomes clear to him one afternoon as the boy comes home from school.

Alexander is not a particularly healthy or athletic or attractive child, and as Macon sees him on the street this day, he sees him clumsy and crying, begging the other children to wait for him. Macon can't hear their response, but he knows the tone — they are mocking Alexander. Two groups of children are jeering at him. So Macon sends his dog to the rescue. Alexander throws his arms around the dog, and together the three of them walk home, in silence. Alexander refuses to talk about what just took place, but as they walk he slips his hand into Macon's.

At that moment, says Anne Tyler, "Macon tightened his grip and felt a pleasant kind of sorrow sweeping through him. Oh, his life had regained all its old perils. He was forced to worry once again about nuclear war and the future of the planet. He often had the same secret, guilty thought that had come to him after [his own son] Ethan was born: From this time on I can never be completely happy."[1]

1. Anne Tyler, *The Accidental Tourist* (New York: Alfred A. Knopf, 1985), pp. 257-58.

"From this time on I can never be completely happy." I expect those words make perfect sense to you parents. No surprise there. No surprise in a parent's involvement in her child's hopes or successes or failures. That *we're* involved like Macon Leary is no surprise at all. The surprise is that God is, too. The surprise is that here, in the prophecy of Hosea, in the part of the Scriptures usually associated with the judgment and anger and vengeance of God, we find, not God the judge, not God the king, not God the ruler of the universe, but God the parent, looking for his child, wondering what to do, suffering himself because of his love for his child. It is a strange thing to see God pacing.

But he is. His people have turned their back on him and looked to other gods, false gods, for protection and prosperity and hope. Things are so bad that he is ready to give up. That's why Hosea is here — to warn Israel that the end has come, that judgment is on the way:

> Like a stubborn heifer,
>   Israel is stubborn;
> can the Lord now feed them
>   like a lamb in broad pasture?
> Ephraim is joined to idols —
>   let him alone.
> When their drinking is ended, they indulge in sexual orgies;
>   they love lewdness more than their glory.
>
> (4:16-18)

So now, nearing the end of the book, with nothing changed in Israel, with exile approaching and Israel still looking to human gods and human kings and human power to deliver them, we don't hear just the voice of Hosea, we also hear the thoughts, the pain, the struggle within the mind of God himself. He knows what Israel is: a rebel, a reprobate, a promiscuous purveyor of the latest religion. But he also knows who Israel is: his own child.

> When Israel was a child, I loved him,
>   and out of Egypt I called my son.
> The more I called them,
>   the more they went from me;
> they kept sacrificing to the Baals,
>   and offering incense to idols.
> Yet it was I who taught Ephraim to walk,

> I took them up in my arms;
>> but they did not know that I healed them.
> I led them with cords of human kindness,
>> with bands of love.
> I was to them like those
>> who lift infants to their cheeks.
>> I bent down to them and fed them.

(11:1-4)

Those don't sound like the words of the ruler of the universe about to send judgment on a disobedient servant — not at all. Those sound like the words of Macon Leary as he remembers teaching his son how to fix a sink or how to throw a ball, or as he considers how frightening it is to raise a child, and how painful it is to lose one. In Hosea 11 God is losing one.

> They shall return to the land of Egypt,
>> and Assyria shall be their king,
>> because they have refused to return to me.
> The sword rages in their cities,
>> it consumes their oracle-priests,
>> and devours because of their schemes.
> My people are bent on turning away from me.

(vv. 5-7)

Everything he's tried has failed. Every piece of advice he's given has been ignored. Every rule he's set down has been broken. Every understanding they've come to has been mocked. So now, having tried everything he can think of, having loved them every way he knows how, having suffered with them and rescued them and searched for them, this parent finally gives up. For seven hundred years he's been raising them, and almost the whole time they've rebelled. The time has come to cut them off.

That's what exile really is. It's losing your inheritance. You see, that land that you leave behind stands for something. It's the result of a promise. It's home. But now Israel is being kicked out. That's the idea. That's what God is thinking — that his child has ended their relationship, that there comes a time when a parent has nothing more to give, that a son can lie and cheat and ignore and betray so much, year after year, that in the end there's no son left.

I know a son like that. For years he abused his parents and took advantage of them, costing them money and pride and pain. His sister died of cancer nine years ago. His father died five years ago last month. It's just him and his mom now. After his dad died she had to hide the insurance papers in the trunk of her car, because he would steal them if he could find them. Today he doesn't know where she is. She's hiding from him. She just wants him out of her life. I told her it was the right thing to do. "Ephraim is joined to idols — let him alone," says the Lord. It's the only way. He's lost his son. It's the right thing to do.

But he doesn't do it: "How can I give you up, Ephraim? How can I hand you over, O Israel?" (v. 8). It is a strange thing to see God pacing, to think of God struggling with what to do over a wayward child, to consider him refusing to give up even though there seems no other way.

> My heart recoils within me;
>   my compassion grows warm and tender.
> I will not execute my fierce anger . . .
> for I am God and no mortal,
>   the Holy One in your midst,
>   and I will not come in wrath.

(vv. 8-9)

Such is the love God has for Israel that he cannot do what he said he would do; he cannot give up on them just because they have given up on him.

There's a scene in the film *Schindler's List* in which Oskar Schindler, growing ever more compassionate toward the Jews, is speaking with Amon Goethe, the local Nazi commandant. Goethe is a cruel man, who kills Jews with a long-range rifle from his balcony as they work, simply to display his power over them, his complete authority. Schindler is gently trying to make Goethe more humane, trying to save a few more Jewish lives. Goethe has been telling him that control is power, that the Jews fear the Nazis because they have the power to kill. To that Oskar Schindler responds, "They fear us because we have the power to kill arbitrarily. A man commits a crime and he should know better. We have him killed and we feel pretty good about it. . . . That's not power, though. That's justice. It's different than power. Power is when we have every justification to kill, and we don't."

It's easy to think of God's power as all threat, because he can do so much. It's easy to think of power as power to judge, power to exile, power to kill. But that's wrong. The power of God is never more evident than it is here in Hosea 11, when he holds on to a son he has every justification for cutting off. "I will not execute my fierce anger, for I am God and no mortal."

There is the hope of Israel. *There* is the gospel. He is God and not mortal. He is God and not a human being. In him there is power not to kill, even when all the circumstances call for it. In him there is power to overcome his anger. Israel will return home, will know him, will have their Father, because that is what *he* has decided will happen:

> They shall go after the Lord,
>   who roars like a lion;
> when he roars,
>   his children shall come trembling from the west . . .
>   and I will return them to their homes, says the Lord.
>
> (vv. 10-11)

"For I am God and no mortal." There is the hope of Israel.

And there is the hope of you and me. We aren't the people of Israel in the eighth century B.C. Although we're regularly tempted to cast our lot with human modes of security, we are not joined to idols. The church has not begun worshiping another god. And yet, we must know that we are not making our own way; we have not earned our place — far from it. As with the idol-worshiping Israelites, it is God that keeps us from being orphans. Even today, even with us, he has more than enough justification to kill, more than enough reason for anger. If we don't believe that, we deceive ourselves.

But it is God that we deal with and no human being, no mortal. It is one with the power *not* to kill. It is one who holds on to his children, who brings them back, who doesn't give up. I know that some of you are praying every day for a mother, a cousin, a friend, a child of your own who has wandered far away from the Holy God. You should pray for them. You should also not despair. You should not let yourself believe that they have counted themselves out, that they have wandered too far, that God will have no more to do with them, that he will give up on them. Do not believe it.

God's people are not business partners with him. They are not acquaintances. They are not commodities. They are children. That's why he's pacing. That's why he's suffering. That's why he refuses to let them die. He is their Father, and this Father is God and no mortal. This parent has the power to forgive, to bring them back, to bring them home.

I don't know exactly how Hosea 11 played out in history. After all, Israel still did go into exile. Some of his children didn't seem to come home. I don't know about that. And Hosea doesn't exactly tell us about that. What Hosea does tell us about is the heart of God. Hosea 11 tells us that we have a God much more like a reminiscing parent who refuses to let go of a wayward child than like a cool, impartial judge. Hosea 11 tells us that we have a God who paces, worrying what will happen to us next, trying to find a way to save us. That's the God of Hosea, a God who loves his people with a fierce and dangerous love.

Whatever we face in the years ahead, and whatever we deserve, we always know the heart of God. He's a God looking for ways to bring his children home, to keep them alive — even if it keeps him up at night, even if it means he must taste death himself.

This is a God we can count on, a God we need to know better, a God we need to stay near. In the name of Jesus Christ, Amen.

Day of the Locust

Text: Joel 1:2-4

Hear this, O elders,
give ear, all inhabitants of the land!
Has such a thing happened in your days,
or in the days of your ancestors?
Tell your children of it,
and let your children tell their children,
and their children another generation.
What the cutting locust left,
the swarming locust has eaten.
What the swarming locust left,
the hopping locust has eaten,
and what the hopping locust left,
the destroying locust has eaten.

Joel 1:2-4

Some books, or plays, or paintings have such depth, such perceptiveness, that they stay with you much longer than you'd ever expect. They play on your mind; they make you think about things. As you may have guessed from other sermons, one of those for me is Kathleen Norris's book *Dakota,* in which a writer chronicles her experience after she moves from New York City back to the small North Dakota town and house of her grandmother, soon after her grandma's death. The book is powerful in its reflection upon the hard, rural life of the American prairie and how the solitude, the economy, and the climate impact the people who live there. Norris points out that there are stories in this way of life, stories that should be told, stories of struggle and sorrow and defeat. But, she says, there are few people who tell these stories — mainly, she thinks, because in this land there are few people who want to hear them.

The people of the plains, the people of Dakota — at least the ones in this town — don't encourage such story-telling, such remembering of the past. They prefer to remember things another way, a way that wasn't so difficult, a way that promised a safe and prosperous future. They like to hear a "good story," as they call it. And "a good story is one that . . . above all doesn't remind us of the bad times, the cardboard patches we used to wear in our shoes, the failed farms, the way people you love just up and die. It tells us instead that hard work and perseverance can overcome all obstacles; it tells lie after lie, and the happy ending is the happiest lie of all." They don't want to remember. So, Norris says, families on the plains have actually "walked away from farmhouses and moved to town, leaving behind not only the oak furniture but old china and handmade quilts, even family photographs. The truth was so painful," she says, "it literally had to be abandoned."[2]

And that is exactly what Joel the prophet is concerned about for the people of Judah: the abandoning of the truth, the erasing of the hard times. He wants them to remember everything, even the pain. That's what makes these first verses of Joel so peculiar. It's not that he calls the elders and everyone who lives in the land to hear him. It's not that he commands them to tell this to their children. The peculiar part of these words is what Joel wants them to say, what he finds so important that it should be passed on from generation to generation. Here it is; here's what Joel wants to be told in Judah from this day forward:

2. Kathleen Norris, *Dakota: A Spiritual Geography* (New York: Ticknor & Fields, 1993), pp. 85-86.

What the cutting locust left,
    the swarming locust has eaten.
What the swarming locust left,
    the hopping locust has eaten,
and what the hopping locust left,
    the destroying locust has eaten.

Remember *that,* says Joel. You see, Joel has the idea that the day of the locust has something to do with the day of the Lord, and that if you forget
the first, you may just miss the second.

But *Day of the Locust?* It sounds like one of those B horror films from
the sixties: *The Grasshopper That Ate Tokyo* or something. And that's just
about what it is, except that it's not a movie, and it's not Tokyo; it's Jerusalem. The locusts Joel is talking about didn't just destroy a few plants or
hurt some farmer's crop. They devastated Judah. They still do.

You see, this part of the world is somewhat prone to locust invasions.
In 1915 an invasion of Jerusalem, Palestine, and Syria was covered by *National Geographic.* The work of the locusts was devastating. Peter Craigie describes it this way: "At the end of February, great clouds of locusts began
flying into the land from a northeasterly direction, so that 'attention was
drawn to them by the sudden darkening of the bright sunshine.' They
came in enormous numbers, settling on the fields and hillsides. There they
laid their eggs in vast numbers (it was calculated that some 60,000 could
come from the eggs planted in thirty-nine square inches of soil . . .). Once
hatched, the new broods started crawling across the ground, at a rate of
400 to 600 feet per day, devouring every scrap of vegetation in their path."[3]

Later on, Joel calls them a large and mighty army. He says,

Before them peoples are in anguish,
    all faces grow pale. . . .
They leap upon the city;
    they run upon the walls;
they climb up into the houses. . . .
The earth quakes before them,
    the heavens tremble.
The sun and the moon are darkened,
    and the stars withdraw their shining.

(2:6, 9-11)

3. Peter C. Craigie, *Twelve Prophets,* vol. 1 (Philadelphia: Westminster, 1984), p. 86.

Think of it: sixty thousand eggs can come from just thirty-nine square inches of ground.

> What the cutting locust left,
> the swarming locust has eaten.
> What the swarming locust left,
> the hopping locust has eaten,
> and what the hopping locust left,
> the destroying locust has eaten.

Joel's not exaggerating. Locusts have destroyed everything in sight. And he wants the people to remember it.

But why? Why does he want them to remember? Why does he want them to tell their children about the locusts that ate Judah? Joel believes that locusts — and cancer and failed farms and earthquakes — as hard as they are to think about, emphasize something important to us. And Joel believes that, if the people of Judah forget about the dreadful day of the locust, they will pay for it on the dreadful day of the Lord.

The easy thing to do here, the natural thing to do, is to call Orkin and get on with their lives. The easy thing is to do their best to make it look like Jerusalem never saw a lightning bug, let alone a few billion locusts. The easy thing — the easier thing, the less painful thing — is to leave this part of their lives behind and tell each other only "good" stories, the stories that don't remind us of the bad times, the stories that lie. It's no fun to remember that a bunch of locusts ate everything you owned, everything you counted on, everything that gave you a chance. But Joel says, "Remember it. Tell it to your children. Don't abandon the truth."

And the truth is that nothing those folks in Judah could do was going to stop those locusts, just as nothing could stop them in 1915. Crises, tragedy, failure, pain, death — they all come. And however advanced, or smart, or strong you are, they'll always win out eventually. There will always come a time when they eat everything you've got. You may figure out a way to ward off the locusts, but something else will take their place, something else will come along to take your crop next year or next decade. So tell your children, says Joel. Tell them about the year that the locusts were everywhere and ate everything and ruined everyone. Tell the children that. But what should they tell them? What should they say about the locusts?

Joel wants them to say that God once used an insect as a call to confession. And it worked. Joel wants them to say that we lost everything in Judah that year to those locusts, but then we remembered how much we need our God; we had been forgetting him, but then we called out to him, and he saved us. Joel wants them to tell their little ones that it's easy to think we keep ourselves alive, we provide our own food, we run things, but the year of the locusts reminded us that none of that is true. We depend on the Lord for it all. Joel wants them to acknowledge that the locusts beat us, the locusts took everything we have, but the Lord delivered us and gave us life again. So remember the terrible locusts, because then you will remember your Lord.

Like almost every prophet that we'll run into, Joel has a warning to announce. And Joel's warning is that the day of the Lord will be a brutal day, a devastating day — even for Judah, even for the church. It'll be a day in which it's more than crops and homes that are destroyed; everything will be at stake, wherever sin has abounded. But it won't destroy you, not if you remember the locusts, not if you remember that there is only one place to turn for help, not if you remember to humble yourself before your God. So don't forget the locusts. And tell your children so they know it, too, so they don't end up at the day of the Lord, never having heard about the hard times, never having heard that you can't make your own way, that you can't count on your own strength.

It's so much easier to tell only "good" stories, stories that don't demand anything, that don't remind us of the bad times, that pretend the day of the Lord will be a snap if we're just basically good people, basically good Americans. So we have to tell about the locusts. We have to tell each other, we have to tell our children, that God's judgment will catch up even his own people when they turn away from him, when they ignore him, when they forget him. We have to tell them that there's only one place to turn in order to live. Tell your children, says Joel.

I worry about that. The ways to tell the children are dwindling. In this day when worship has lost much of its priority, when Sunday school is optional, when lives are full of everything but reading the Scriptures, when Christian education — at any level — is deemed less and less important, I worry. How are we telling our children? It's a bit sad that so few of us know that the locusts once devastated Judah and that Joel used that event as a reminder that the day of the Lord is coming. That's sad. But there are a lot more common, more basic biblical ideas than locusts that few of us spend any time on at all, that we're not trying to understand ourselves, let alone explain to our children. Let's not be so foolish as to believe that faith — or we — will stay alive because we pay some lip service to it.

We need to tell our stories. We need to say what the priorities are. Our children need to know them like they know their aunts and uncles. They need to know how God stepped into the world and grabbed a man named Abraham and said, "It's you and me now." They need to know that that's our ancestor; that's our family tree we're talking about. Let's remember it. Let's remember the locusts, too. That's a promise we make at baptism — a vow. Take it seriously. Don't let others, don't let your children, believe that basketball games or waterskiing or television or money is more important than belonging to this Lord, than telling the stories about him. As awful as it was, the locusts gave Jerusalem a chance to set itself right, to give the Lord once more the place he deserves. Remember the locusts.

So Joel calls our attention to the crisis, but he doesn't stop there. He begins by saying, Repent, turn to God, remember your place, tell the children. And then he envisions a new day, a day when God's Spirit will be poured out, when sons and daughters will prophesy, when anyone who calls on the name of the Lord will be saved. Joel envisions a day when the Lord will pardon the sin of his people. In Joel 2:25 the Lord says, "I will repay you for the years that the swarming locust has eaten." We're so close to that time, so close to the end — Jesus Christ has died in our place, the Spirit has been poured out, and our children have been baptized, our sons and daughters *have* been declared prophets, and priests, and kings. Joel's words are being fulfilled. The day of the Lord can come at any time. And for those who remember the locusts, who remember their place, that's not a problem.

At another point in *Dakota,* Kathleen Norris says that some people on the plains do tell stories, true ones. She says that, while a lot of the rest of us neglect stories of the past, native Americans do not. Native Americans, she says, have learned that people who are going to survive encroachment by another culture need story. If they're going to remain who they are, they need to tell their stories.

And, if we're going to remain who we are, so do we. That's why the Scriptures are full of words like these from Joel: Tell it to your children. Tell them what the locusts did. And tell them what the Lord will do. Tell them that a day is coming — it's almost here — which will be the day of the Lord. And on that day every knee, all people, will bow before Jesus Christ. And there won't be a locust in sight.

Damaged Worship

Text: Amos 5:18-27

Is not the day of the Lord darkness, not light,
  and gloom with no brightness in it?
I hate, I despise your festivals,
  and I take no delight in your solemn assemblies.
Even though you offer me your burnt offerings and grain offerings,
  I will not accept them;
and the offerings of well-being of your fatted animals
  I will not look upon.
Take away from me the noise of your songs;
  I will not listen to the melody of your harps.
But let justice roll down like waters,
  and righteousness like an everflowing stream.

Amos 5:20-24

The book of Amos begins, "The words of Amos, one of the shepherds of Tekoa." It is as if Amos wants to make sure, right from the start, that everybody knows this wasn't his idea. He's just a shepherd — he never made it to seminary. Later he says, "I am no prophet, nor a prophet's son, but I am a herdsman, and a dresser of sycamore trees, and the Lord took me from following the flock, and the Lord said to me, 'Go, prophesy to my people Israel'" (7:14-15). It wasn't Amos's idea at all.

And if I were Amos, I think I'd want to get that straight, too, because what Amos has to say Israel does not want to hear. And they have no idea that it's coming. Things are really going pretty well in Israel right now: the kingdom is stretching as far as it did in the days of Solomon; nobody is pressing their borders or getting them to pay tribute to foreigners. There is success and prosperity in Israel, and there is even worship of the Lord going on. It hardly seems like a prophet is even necessary these days. Maybe that's why God grabbed a shepherd.

So Amos comes strolling into town, in these golden days in Israel, when nobody who's anybody thinks the Lord is upset with them, and the first words out of his mouth are, "Thus says the Lord: 'For three transgressions — *sins* — of Damascus, and for four, I will not revoke the punishment." And from Damascus Amos turns to Gaza, and from Gaza he turns to Tyre, and from Tyre he turns to Edom — one by one Amos pronounces judgment upon the enemies of Israel, and it all makes so much sense. After all, Israel is worshiping the Lord, and they're bubbling over in prosperity — God must be happy with them. So of course it's the enemies of Israel that Amos has come to prophesy against.

And on and on Amos goes: "For three transgressions of the Ammonites, for three transgressions of Moab, for three transgressions of Judah, and for four, I will not revoke the punishment." On seven countries, seven enemies of Israel, Amos calls down the judgment of God. And in Israel nothing could make better sense. Finally, a prophet who understands things. All of our prophets should be shepherds.

But wait — he isn't done yet. Even though seven is the number of completeness in Hebrew thought, even though Amos has probably never heard an *eight*-point sermon in his life, even though this is the time to quit while he's ahead, Amos the shepherd-prophet has one more thing to say:

> Thus says the Lord:
> For three transgressions of Israel,
>   and for four, I will not revoke the punishment;
> because they sell the righteous for silver,
>   and the needy for a pair of sandals —
> they who trample the head of the poor into the dust of the earth,
>   and push the afflicted out of the way.
>
> (2:6-7)

On and on Amos goes, his eighth point lasting three times as long as any of the previous seven. It's for Israel that Amos has been made a prophet.

And that's what Amos is addressing here in chapter 5, because all the prosperity and the power and the exciting worship have gone to Israel's head, and here is what God has to say through Amos the shepherd:

> Alas for you who desire the day of the Lord!
>   Why do you want the day of the Lord?
> It is darkness, not light. . . .
> I hate, I despise your festivals,
>   and I take no delight in your solemn assemblies.
> Even though you offer me your burnt offerings and grain offerings,

> I will not accept them. . . .
>
> I will not listen to the melody of your harps. . . .
>
> I will take you into exile beyond Damascus, says the Lord,
>> whose name is the God of hosts.
>
> (5:18-27)

So much for things looking up in Israel.

And I don't think the main problem here is that Israel is worshiping other gods. Some of that's going on, but the real problem is not that they're worshiping Baal, but that they're worshiping the Lord the same way that they worship Baal. You see, with an idol, religion is fairly simple. You worship it, you make offerings to it, you honor it, and then you see if it worked by how well your life goes. Worship well, live well — with idols. But with the living God it doesn't work that way. With the living God, just because you're worshiping and just because life is pretty good doesn't mean you're doing it right; it doesn't mean you have his blessing. With him it's not just a matter of burning offerings and bowing down and making nice. You can't buy off this God.

In his book *Yearning*, Craig Barnes talks about a legend that is well known in the mountains of Nepal.

> According to the legend, in the cool air of a mountaintop a huge wax god sat in solitary splendor. Generations of villagers from the valley below made their way up the mountain to worship at the shrine. There came a time, though, when some decided to bring the god down from his chilly citadel and establish him in the center of their marketplace. He was convenient then, and worship was not such a bother.
>
> But in the heat of the following days, the wax god softened and sagged. And the villagers realized that they could now make a few changes in their god. Those who thought his countenance too stern molded a delightful smile on his face. Soon the god looked just the way they wanted him to look.
>
> In the heat, though, he continued to sag. Little by little, the people began to take away pieces of the wax to light their homes. Soon all of the wax — and all of the god — was gone.

Barnes's point is this: "When we mold God into our image and use him to fill our own needs, we soon find that we have no god at all. True worship does not bring God down into conformity with what we've always wanted him to be. True worship invites us up to a fearful encounter with the sacred Creator of our lives."[4]

Israel had moved their God down from the mountain. He wasn't molding them; they molded him. They fit him into their routine. Sure, they still did their sacrifices, but that was all they really wanted to hear from him. And they didn't hear from him, until Amos came along. Their kingdom was growing, their boundaries were secure, life seemed to be great. God was on their side. They were enjoying a little taste of the day of the Lord, when Israel would really be on top of the world. But then Amos came along. Don't look for the day of the Lord, he said. That will be the day you die.

I've mentioned before the importance of remembering that you are not Israel and I am not Hosea. You're not worshiping idols instead of the God of Jacob, and I am no prophet, certainly not in the sense of being able to discern the times and see some divine judgment coming our way. There's a certain distance between us and these books that we can't do away with, and probably that distance helps us as we read them; it softens the blow of words like "I will destroy you, O Israel; who can help you?" from Hosea 13. There's a buffer between us and these prophets.

But we don't have the comfort of the same sort of distance with the prophecy of Amos, especially Amos 5, because in Amos 5 we're not talking so much about worshiping other gods or about God's people making deals with Assyria or bowing to Baal. In Amos 5 we're talking about worship that is aimed in the same direction as ours; we're talking about people who know God, our God, people who are in the habit of thinking something like "Come quickly, Lord Jesus." And to these people, gathering in his worship and looking for his return, our God says, "Alas for you who desire the day of the Lord." To worshipers like us, our God says, "I hate, I despise, your festivals; I take no delight in your solemn assemblies. Take away from me the noise of your songs! I will not listen to the melody of your harps."

I wonder, how possible is it that such words could be directed at us? "I hate, I despise, your prayers of confession. I will not listen to your hymns or your instruments. I refuse to look upon your sacraments. I will not accept your worship." We'd better pause before we declare that that cannot be the case. In one of his books Eugene Peterson says that deception is nowhere more common than in religion. "The commonest forms of devil-

---

4. M. Craig Barnes, *Yearning: Living Between How It Is and How It Ought to Be* (Downers Grove, IL: InterVarsity Press, 1992), pp. 104-5.

inspired worship do not take place furtively at black masses with decapitated cats but flourish under the bright lights of acclaim and glory, in a swirl of organ music."[5] That's Amos's Israel; but it just could be us, too.

When Israel moved God from the mountain, when he stopped being the Creator of their lives and instead became something they could mold to their liking, two things changed: (1) they assumed that he was on their side, that his day would always be their day; and (2) they thought just doing the worship was enough, that sending up an offering would appease him, that he could be bribed like a Baal, that he didn't care about anything else. That's what happened. That's what made God put in the ear plugs when they began the prelude.

Is that the church of today? Is it us? It can be. It can be, if we're just here, saying the words, taking the sacraments, to take care of God, to get him off our backs, to appease him with an offering. What we do here is very important; it is vital; it is declaring that the earth is the Lord's and everything in it. But these vital acts mean something only if from them flow justice and righteousness, only if from them arises a concern for those the world likes to push down and knock over.

"I don't want your worship. I want justice to roll down like waters and righteousness like an everflowing stream." It's easy to talk about God, to sing hymns to him, to write a check for eight percent of our income and then to go home and never spend a thought, a dime, or a minute on the things God says matter to him most. It's easy to pray for the poor, give some dollars we don't need, and then vote our pocketbooks, vote for those who will make our situations better, without ever a thought about the situations that matter to the one we worship. "Take away from me the noise of your songs . . . but let justice roll down like waters!"

It is not simple to do justice and righteousness today — though a certain segment of the church seems to think it is and claims to know God's mind on trade agreements and tax cuts and even automatic weapons. It's not that simple. But that's not the point. The point is, Is justice flowing through us? And those waters cover all kinds of territory: they pour through us when we treat an aging parent or a struggling adolescent with love and respect. They flow in torrents when we give our time to hospice and AIDS centers and foster care. Where our money goes, who we'll be seen with, how we vote — these are all places where justice and righteousness can swirl and stream, or where they dry up. When we worship right,

5. Eugene H. Peterson, *Under the Unpredictable Plant* (Grand Rapids: Eerdmans, 1992), pp. 14-15.

we will not forget those poor and sick and small and weak ones that God remembers so well.

"But let justice roll down like waters, and righteousness like an everflowing stream." They're powerful words. No wonder they meant so much to Martin Luther King. They couldn't have been more appropriate. Richard John Neuhaus, a Catholic churchman, tells of a scene during the civil rights confrontation at Selma, Alabama. In the middle of everything, an Episcopal priest celebrated mass along the dusty roadside. It wasn't a "civil rights mass"; it didn't have any special litany or way of doing it. It was just the same act of worship he did all the time. And yet it was an act of power, too, because there was the church, worshiping and seeking justice, worshiping and speaking up for those who are pushed down, letting everyone see that one has a lot to do with the other, that this sort of thing is less our mission than it is God's.

That's what Amos is looking for. The worship of God's people doesn't have to do with telling God what he wants to hear and getting rich as a result; it has to do with belonging to a God who cares for his world and not just for his worship. That worship has something to do with the homeless and the sick and the poor and the invisible. It means that those who love God also know whom God loves. And that worship is a long way from Baal, but it's right at the heart of Amos the shepherd.

When a Brother Laughs

Text: Obadiah

On the day that you stood aside,
*   on the day that strangers carried off his wealth,*
and foreigners entered his gates
*   and cast lots for Jerusalem,*
*   you too were like one of them.*
But you should not have gloated over your brother
*   on the day of his misfortune;*

you should not have rejoiced over the people of Judah
  on the day of their ruin; . . .
you should not have looted his goods
  on the day of his calamity.
You should not have stood at the crossings
  to cut off his fugitives;
you should not have handed over his survivors
  on the day of distress.

Obadiah 11-14

In his novel *The General's Daughter,* Nelson DeMille tells the story of a young woman, the daughter of a high-ranking military officer. This woman follows in her father's footsteps and herself enters the nation's finest military academy, where she proves to be an outstanding cadet. One day, however, during her time at the school, a terrible crime is committed against her by some other students. She is humiliated and shamed; and, if the event becomes public, the academy will be, too. Faced with the opposing concerns of the military's reputation and his daughter's retribution, the officer-father chooses his career. He allows a cover-up. His daughter must recover alone.

But none of that is DeMille's story. It's only the background. The story is of a young woman who never forgave her father for the choice he made, a young woman determined to destroy him as completely as he had destroyed her. The story is of a woman who took these words of Friedrich Nietzsche as her favorite saying: "Whatever hurts you makes me stronger." Betrayal had turned into utter hatred.

I wonder if that ever happened to Esau. You recall Esau from the book of Genesis, Isaac and Rebecca's oldest son, Jacob's twin brother, the poor sap who again and again was hoodwinked by his brother's dirty tricks. One day he lost his birthright because he was so famished for some of Jacob's soup that he gave in to extortion — your inheritance in exchange for a meal. Another day he missed out on his father's blessing because Jacob snuck to the old man's side disguised as Esau and Isaac fell for it. Jacob got out of town before Esau could catch him — could shout him down or slap him around a bit — all because Jacob the swindler was always one step ahead of him. Even years later, when they run into each other again and have a peace-making in the desert — Jacob and his whole family, Esau and his — even then, when they agree to meet up later, Jacob can't be trusted. He goes back on his word again, he sneaks off, figuring that Esau is just as much a cheat as he is, and so he'd better get away while he can.

I've always been so disappointed in this story, especially when Esau is lied to the last time, duped again because he thought his brother would do what he said, would be faithful, would live up to his word. According to his mother Rebecca, at one point Esau consoled himself with the thought of killing Jacob, and who could blame him? Who could blame him for blaming his brother for all that had gone wrong in his life? Who could blame Esau for letting betrayal turn to hatred, for taking the words of Nietzsche as *his* gospel: "Whatever hurts you makes me stronger"?

But that's all we read about Esau. There's no word of Esau taking any revenge or being driven by any Nietzschean philosophy, no retribution, no payback. All we find in the last word about the life of this man is the list of his descendants and the note that "This was Esau, the father of the Edomites."

Maybe Esau never got his revenge. Maybe as far as he was concerned the whole thing was settled, water over the dam. Maybe he figured that his line and Jacob's line belonged to the same family, the only family he had, and a feud wasn't the way a family should do things. And then again, maybe he thought something else. But whatever *Esau* thought, the battles between him and Jacob were not over. And that was never more clear than on the day in the year 586 B.C. when Nebuchadnezzar the Babylonian took over Jerusalem — because that was the darkest day in the history of the people of Jacob, and that was the day the Edomites were holding their bellies, they were laughing so hard.

And so the prophecy of Obadiah is a word to Edom. It's a word to a people gaining strength from the pain of somebody else, from the pain of their own brothers and sisters. And so the prophecy of Obadiah is a word of judgment, from God to Edom:

> I will surely make you least among the nations;
>> you shall be utterly despised.
> Your proud heart has deceived you,
>> you that live in the clefts of the rock,
>> whose dwelling is in the heights. . . .
> Though you soar aloft like the eagle,
>> though your nest is set among the stars,
>> from there I will bring you down, says the Lord. . . .
> For the slaughter and violence done to your brother Jacob,
>> shame shall cover you,
>> and you shall be cut off forever.

(vv. 2-4, 10)

The day of Jerusalem's pain was a holiday in Edom, a time to jeer, a time to revel in their own circumstances, in the fact that they are safe and sound in the mountains of Edom, while Jerusalem is being dragged off to Babylon. But that they should not have done:

> You should not have gloated over your brother
>   on the day of his misfortune; . . .
> You should not have entered the gate of my people
>   on the day of their calamity;
> you should not have joined in the gloating over Judah's disaster
>   on the day of his calamity;
> you should not have looted his goods
>   on the day of his calamity. . . .
> For the day of the Lord is near against all the nations.
> As you have done, it shall be done to you;
>   your deeds shall return on your own head.
>
> (vv. 12-13, 15)

For celebrating Jerusalem's destruction, Edom itself will be destroyed.

And that would make good sense if Judah had been the faithful people of God. It would make good sense if Jacob was a fair and proper brother. It would make sense if Edom had no reason to want Judah's downfall. But they do have a reason. Jacob was a lousy brother — a lying brother. And Judah hasn't been faithful to God, either. In fact, the very destruction of Jerusalem that the Edomites are enjoying was sent by God himself, because the Jews were disobedient, because they deserved to be punished, because they had abandoned the Lord. And yet none of that matters — none of those things is reason to celebrate when Judah goes up in smoke.

And it all comes down to one little verse of Obadiah, verse 11: "On the day that you stood aside, on the day that strangers carried off his wealth, and foreigners entered his gates and cast lots for Jerusalem, you too were like one of them." That's the problem with Edom: "You were like one of them." But they weren't one of them. They weren't strangers or foreigners. They were neighbors. They were brothers. The day that strangers and foreigners came and overwhelmed Jerusalem, terrorized its children and made off with its possessions — that day when they needed a brother the most — Edom was nowhere to be found, because Edom was "like one of them," like a stranger. Edom was laughing. Edom was terrorizing. Edom was making off with Jerusalem's possessions, too.

And so Edom will die, because Edom didn't know their brother, or didn't care. And that is the word of the Lord for us this morning. That is the message that the people of God have considered holy and inspired, worth hearing as part of their worship until the end of time: Jerusalem's Mount Zion will be raised up; the proud and lofty mountains of Edom will be made low. "And the kingdom shall be the Lord's" (v. 21).

Without that last line Obadiah would seem just like the angry words of one bitter enemy to another. But Obadiah doesn't end with the destruction of Edom or the glory of Jerusalem; it ends with "And the kingdom shall be the Lord's." That's what matters. It doesn't matter that Edom has some old score to settle or some reason to cheer on the pain in Judah. What matters is that the kingdom will ultimately be, not Edom's or Judah's or Babylon's, but the Lord's, and in the Lord's kingdom you always remember your brother and your sister. In the Lord's kingdom only destruction follows those who seek pain, even when they have a reason.

DeMille's young woman ends up destroyed, too. "What hurts you makes me stronger" may have been her theme, but another quote she knew from Nietzsche proved to be the one that she should have heeded: "Whoever fights monsters should see to it that he does not become a monster. And when you look long into the abyss, the abyss also looks into you." A sure way to destruction is to celebrate misery, is to forget brothers, is to be like one of them. God has a different way.

And that way is one of grace, one of rejoicing with those who rejoice and mourning with those who mourn, one of loving a neighbor as we love ourselves. And who is Edom's neighbor? The answer for Edom began with Judah and Israel, their old brother. For us the answer comes from Jesus. When he was asked, "Who is my neighbor?" he reached for the most distant, despised person he could find and said, "That is your neighbor. Your love is to reach even there. Because that is how the Lord's kingdom works." It is love that doesn't celebrate misery or pay back wrong but looks with compassion and is full of mercy.

A few years ago Philip Yancey wrote in *Christianity Today* of his experience walking in a gay-rights parade. A gay friend had asked Yancey to join him, and he agreed. During the walk Yancey says he was greeted with signs and chants from the sidewalks, from those calling themselves Christians, saying things like "AIDS is gonna get ya" and "Hell will be your home." Yancey was really puzzled by all of this. He wasn't seeking to condone homosexual behavior, but he sure found it hard to bless the "Christian" response there, either. What Yancey finds hard to bless the prophet Obadiah curses in the name of God. And that is so whether or not AIDS is

God's judgment, which we do not know. Citizens of the Lord's kingdom do not celebrate the misery of their neighbors.

Germans have a word for such a thing: *schadenfreude*, from the words for "damage" and "joy" — that is, enjoying what damages someone else. Obadiah says we must not do that, even if the damage is from the Lord. We must remember that the day of the Lord is near for all of us.

It's amazing how easy it is to enjoy the pain. Even nobler events like the Olympics are tainted with it. I suppose that's not surprising. In the case of nations it may be true that what hurts others makes ours stronger. Nietzsche may be right there. But only for a little while, only until the day of the Lord comes for all nations — Edom, Judah, the United States. We who today share the patriotic pride of the Edomites would do well to remember that.

But of course it's not just nations. It is a difficult thing, as much in the church as out, to rejoice with those who rejoice and mourn with those mourn. It's easier the other way around. Someone who knew that once said, "With every success of my friends, a part of me dies." It comes more naturally that way. But it must not stay that way. We must not be like that to each other. We must not be like one of them — foreigners and strangers. We are not that. We are neighbors. We are brothers and sisters. The Edomites forgot.

This wasn't the last time they forgot, either. As a matter of fact, it wasn't the last time Edom took part in a Jewish massacre. The next one, at least the next one that's recorded, happened almost six centuries later, in the year 5 B.C. That was when a king, an Edomite named Herod, ordered all the male babies in the town of Bethlehem to be killed. He, too, believed in Nietzsche: "What hurts you makes me stronger." It didn't work out for Herod, either.

Jesus Christ said again and again, "If you want to find your life, you have to lose it." That wasn't Nietzsche, or Herod, or Edom, or Judah itself, for that matter. But it is the way of God; it is the way of his kingdom. You find your life when you stop trying to protect it, to make it stronger, to step on somebody else. You find your life when you see your brothers and sisters.

Things didn't work out for Edom. They didn't work out for Judah, either. Both nations pretty much disappeared. Jacob and Esau never quite got it right. But that doesn't really matter — at least, it doesn't have to, not if we follow the way of Jesus Christ, not if we live as citizens in God's kingdom, not if we refuse to be like one of them, like strangers.

A preacher of a generation ago, Frederick Neumann, summed it up this way: "Jacob is dead, let him be dead, for the true Israel lives. Edom is dead, let him be dead, for true brotherly love continues." Praise God that it does. Praise God *when* it does. Praise God that the kingdom is the Lord's. In the name of Jesus Christ, Amen.

The Prayer

Text: Jonah 2

Then Jonah prayed to the Lord his God from the belly of the fish, saying,
"I called to the Lord out of my distress,
and he answered me;
out of the belly of Sheol I cried,
and you heard my voice. . . .
As my life was ebbing away,
I remembered the Lord;
and my prayer came to you,
into your holy temple.
Those who worship vain idols
forsake their true loyalty.
But I with the voice of thanksgiving
will sacrifice to you;
what I have vowed I will pay.
Deliverance belongs to the Lord!"
Then the Lord spoke to the fish, and it spewed Jonah out upon the dry land.

Jonah 2:1-2, 7-10

Well, it's not what I would have said. Not now. I mean, ten minutes ago Jonah was sitting on the ship's deck sipping iced tea. Now, as Aldous Huxley put it, "he's seated upon the convex mound of one vast kidney." Just like that Jonah's life has taken its strangest twist — he's thrown into a raging sea, tossed and turned and terrified by the troubled water, then ingested by some sea monster, some gigantic fish that, fortunately for Jonah, is more interested in swallowing than chewing. So here he is, perched on that vast kidney, inside the belly of this overgrown guppy, with no idea what to do next.

Except, of course, pray. When you read the first verse of chapter 2 about Jonah praying, you may be cynical. You may think that this wayward prophet, this man of God who was assigned to fly to Nineveh but instead went right to the dock and bought passage in the other direction, you may figure that Jonah is the ultimate fox-hole believer — the kind that seeks out God at the first sign of trouble but then is running off to Tarshish again as soon as things quiet down. Of course he's going to pray; of course he's going to turn to God now; of course he's going to look for help anywhere he can get it; of course he's going to do that, because that's Jonah. He looks for the easy way out. But you think that only until you learn what Jonah prays.

As I studied this most unusual minor prophet, I was drawn to Jonah's prayer for our text this morning, because in that prayer is something I'd never known before.

As I said, if this were me, and probably if it were you, sitting in Jonah's place inside this early version of Moby Dick, I'd be praying, too. I'd pray, "Help!" I'd speak of my fear. I'd say that I never should have tried to run to Tarshish in the first place and now I've learned my lesson. I'd beg God to save my life. I would say everything I was feeling, everything I was wishing, everything I was suffering. That's what I would pray — but that's not what Jonah prays.

Jonah doesn't pray out of his fear, and he doesn't pray out of his desires, and he doesn't pray out of his feelings. Jonah prays out of his past. Jonah's prayer doesn't come from his emotions, it doesn't come from his thoughts at the moment. It comes from the prayers of his people, it comes from the Psalms. So it doesn't sound exactly like somebody in a fish. You don't notice it at first, but every part of this prayer originates in the Psalms. "I called to the Lord out of my distress, and he answered me" comes from Psalm 120. "Out of the belly of Sheol I cried, and you heard my voice" is from Psalm 30. "You cast me into the deep" is from Psalm 69. "All your waves and your billows swept over me" is from Psalm 42. "I said, 'I am driven away from your sight'" is from Psalm 31. On and on it goes. This prayer hasn't been written by Jonah; it's been written by the writers of Psalm 5 and Psalm 69 and Psalm 18 and Psalm 103. They're the ones who wrote this prayer. Jonah's praying their words.

And that's made many readers believe that Jonah's prayer doesn't really belong in the story. They figure that it was put here by the last person who edited the book before it became part of the Scriptures, that the prayer of Jonah was forced in here after the fact. And these folks have noticed that, if you go from verse 17 of chapter 1 right to verse 10 of chapter 2, it doesn't seem like anything's missing: "But the Lord provided a large fish to swallow up Jonah, and Jonah was in the belly of the fish three days and three nights. . . . Then the Lord spoke to the fish, and it spewed Jonah out upon the dry land." We can skip Jonah's prayer entirely and not miss a beat. So plenty of interpreters suggest doing just that, because Jonah's prayer doesn't sound like the prayer of somebody in trouble like Jonah is in trouble, because Jonah's prayer doesn't fit the story of Jonah very well at all, and because Jonah's prayer doesn't come from Jonah, at least not originally.

And when we listen to what they're saying, when we think about the problems they raise, we wonder about this prayer too. Maybe it doesn't belong here; at least, it seems kind of strange, because Jonah's prayer isn't what we think of as true prayer, genuine prayer, ideal prayer. It surprises us that Jonah doesn't speak his feelings or his fears or his desires to God. It seems strange to us that Jonah doesn't cry out, "Lord, save me from the digestive tract of this fish!" It's odd that Jonah prays somebody else's words.

But what we forget, what many of Jonah's interpreters forget, is that it's not odd for Jonah. Jonah, in his prayer from the fish's belly, is truer to his faith than he is anywhere else in the entire story. Here Jonah prays just as he's been taught. He uses the prayer book of his people. In the strangest moment of his life, in the most desperate time he's faced, Jonah turns to the Psalms. Jonah remembers the Psalms. Jonah prays the Psalms.

And that is what they are for. In his sermon on Jonah 2, John Timmer points out that over fifty psalms have a heading like "To the choirmaster" or "For the director of music." Those psalms are written so that the worship leaders can teach the people how to pray, how to speak to God. Timmer says that, for the Old Testament people, the Psalms is the school of prayer. "It's as though the book of Psalms says to Jonah, 'Here, pray these words of mine and you will yet learn how to pray.'"

When we use the Psalms to pray, when the Psalms serve as our guide in conversation with God, when we let them teach us, our own prayers will be more godly. Eugene Peterson says that this idea "contrasts with the prevailing climate of prayer. Our culture presents us with forms of prayer that are mostly self-expression — pouring ourselves out before God or lifting our gratitude to God as we feel the need and have the occasion. Such prayer is dominated by a sense of self. But prayer, mature prayer, is dominated by a sense of God. Prayer rescues us from a preoccupation with ourselves and pulls us into adoration of and pilgrimage to God."[6]

You see, if prayer is controlled by what we feel, then it will occur only when we feel like praying, it will say only what we feel like saying, and it will last only as long as our feelings concern God. To pray from our feelings is too much for us to handle. We think that we have to pour out our feelings, that a good prayer life is determined by how well we describe everything we feel, that real prayer is always spontaneous, from the heart, made up as we go. But we can't handle that. We can't handle it because our feelings are just too much for us to control — to direct always toward God, to keep under his power. We can't handle it because our feelings are often wrong — they deceive us and seduce us and overwhelm us. And we can't handle it because, as Eugene Peterson says, that kind of prayer is dominated by a sense of self. Prayer written by our feelings is prayer in which we have the starring role. Prayer to our God must give that role to him.

And Jonah does that surprisingly well. There are different types of psalms. From the belly of that fish we'd expect him to pray a lament type of psalm. We'd expect him to pray something that speaks of all his suffering and sorrow and asks for salvation from God. But that's not the kind of psalm Jonah prays. He prays a psalm of thanksgiving. He prays as if he's already been saved, as if God has already responded. You see, Jonah's prayer is occasioned by the way he feels, but that's only where it begins. That's only *why* he prays. *What* he prays is determined more by who God is than by where Jonah is. *What* he prays is as much a statement of faith as it is a prayer to God. So his prayer ends by saying, "I with the voice of thanksgiving will sacrifice to you. . . . Deliverance belongs to the Lord!" Jonah knows that psalms can be written in different situations and by different persons who had different feelings, but they still address the same God. So there is his comfort: he knows this God, even if he doesn't know this fish.

And that's what God's people have always known: their God. The prayers of God's people then can be the prayers of God's people now because he does not change, and prayer is more about him than it is about us — even in the belly of a great fish, and in the aftermath of a great sin, and in the joy of a great message. That's where Mary is in the first chapter of Luke, and her response to God is a psalm from the Old Testament. So is

6. Peterson, *Under the Unpredictable Plant,* pp. 102-3.

Zechariah's. It's always been that way for God's people. In the moments of life that call for prayer, the Psalms give the words and the form and the focus for speaking to God. And God's people have always known that, even in the church.

From Augustine to Martin Luther to John Calvin to French Protestants tortured to death in the days of the Reformation to Jews on their way to the gas chamber in the days of the Holocaust — in the times of real pain, when prayer was all they could do, it was the Psalms they prayed. Luther said, "Whoever has begun to pray the Psalter seriously and regularly will soon give a vacation to other little devotional prayers and say: 'Ah, there is not the juice, the strength, the passion, the fire, which I find in the Psalter.'" John Calvin said that the Psalms are "the design of the Holy Spirit . . . to deliver to the church a common form of prayer."

"A common form of prayer" — binding Jonah to his people, binding the church across time and space, binding all of us to God, through one common form of prayer, one method of addressing him, true of a Hebrew in the eighth century B.C. and a Chinese Christian in the eighteenth century A.D. Until a couple of hundred years ago you wouldn't have thought it odd to read the story of Jonah, to imagine him in the most frightening predicament of his life, and to find a psalm as his prayer, because all these centuries the Psalms have been the way God's people pray. Psalms have given us the words we use; they have been the school where we learn to speak to God — and not the anonymous God they pray to before Congress, but the God of Abraham and Isaac and David and Jonah and John the Baptist and Peter, the God who promised a Savior to those sinners of the Old Testament and provided one for those sinners in the New. If you want to learn how to speak to that God, turn to his prayer book. Turn to the Psalms.

In this day, which has traded in the prayers of God's people for more romantic and emotional and uplifting ones, in this day when prayer is so often a means for getting what we want, whether it be healing or money or a new job or rescue from the belly of something that's got hold of us, the church needs to learn from Jonah. We need to learn how to call upon the God who saves. The Psalms are how. The Psalms can teach us how to pray.

In another place Eugene Peterson says, "If we are willfully ignorant of the Psalms, we are not thereby excluded from praying, but we will have to hack our way through formidable country by trial and error and with inferior tools. If we dismiss the Psalms, preferring a more up-to-date and less demanding school of prayer, we will not be without grace, but we will miss the center where Christ worked in his praying."[7] He's right. Jonah and Mary and Martin Luther aren't the only ones who remembered psalms in prayer. At the end of his career, on the cross, when our Lord spoke to his Father, he turned to two psalms. The prayers that speak best know the God they're addressing; they have been formed by the prayer book of God's people; they are bigger than the people who pray them. May none of us forget the words that Jonah remembered. May none of us forget the Psalms. And may we also never forget to pray, "Not to us, O Lord, not to us, but to your name give glory, for the sake of your steadfast love and your faithfulness" (Psalm 115:1). Now there's a prayer for wherever you're seated.

How to Turn Off God

Text: Micah 3

Hear this, you rulers of the house of Jacob
*   and chiefs of the house of Israel,*
who abhor justice
*   and pervert all equity,*
who build Zion with blood
*   and Jerusalem with wrong!*
Its rulers give judgment for a bribe,
*   its priests teach for a price,*
*   its prophets give oracles for money;*
yet they lean upon the Lord and say,
*   "Surely the Lord is with us!*
*   No harm shall come upon us."*
Therefore because of you
*   Zion shall be plowed as a field;*

7. Eugene H. Peterson, *Answering God: The Psalms as Tools for Prayer* (San Francisco: Harper & Row, 1989), p. 4.

> *Jerusalem shall become a heap of ruins,*
> *and the mountain of the house a wooded height.*
>
> Micah 3:9-12

Well, this is sort of a strange place to wrap up, but this is it: we're through the first half of the minor prophets — there's even a symbol in the Hebrew at the end of chapter 3 to mark this point as the close of the first half of the book of the twelve minor prophets. That's what it's called in Hebrew: the book of the twelve. But, even here, even seven sermons into this book, we're reminded how much we struggle with these strange voices from God. We still struggle with wondering what these words about Israel and Jerusalem and exile mean for us today. How does the word of Micah to the leaders of Jerusalem, this message of doom to elders and governors in a time that is so foreign to ours, also serve as a message now, to you and me? What does the corruption of Judah's leaders and the silencing of its prophets and the coming destruction of Jerusalem have to do with us?

Well, not much, actually — not directly, anyway. And we have to remember that, because that's such an easy mistake to make. I remember a time as a seminary student when I and a couple of others were in a small sermon-critique group with an experienced minister. The four of us met together in this man's office. One of the other students went first. His passage was the story in Luke of the woman who anoints Jesus' feet in the house of Simon the Pharisee. The issue there is the Pharisee's unwillingness to receive sinners like this woman into the kingdom of God. Well, at a climactic point in his sermon, after he laid out the story for us, my friend paused and announced, "We are the Pharisees." At that, the preacher who had agreed to mentor us stopped him and, with much exasperation, asked my friend why he would say such a thing, why he'd call people gathered for worship of Jesus Christ today "the Pharisees." He didn't understand. I sat there also looking disappointed in my friend's mistake, all the while pretty sure that I had a sermon on that same passage with a line pretty close to, "We are the Pharisees."

But the truth is we aren't the Pharisees any more than we're Jesus. We can forget that too, sometimes. But we're not. And we're not the leaders of Jerusalem, either. And our preachers are not prophets, not these prophets. And we have to remember that, because in our haste to make these words work for us or be relevant to us or support us, the easiest thing to do is to skip over figuring out who's who and get right to the point. And then the point of Micah 3 is that the Lord is going to remove himself from those who have put down his people.

And then our preaching gets really dangerous, because then this passage applies to anybody who puts us down; anyone who speaks against or disagrees with or is on the other side of our group of Christians becomes the oppressor that prophets like Micah condemn. When Christians or the church or American evangelicals become today's version of Micah's people, then our preaching gets dangerous, because then all the prophets will ever do is call down the judgment of God upon those we would like to see judged. And that is a long way from Micah 3, and we are a long way from being Micah's people.

You see, when Micah says to the officials in Jerusalem, "Should you not know justice? — you who hate the good and love the evil, who tear the skin off my people, and the flesh off their bones" (3:1-2), when he talks about his people, he's not talking about all the people of God, or just anyone who happens to live in Israel; he's talking about *his* people, *Micah's* people, the people of Moresheth, his home town. That's who the leaders in Jerusalem are abusing. The big-city power brokers are oppressing Micah's neighbors and friends, and Micah's had enough.

Moresheth, where Micah's from, is twenty miles from Jerusalem, but it's in a high-traffic area. It happens to be on the way to several important places, so the leaders and officials of Jerusalem pass through there regularly. And along the way it's not unusual for them to drag some of the citizens off to Jerusalem to work on the estates of rich Jerusalemites or on official government construction projects. It's those people, Micah's neighbors, who have lost their voice, who have been taken from their little lives to help lavish luxury on the lives of the wealthy and important people of Jerusalem — those are the ones Micah calls "my people." They are the ones God will remember. They are the reason God will pull out of Jerusalem.

And that is exactly what is going on here. Micah is announcing the Lord's evacuation of the capital city. And it is all "because of you," he says to the officials and the prophets and the rulers in the house of Israel. It is because the leaders walk all over the people, "chop them up like meat in a kettle" (v. 3). So when these leaders call out to the Lord, he will not answer them. He will hide his face from them because of the evil they have done.

And then Micah turns to the prophets, because they're part of the problem, too. They're at the center of the problem, because they're the ones who should be proclaiming the word of the Lord in Jerusalem, but instead they're proclaiming whatever pays the best. Their messages are for sale: "they cry 'Peace' when they have something to eat, but declare war against those who put nothing into their mouths" (v. 5). Therefore, says

Micah, it will be dark for the prophets of this city — the Lord will have nothing to say to them, no visions for them to describe, no message to proclaim: "They shall all cover their lips, for there is no answer from God" (v. 7).

And then Micah turns back one more time to the rulers and the administrators in Jerusalem, the ones "who build Zion with blood and Jerusalem with wrong."

> [Jerusalem's] rulers give judgment for a bribe,
>   its priests teach for a price,
>   its prophets give oracles for money;
> yet they lean upon the Lord and say,
>   "Surely the Lord is with us!
>   No harm shall come upon us."
>
> (vv. 10-11)

But they are wrong, says Micah. Because of you, he says to these leaders, not only will God not answer *you,* not only will he shut off his word to the *prophets,* but he will also remove himself from the city: "Zion shall be plowed as a field, Jerusalem shall become a heap of ruins." That's what Micah sees coming: leaders with no answer from God, prophets with no access to the Lord, the holy city deserted. God will turn himself off.

Micah sees silence coming — a time when the leaders of Judah will expect guidance from the Lord, but nothing will happen; a day when the prophets in Jerusalem will go to their rooms, open their Scriptures, and look for a word from God, but they will get nothing; a day when Jerusalem, a city full of activity, will be a heap of rubble, deserted, weeds growing in the temple, voices and carts and shops all stopped, all boarded up, all gone — because the Lord has turned himself off.

But now what are *we* to do with this information? If we are not Israel, if Micah is not speaking to us, then what should we hear in these words?

We should hear that the good will of the Lord is no sure thing just because we hang out at the temple. We should hear that one time a prophet of the Lord said all of Jerusalem would pay because its leadership misplaced their job descriptions. We should hear that one time, when the leaders of God's people, in his capital city, placed wealth above justice, when their politics were determined by their bank books, when their religion was used to help out the big shots, then at least one time, God turned himself off. We should hear that, and we should let it speak to us. We should hear that when the leaders of Jerusalem lived on the backs of the poor people from Moresheth, Jerusalem turned into a scrap heap. Before we assume that God's blessing is upon us, before we assume that his voice is with us, before we step into a voting booth next year, we should think about Micah 3, we should remember the book of the twelve.

And that doesn't mean I know what decisions you should make in those voting booths. I don't. Micah might, but I don't. What it means is that God's interest, the recurring theme in the prophets from Hosea to Micah, is that there be justice. And if our vote, if our voice, if our support for any person or any party is a vote for our bank accounts, then *we* are doing the work of those rulers who misplaced their job descriptions. When Micah is summing everything up in Jerusalem, he says, "Its rulers give judgment for a bribe, its priests teach for a price, its prophets give oracles for money." The problems are across the board: from prophet to priest to king. So God turned himself off. Let's not let it happen again.

In God's plan, the people of Jerusalem care for the welfare of the little people of Moresheth. But that's not always a natural concern. We all have our own plans, our own problems, our own houses to build and streets to pave, but we're called to something higher. We're called to seek justice, and justice begins with the ones who have no voice, no vote, no food. Those are the ones God keeps a special eye on, just like Jesus receiving that disgusting sinner in the Pharisee's house. We're not the Pharisees. So let's be sure we don't act like them.

When Micah compares himself to these prophets-for-hire, he says:

> But as for me, I am filled with power,
>   with the Spirit of the Lord,
>   and with justice and might,
> to declare to Jacob his transgression
>   and to Israel his sin.
>
> (v. 8)

That's what Micah's out to do — declare to Israel his sin. Micah the prophet is out to tear off all the shiny veneer and the beautiful facades and the wonderful religious festivals and expose sin. Not in other nations, not in pagan types, but in God's own people. That's what Micah's after — to declare to them their sin. Let's take that with us, not only into our politics but into the fabric of our lives. Let's take that with us as we leave the minor prophets: a determination to declare sin, not first in others, but in ourselves, sin in Israel, sin under the name *Christian*.

In his book *Under God: Religion and American Politics,* Garry Wills notes that, somewhere along the line, this country has lost the old Augustinian notion of sin as something to find in oneself and in one's motives as well as in others. In Protestant America, instead, sin is what we find in someone else; it's something to protect ourselves against, to oppose with the force of God.[8] Now sin is "over there."

Let's not be that American. Let's get back to Augustine. Let's practice claiming our sin, recognizing it, repenting of it, and from there speaking — in our families, in our churches, in our nation — the word of God as best we can, knowing that God's people themselves are objects of grace and that judgment begins in Jerusalem.

It's a strange place to end the book of the twelve, but it's only part 1, of course. Part 2 is still coming — Nahum, Habakkuk, and so on through Malachi. But of course this book doesn't really end even there. This book of pain and warning and judgment and threat doesn't really end until the curse is complete, until it all focuses on one single human being, until God stands completely silent while death and hell have their way. And the miracle there is that, in that same silence, Jerusalem and Moresheth both are made alive.

In the name of Jesus Christ, Amen.

Waging Peace

Text: Micah 4:1-5

In days to come
 the mountain of the Lord's house
shall be established as the highest of the mountains,
 and shall be raised up above the hills.
Peoples shall stream to it,
 and many nations shall come and say:

8. Garry Wills, *Under God: Religion and American Politics* (New York: Simon and Schuster, 1990), p. 72.

> *"Come, let us go up to the mountain of the Lord,*
>   *to the house of the God of Jacob;*
> *that he may teach us his ways*
>   *and that we may walk in his paths."*
> *For out of Zion shall go forth instruction,*
>   *and the word of the Lord from Jerusalem.*
> *He shall judge between many peoples,*
>   *and shall arbitrate between strong nations far away;*
> *they shall beat their swords into plowshares,*
>   *and their spears into pruning hooks;*
> *nation shall not lift up sword against nation,*
>   *neither shall they learn war any more;*
> *but they shall sit under their own vines and under their own fig trees,*
>   *and no one shall make them afraid;*
>   *for the mouth of the Lord of hosts has spoken.*
> *For all the peoples walk,*
>   *each in the name of its god,*
> *but we will walk in the name of the Lord our God*
>   *forever and ever.*

Micah 4:1-5

This morning, even though we are in the middle of a sometimes strange and not very well known part of Scripture, even though we are a long way from the New Testament and the life of Jesus, nonetheless we are near the very heart of the gospel. But to appreciate that, we need to remember our past reading of the book of the twelve minor prophets. We opened that book some time ago and proceeded to hear from Hosea and Joel and Amos and Obadiah and Jonah and Micah. That's all we had time for. We stopped at Micah 3, and we stopped there for a reason. We stopped there because in the Hebrew text there is a mark indicating that this point — the end of Micah 3 — is halfway through this book of prophets; it's the end of volume 1 of the book of the twelve.

Volume 1 does not end well. As a matter of fact, it seems to end everything, at least as far as Jerusalem is concerned. It seems that Micah 3 is the last word from the Lord, because at the end of Micah 3 Jerusalem — the city of David, the home of God's temple, God's very presence — is destroyed: "Therefore because of you," says Micah — because of you prophets and rulers of my people, because of your greed and dishonesty and corruption — "Zion shall be plowed as a field; Jerusalem shall become a heap of ruins, and the mountain of the house [that is, the temple hill] a wooded height" (3:12). Zion will be *plowed,* Jerusalem will be *in ruins,* the temple hill will be *full of trees.* And that concludes volume 1 of the book of the twelve prophets.

And that's why this morning we have come close to the very heart of the gospel. The gospel is about life coming to something — some person, some town, some race, some world — that has been overwhelmed by, swallowed up in, death. And that is what we have in Micah 4, the beginning of volume 2 of the book of the twelve. Jerusalem the city of the Lord and Zion the mountain of the temple of the Lord — they are raised from the dead of Micah 3 and made gloriously alive in Micah 4. In spite of the judgment they deserve, in spite of the judgment they still will receive, in spite of the faithlessness of their leadership and the godlessness of their lives, "In days to come," says Micah, "the mountain of the Lord's house shall be established as the highest of the mountains."

That's a funny thing to say, not only because the last thing we heard about Mt. Zion is that it would be turned into a plowed field, but also because Mt. Zion's not the kind of mountain that's the highest of anything. It's only about two thousand feet high when it's not plowed — not exactly a peak to inspire poetry or rock-climbs. But little, plowed Mt. Zion is going to be the highest mountain, Jerusalem will bustle again, and the Lord will be in his temple. Everything that was stilled and silenced and shut up in chapter 3 will flourish and prosper and thrive again, according to chapter 4. And the whole world will be drawn to it.

The strange thing is that this entire reversal takes place without a single human being having one thing to do with it. Zion and Jerusalem and the temple are brought down in chapter 3 because the leaders of Jerusalem forget about God and spend their energies lining their own pockets. Zion and Jerusalem are brought down because of human sin and human greed and human corruption and human-created injustice. The downfall of Zion is brought about by human beings. So you would expect that the salvation of Zion could come only with some human effort, that it would take place only when these priests and prophets and kings straighten out their acts and fly right, treat the poor well and seek to worship the Lord. You'd think that only when those things happen — if even then — would Zion be a mountain again. But it's not so.

None of that happens. There's not a word about leaders repenting or prophets studying the word of the Lord or anything else. We go right from the ruins of Zion and Jerusalem to Mt. Zion being the highest mountain and Jerusalem the center of the world. And so we are that close to the gospel itself today, because the good news of the gospel is that life does not come because we deserve it; it comes as the work, the mission, the gift of God. So Zion is destroyed because its leaders are corrupt; but Zion is exalted, raised up, and glorified because *God* has made it so. And that is good news. That is the mystery of grace. And that is the church as well.

In spite of the guilt that *we* in the church bear in our souls, in spite of the death we deserve and the corruption in the church today, in spite of all that, this is the place of God's presence, and this is the place from which God offers life to the nations. If it were not a work of God, everything would stop where chapter 3 stops — God's temple a shambles, overrun by weeds; his people getting exactly what they deserve for their greed and dishonesty and sin. But God had another plan. He took the guilt and bore it himself on the cross in the person of Jesus Christ. And so now it's not a matter of getting what we deserve; it's a matter of receiving what God has to give. It's a matter of seeing what Micah sees: that God will use even corrupt, little Zion to gather in the nations of the world.

Micah sees a time when people from every place and nation will stream toward his God saying, "Come, let us go up to the mountain of the Lord, to the house of the God of Jacob." Micah sees a time when the word of the Lord will go out from his temple and the world will listen to it. He sees a time when there will be justice on the earth with all people enjoying the earth and unafraid, so that swords and spears will have to find new occupations, because waging war and drawing blood will be out of style. What Micah sees, centered around Jerusalem, is a world in which the Lord is God, where every person receives respect and dignity, where all nations are at peace.

That's what Micah sees: a time when the house of the God of Jacob will be the source of truth and grace, hope and life, where all peoples will go to worship. God's house isn't a place anymore; now it's a people. And that people is made up of everyone who belongs to Jesus Christ; that people is the church. No matter what things look like today, no matter what poor shape the church may be in now, Micah sees a time when all the world will drop their weapons and head for its doors.

And that will be a time of peace. More than anything else, what our God brings to the world is peace — peace between us and God, peace between us and each other. There probably was an ancient battle cry in which people would yell to their countrymen in time of war, "Beat your plowshares into swords and your pruning hooks into spears." Micah sees a time when the opposite will take place, when swords and spears are the last thing we'll need.

And even though it doesn't look much like it now, even though the earth today remains full of war and violence, idolatry and injustice, Micah sets a different path for the ones who belong to Zion, the ones who belong to Jesus: "All the people walk each in the name of its god, but we will walk in the name of the Lord our God forever and ever." That's what we do — we live out Micah 4 right now; we learn the ways of the God of Jacob right now; we work for peace right now; we walk in the name of the Lord our God today as well as forever.

And that's important for us to remember at a time like this, in a land that places loyalty to country right up there with loyalty to God. As we take pride in our history and heritage and government, let us make certain that all of it submits to our walking in the name of the Lord, to proclaiming his word, to waging peace.

In our denomination's contemporary testimony, which is in the back of our hymnals, we declared: "Following the Prince of Peace, we are called to be peacemakers, and to promote harmony and order. . . . We deplore the arms race. . . . We pledge to walk in ways of peace, confessing that our world belongs to God." I hope that's true — I hope that we are peacemakers, not enjoying war or savoring victory but waging peace. In the one war I've seen this country participate in, I'm not sure that was true. When it is true, it sets us apart, it turns things upside down. As the rest of our land and our world walk in the name of their gods, they will not produce peace. Peace comes from the Lord. And one day it will come in abundance.

But of course that day is not here yet. And that's the trouble. What's in front of us is more Micah 3 than Micah 4. We don't see the world streaming into the church to hear the word of God, not regularly. And we don't see many missiles being turned into grain silos or M-16s into can-openers, not like Micah saw it. We see countries and factions; we see gods named money and power. We don't see this day of peace and faith, and often we find it hard even to imagine. And that's why we must keep Micah 4 before us, why we can never forget what is the heart of the gospel.

In *Finding God in Unexpected Places,* Philip Yancey reflects on the size of the universe. He talks about how our galaxy, the Milky Way, holds 500 billion stars and that there are a hundred billion galaxies, and that some of these are moving at 30 million miles a day. The time he saw the Milky Way most clearly, he says, he was in Somalia during its ugliest days. He was there interviewing relief workers. "After three days of hearing tales of human misery," Yancey says, "I could not lift my sights beyond that refugee camp situated in an obscure corner of an obscure country on the horn of Africa. Until I saw the Milky Way. It abruptly reminded me that the present moment did not comprise all of life. History would go on. Tribes, governments, and whole civilizations may rise and fall, trailing disaster in their wake, but I dared not confine my field of vision to the scenes of suffering around me. I needed to look up, to the stars."[9]

So do we. Philip Yancey reminds us that we need to look up like Micah; we need to remember that there is so much more than the present, so much more on the way. We need to remember that after Micah 3 comes Micah 4. Otherwise, all we see is what's around us, what's going on right now — we see only that we're suffering or that we're at war or that we're Americans. Micah looks up; he has a bigger picture for us, a picture that includes a time when none of that will be true, when none of us will be suffering, when none of us will be at war, when none of us even will be Americans, not like we are now. Micah has a picture of peace, and when we see that picture — when we see by faith, when we unite ourselves with the body of Christ — then we are at the heart of the gospel, then God will bring peace to us and through us, even now, and then we will walk in the name of the Lord our God forever and ever.

God the Enemy

Text: Nahum

The Lord is slow to anger but great in power,
*   and the Lord will by no means clear the guilty.*
His way is in whirlwind and storm,
*   and the clouds are the dust of his feet. . . .*
The Lord has commanded concerning you [Nineveh]:
*   "Your name shall be perpetuated no longer;*
from the house of your gods I will cut off
*   the carved image and the cast image.*

9. Philip Yancey, *Finding God in Unexpected Places* (Ann Arbor: Servant Publications, 1997), p. 22.

I will make your grave, for you are worthless."
Look! On the mountains the feet of one
  who brings good tidings,
  who proclaims peace!
Celebrate your festivals, O Judah,
  fulfill your vows,
for never again shall the wicked invade you;
  they are utterly cut off.

Nahum 1:3, 14-15

Several years ago J. B. Phillips wrote a fine little book called *Your God Is Too Small*. I think that today, if he were interested in writing a sequel, the title perhaps should be *Your God Is Too Nice*. The God of our day, who is so often thought of as one who tolerates anything that gives worshipers a good time, who requires next to nothing from his disciples' behavior or priorities or wallet, whose main concern is that all human beings be personally fulfilled — that God is just too darn nice.

Neal Plantinga has spent a lot of time considering the question, Where has sin gone? What's happened to it? How come, even in the church today, sin is sort of a dirty word? A large part of the problem, he says, is that we have changed our image of God so that now, in our egalitarian culture, we have an egalitarian God. A God who is our equal, a God who is our chum — a God who is nothing but nice.

Well, this morning, like it or not — and we may not — we have a different image of God before us. And this image is not God the equal, it is not God the chum. It is God the righteous Judge, God the sovereign King, God the Enemy. Nahum presents us with a picture of a God who has had enough, a God who will wait no more and be gracious no longer, a God who is out to destroy the ones who refuse him.

We may not realize it at first when *we* read it, but this violent, terrible prophecy is actually a word of good news to Nahum's people. His name even means "comforter," and that is exactly what he is to the people of Judah, because Judah has been getting tossed around by Assyria for over a hundred years. And "tossed around" is putting it mildly, because Assyria was the most vicious conqueror in the history of the ancient Near East, and the people of Judah had seen that viciousness up close. They had seen the ten tribes that made up their sister nation Israel deported by Assyria, wiped out forever, never to be heard from again. Around that same time they had seen their own nation made a vassal of the empire. And when in Hezekiah's time the people of Judah revolted, they had to watch forty-six of their cities be destroyed before the armies of Sennacherib, and they avoided Israel's fate only by stripping themselves of their treasure to pay a heavy tribute to the capital in Nineveh.

The worst they had seen, however, probably took place under King Manasseh. He survived on Judah's throne only by selling himself and his reign to the Assyrians. During his time Nahum's people watched Assyrian gods and goddesses set up in their temple; they beheld child sacrifice in their land; they saw their prophets persecuted and killed; they witnessed their own royal officials going around in Assyrian dress and practicing Assyrian customs. To Nahum's people Assyria represented a hundred-year nightmare.

So how can a book full of devastation and destruction be the words of Nahum, the comforter? How can it bring good news? By ending a century of brutality, a century of arrogance and pride. The Assyrian rulers loved to brag about their acts of destruction and inhumanity. Now, Nahum says, it is *their* destruction that will be celebrated, it is Assyria that will be wiped out. And for the people of Judah, no music could sound so sweet.

Those few words of grace and goodness in chapter 1 seem so out of place in this book: "The Lord is good, a refuge in times of trouble. He cares for those who trust in him . . ." (v. 7). But for Judah they make perfect sense just where they are, because for Nahum's people, the way for the Lord to be good, to be a refuge in trouble, to care for those who trust in him at *this* time is to destroy Nineveh, to overwhelm Assyria, to kill his enemy.

But that makes things only a bit easier on us, because the truth is that a nice God is never God the enemy, a nice God is always giving one more chance, always bargaining and cajoling and pleading with those who refuse him to turn around and give him a little attention and live happily ever after. A nice God never says no, let alone something like "I will prepare your grave, for you are vile." And that's why Nahum is just as meaningful a word to us as it was for ancient Judah — just for different reasons.

For Judah the destruction of Nineveh was a reminder that, no matter how slow he is to anger, no matter how patient he is with his world, no matter how long he may take to do it, the Lord will not leave the guilty unpunished. Judah needed to know that no matter how things looked, no matter what idols were being worshiped and what godly people were being killed, evil would not win out. It would not last. It would not go unpunished. God's patience may grant a hundred years, but it will not grant forever, and the Judge of all the earth will see to it that things are put right. For Judah the message of Nahum is a message of hope.

For us of course it doesn't sound that way; for us the book of Nahum is a little harder to take. Unless we're talking about some group we love to hate, like homosexuals or abortionists, we don't like to think much about God's rejecting those who reject him. We don't like to think that people we like, people who have done pleasant things for us, have God against them because they have refused his lordship. Today the church is expected to be a nonjudgmental place, where every opinion, every behavior, every person is received on whatever terms they choose. J. B. Phillips was right, our God *is* too small, but he's also too nice.

> The Lord is slow to anger and great in power. . . .
> The Lord cares for those who trust in him,
>   but with an overwhelming flood
> he will make an end of Nineveh.
>
> (Nahum 1:3, 7-8, NIV)

Nahum makes it very clear: to those who defy his lordship, God is an enemy. We don't usually think that way; we don't count on God's judgment as part of our hope.

But maybe we should — not because we enjoy the suffering of those who walk a different path; there's too much of that in the church as it is. We should take hope from these words of Nahum because they remind us that — however long it takes, however much suffering there is in the meantime, however much it seems that evil has won the day or will never be destroyed — the forces that stand against God and work contrary to his will and his mission will be destroyed. The Lord has not given up his world to its present state — its corruption, its violence, its inequity. He will set it right; he will destroy what is wrong; he will defeat his enemies. Even if you find yourself waiting the better part of a century, don't ever believe that it won't happen. "The Lord is slow to anger but great in power; the Lord will not leave the guilty unpunished." That picture is reason for hope, because we know the Lord will show himself indeed as a refuge for those who trust in him. Nineveh will not have the final say, ever. Count on it.

But of course there's also something frightening about that. Maybe that's why today's God is too nice, too small. It's frightening to read the words of Nahum and know who you are, know what goes on in your own heart, in your own mind, in your own life. It's frightening to have a God who is God, a God who destroys evil and punishes wrong, because that God should then come to punish me. It's really much easier when your God is too nice. But that's not the God of Nahum. Biblical scholar Elizabeth Achtemeier writes, "The God portrayed here is really God, different from all lesser imitations, and different too from those impotent idols that we often project upon our universe."[10] The God of Nahum is really God, Master of his creation, Avenger against his enemies, Judge of the earth.

Let me suggest to you that if you haven't taken him seriously so far, now's the time. He is slow to anger, but his anger is real. Let's face it: some of us don't believe that, some of us don't bow to his lordship at all; we just play around the edges of the faith and figure everything is going to be fine. The prophet Nahum should make us shudder then. Remember: Assyria doesn't get another chance; the decision's been made, and time has run out. And that should make *all* of us shudder.

Today the church, in its political posturing, has this habit of using passages like this and self-righteously applying them to those who disagree. That's not how John Calvin responded to Nahum. Calvin's response was to be humbled, to repent, to pray. This is his prayer: "Grant, Almighty God, that as you set before us here as in a mirror how dreadful your wrath is, we may be humbled before you, and of our own selves cast ourselves down, . . . and be cleansed from our vices, until we shall at length appear in confidence before you, and be gathered among your children." When we see God portrayed as really God, when we look at ourselves for what we really are, humility and repentance are all that any of us have.

Heinrich Heine is noted for saying, "I like to sin. God likes to forgive. Really, the world is admirably arranged." His god is too nice, and he's not the God of Nahum. "I am against you," declares the Lord Almighty to Assyria. "Nothing can heal your wound. Your injury is fatal." We who have assumed that we are receiving the promise from God, "I am with you," must ask ourselves, is it possible he's actually saying, "I am against you"?

C. S. Lewis has written a marvelous little book about a fantastic bus ride from hell to heaven. It's called *The Great Divorce*. Among all the different kinds of people you encounter in the book, you find some surprises — murderers who have ended up in heaven, teetotalers destined for hell. But then you realize that the destination of every last one of them comes down to one thing. In the book our guide through heaven sums it up: "There are only two kinds of people in the end: those who say to God, 'Thy will be done,' and those to whom God says, in the end, '*Thy* will be done.' All that are in Hell, choose it."[11]

---

10. Elizabeth Achtemeier, *Nahum–Malachi*, Interpretation (Atlanta: John Knox, 1986), p. 8.

11. C. S. Lewis, *The Great Divorce* (New York: Macmillan, 1946), p. 72.

That's what it's about — not the amount of guilt we have, but who is Lord. Those who belong to Nahum's people, God's children — their guilt he took out on an innocent man two thousand years ago; that cup of anger was swallowed by God's own Son. Those who insist on running their own lives, who refuse a God who is really God, who challenge the Lord's rule of his earth — them God will not let stand in his way, just as he wouldn't let Assyria.

One way or another, he will be Lord, and his people will live in peace. May every one of us belong to that people, and so may these words of Nahum be indeed words of the comforter — not because God is nice, but because God is God, slow to anger but great in power. In the name of the Father and of the Son and of the Holy Spirit, Amen.

In the Meantime

Text: Habakkuk

Though the fig tree does not blossom,
and no fruit is on the vines;
though the produce of the olive fails,
and the fields yield no food;
though the flock is cut off from the fold,
and there is no herd in the stalls,
yet I will rejoice in the Lord;
I will exult in the God of my salvation.
God, the Lord, is my strength;
he makes my feet like the feet of a deer,
and makes me tread upon the heights.

Habakkuk 3:17-19

At the beginning of the film *Grand Canyon,* the main character, an immigration attorney, is driving home late at night from a Lakers' game. Frustrated with the slow-moving traffic, he turns off onto a side street. But the area quickly grows deserted and darker. Then he hears the dreaded noise in the engine; it cuts out and he is stranded, stranded in his expensive car in one of those places ruled by teenagers and guns. He does manage to phone for a tow truck, but before it arrives five young street toughs surround his vehicle and promise him some serious problems. But just then the tow truck shows up and its driver — an earnest, pleasant man — begins to hook up the disabled car. The toughs protest: they've got dibs here; this is *their* customer. And the tow truck driver takes the leader of the group aside and speaks a little prophecy to him. "Man," he says, "the world ain't supposed to work like this. Maybe you don't know that, but this ain't the way it's supposed to be. I'm supposed to be able to do my job without askin' you if I can. And that dude is supposed to be able to wait with his car without you rippin' him off. Everything's supposed to be different than what it is here."

It's prophecy, I say. But that tow truck driver wasn't the first one to speak it, of course; that would have been somebody like Habakkuk. And for Habakkuk, the fact that things aren't the way they're supposed to be — that streets are ruled by guns and cities by violence, that government influence is sold to the highest bidders and the poor lose their voice, that sin is rewarded and righteousness comes at a price — is not just something that gets in the way of his job, it's not just something that he is sadly resigned to. For Habakkuk, the fact that things aren't the way they're supposed to be and he can't see them changing is a burden that weighs on his soul. Habakkuk knows two things in his heart: he knows that God is on a mission of life and peace in this world, and he knows that the world is nothing like it's supposed to be. So his challenge, his burden, is to determine how those two truths can coexist, how the plan of God and the terrible brokenness of the world can go on at the same time.

> O Lord, how long shall I cry for help,
>   and you will not listen?
> Or cry to you, "Violence!"
>   and you will not save?
> Why do you make me see wrong-doing
>   and look at trouble?
> Destruction and violence are before me;
>   strife and contention arise.
> So the law becomes slack
>   and justice never prevails.

(1:2-4)

Habakkuk doesn't understand how, in God's world, things can remain so far from what they're supposed to be. And the answer he receives doesn't do much to clear up his confusion.

Let's set the scene here. It's about ten years after the fall of Assyria, a nation that had tormented Habakkuk's nation, Judah, for a hundred years. So Assyria's gone, but Judah is on the brink of being overrun again, this time by the Babylonians (the Chaldeans they're called) and this time permanently. One of these days Judah is going to be wiped out.

Not long before this, Judah had experienced a revival, a time of re-form, a time of returning to the Lord, under King Josiah. But those days are over, and now things are back to "normal" in Judah: people are disre-garding the ways of the Lord, the king has forgotten that he is the servant of the Lord, violence and injustice and wickedness run rampant in the land of the Lord. So Habakkuk wants to know from God, Why do you put up with this? If this is your world, why does it look like it does? Why aren't things the way they're supposed to be?

And then Habakkuk receives the last answer he would ever expect.

> Be astonished! Be astounded!
> For a work is being done in your days
>> that you would not believe if you were told.
> For I am rousing the Chaldeans.

(1:5-6)

The Lord's answer to Habakkuk's call for justice is the Chaldeans, the Babylonians, a people that worship only strength, that are interested only in their own honor, that destroy cities and overwhelm nations. I am rais-ing up the Babylonians, says the Lord.

And with that answer Habakkuk's confusion becomes utter baffle-ment. His question had been, Why do I not see the life and peace you promise flourishing around me? Why do you allow wrong to have its way in your world? And God responds, My answer to the violence of Judah will be the greater violence of Babylon; that's how I am going about my plan: the Babylonians are coming. And Habakkuk is baffled. "Your eyes are too pure to behold evil," he says, "and you cannot look on wrongdoing; why do you look on the treacherous and are silent when the wicked swallow those more righteous than they?" (1:13).

J. D. Eppinga, a retired minister in our denomination, once told a lit-tle story of a dream he had. In his dream he's being led around town by a guide, an angel. They come to a church, one of cathedral-like grandeur.

Inside are beautiful wooden pillars reaching to the rafters. As they stand there, a man with a bucket of paint walks by; there's a button on his coveralls that reads, "Quiet! Genius at work." And the man places a ladder alongside one of these wonderful pillars and slops paint on it. Eppinga is stunned. The beauty of the place will be ruined.

Well, he and his guide move on. On the sidewalk they come to an artist working on a scene of the town. They look over her shoulder while she works. She too has that button, "Quiet! Genius at work." But what she's painting makes no sense — it says nothing, it looks nothing like the scene in front of her. He's disappointed.

They go on again. They come to a diner. In the window is a sign, "Quiet! Genius at work." Through the window they see a chef working on a sort of stew. But what he puts in there and the amounts of spice and sauce make no sense, and the smell is strong and unappealing. Still, at his guide's encouragement they decide to stay and eat. To Eppinga's surprise, the meal is excellent, one of the best he's ever had. He is duly impressed.

Back on the sidewalk, they come across the artist. She's almost finished. Again they look at her work, and this time he's stunned by it. It says more about that place than any words or picture could express.

Finally, they return to the church, where the pillars are now a rich black. And it is glorious. He is drawn to worship. But, he wants to know, what about that sign, "Quiet! Genius at work"? Oh, that, says his guide, that's Psalm 37:7: "Be still before the Lord and wait patiently for him."

That's really the answer Habakkuk receives as well. It is an ugly thing that will happen to his people, not to be compared to a strange recipe or a painter in mid-work. There is nothing pretty about Babylon, and the suffering it will produce will be felt for centuries. But there *is* someone at work, and there *is* a plan in mind. The Lord *will* work his purpose out. So the response to the prophet's complaint is really the same: Be still and wait.

> For there is still a vision for the appointed time;
> > it speaks of the end, and does not lie.
> If it seems to tarry, wait for it;
> > it will surely come, it will not delay.

(2:3)

And that's why Habakkuk, as much as any prophecy in the book of the twelve, is a word for us. It slides so easily into our time, into any time, because faithful people are forever asking Habakkuk's question: Where is the plan of God amid all this evil? Why are things still so far from the way they're supposed to be? And so the word of the Lord to Habakkuk is the word of the Lord to every person who has prayed to him for peace and experienced only war, who has worked for justice and seen only corruption, who has asked for healing beside a sickbed only to experience death.

The word of the Lord to Habakkuk is the word of the Lord to every person who knows that this is their Father's world but at the same time knows just as well that the way things are is not the way they're supposed to be. Habakkuk is about living in the tension of those two truths. It's about seeing destruction and violence but knowing the God of hope and peace. Habakkuk is about living in the meantime.

And the way to do that, the way to live between the promise of God and its full display, is also found in Habakkuk:

> Look at the proud!
>   Their spirit is not right in them,
>   but the righteous live by their faith.
>
> (2:4)

Faith is the way to live in the meantime. Faith, says the writer of Hebrews, shows us what we cannot yet see. Faith is what allows the psalmist to remember the great deeds of the Lord and meditate on his goodness even in the day of trouble, even when he is weary with sorrow. Faith gives us hope, so that, even when the wrong seems so very strong, we know this is our Father's world. Even when violence and inhumanity seem to be all we can find, we know that the God of this place is a God of peace and justice. Even when wickedness seems to flourish, we know that the Lord does not reward evil but puts it down, even now, even as he used pagan Babylon to put down faithless Judah. Living by faith has to do with trust, trust in the Lord, trust that he is at work, trust that he is good and loving and present, trust that he knows exactly what he is doing, trust that he will work his purpose out. That's what we want to show our children, right from the start: we must trust the Lord, no matter where the world seems headed today.

Life was certainly not what it was supposed to be for Dietrich Bonhoeffer. Bonhoeffer was a young German pastor arrested by the Nazis for his role in a plot to assassinate Adolf Hitler. For Bonhoeffer, though, as he sat in prison, the issue was not, Why is Hitler out there and I am in here? For Bonhoeffer the issue was trusting that God was still at work. So three days before Christmas, 1943, he wrote these words to his closest friend: "I must be able to know for certain that I am in God's hands, not in men's. . . . Then everything becomes easy, even the severest privation. . . . All we can do is to live in assurance and faith — you out there with the soldiers, and I in my cell. — I've just come across this in the *Imitation of Christ:* 'Take good care of your cell, and it will take care of you.'"[12]

"Take good care of your cell, and it will take of you." That is the faith of the righteous, the faith of the psalmist, the faith of Habakkuk. The answer Habakkuk receives from God isn't the one he was looking for. He's not given an explanation; he's not told a date when God will make everything the way it's supposed to be. What the Lord tells him is, I am at work; I will keep my promise; I will accomplish my purpose; and right now I am raising up the Babylonians to overrun Judah. And this is how Habakkuk finally handles that answer:

> I hear, and I tremble within;
>   my lips quiver at the sound. . . .
> I wait quietly for the day of calamity
>   to come upon the people who attack us.
> Though the fig tree does not blossom,
>   and no fruit is on the vines;
> though the produce of the olive fails,
>   and the fields yield no food;
> though the flock is cut off from the fold,
>   and there is no herd in the stalls,
> yet I will rejoice in the Lord;
>   I will exult in the God of my salvation.
>
> (3:16-18)

Dietrich Bonhoeffer was executed in 1945. Habakkuk was almost certainly killed or run off to Babylon. Yet they, and *everyone* who lives by faith, could endure those things even with joy — not because this is the way it's supposed to be. Of course not. They could write and speak and live with joy because they know whose world this is. They know that God is at work here. And they know that in the end all his children will have life and have it more abundantly than ever before.

Every one of us looks around and sees — in our society, our families, our health, our church, our hearts — things different from the way they're

---

12. Dietrich Bonhoeffer, *Letters and Papers from Prison* (London: SCM Press, 1971), pp. 174-75.

supposed to be. But we know the God of this place; we are his children. We must trust him. We must trust his love. We must trust his work. We must trust him with our future. And then we can rejoice in the Lord, even here, even now.

The End of Zephaniah

Text: Zephaniah 1

> On that day, says the Lord,
>   a cry will be heard from the Fish Gate,
> a wail from the Second Quarter,
>   a loud crash from the hills.
> The inhabitants of the Mortar wail,
>   for all the traders have perished;
>   all who weigh out silver are cut off.
> At that time I will search Jerusalem with lamps,
>   and I will punish the people
> who rest complacently on their dregs,
>   those who say in their hearts,
> "The Lord will not do good,
>   nor will he do harm."
> Their wealth shall be plundered,
>   and their houses laid waste.
> Though they build houses,
>   they shall not inhabit them;
> though they plant vineyards,
>   they shall not drink wine from them.

Zephaniah 1:10-13

I was a bit concerned when we began this foray into the book of the twelve minor prophets. I was concerned that maybe it would be just too much doom and gloom in one sitting; maybe all we would hear about, week after week, would be Israel's idol-worshiping ways and their abuse of the poor and then God's response: how his patience had run out, how his pleading and seeking after his people was over, how judgment was coming. And so I wondered if that was the kind of thing we'd want to spend the summer talking about. Maybe a series on "family reunions" or "outdoor activities from the Bible" would make more sense.

But of course that wouldn't make sense, not even in summer — not if we want to be a people molded and renewed by the word of God. And the irony is that the word we've heard from these prophets has been remarkably balanced. They've spoken of the Lord's inner turmoil as he waits up for his wayward child, pacing the halls, looking for the first sign that Israel has come back to him. They've described a God who destroys weapons, a God whose plan for the earth is a plan for peace. And when they've spoken in anger, it's anger at injustice and unrighteousness — it's anger that many of those made in God's image have no chance or hope for a decent life; it's anger at those who celebrate the misery of others — because ours is a God who calls for love, even toward enemies. So, although it isn't exactly "summer fun in the Bible," we've seen an amazingly rounded picture of God develop from the book of the twelve. We've seen a God as committed to the love and future and prosperity of his people as ever.

We have to admit, though, that the doom and gloom increase when we read the book of Nahum. In Nahum we have God at war. There are startling and unrelenting pictures of God when he's had enough, when he's out to destroy sinners, when he's become an enemy. We could try to make light of that. After all, we could say, some folks think the book of Nahum shouldn't even be in the Bible, and that certainly it shouldn't be emphasized. And after all, we could go on, in Nahum God's anger is directed at an evil empire, the Nazis of their day, a people totally without any redeeming value, any possibility of salvation — the Assyrians. We might argue that God had no choice but to exterminate them.

And maybe all that would help us get through the doom and gloom of Nahum. But then, two prophets down the line, we get to Zephaniah, and Zephaniah also has an end in sight. But Zephaniah's end isn't just for the Assyrians, just for those monstrously evil countries with reputations for slaughtering infants and spitting on altars. Zephaniah prophesies an end for us *all*.

The word of the Lord that came to Zephaniah. . . .
I will utterly sweep away everything

from the face of the earth, says the Lord.
I will sweep away humans and animals;
    I will sweep away the birds of the air
    and the fish of the sea.
I will make the wicked stumble.
    I will cut off humanity
    from the face of the earth, says the Lord.

(1:1-3)

Zephaniah sees not only the end of Assyria; he sees the end of everything. He sees creation thrown into reverse by a God who can do it. And then, just in case his audience somehow gets the idea that God's own people are excused from this catastrophe, he goes on:

I will stretch out my hand against Judah,
    and against all the inhabitants of Jerusalem.

(v. 4)

This is the word of the Lord, but it's hard to respond this time, "Thanks be to God." When we read about the end Zephaniah prophesies, about his "de-creation," it's hard to imagine that there is a gospel to be found here, that Zephaniah can offer us any hope whatsoever. And we certainly wouldn't be the first ones to hear these words and feel that way.

In 1939 a British preacher named W. E. Bowen preached a sermon on Zephaniah 1:2 entitled "Black-Robed Years." In that sermon Bowen read two verses of Scripture — first Zephaniah 1:2, "I will utterly sweep away everything from the face of the earth, says the Lord"; and then John 3:16, "For God so loved the world that he gave his only Son, so that everyone who believes in him may not perish but may have eternal life." And Reverend Bowen asked, "Can we who profess and call ourselves Christians doubt which of these sayings is from a spiritual standpoint the finer of the two? . . . There is surely nothing in [Jesus'] teaching to justify the supposition that he would have endorsed such a prophecy."

Of course, it's that kind of thinking that would have us ignore Zephaniah and Nahum and other fairly large chunks of the book of the twelve. It's that kind of thinking that would have us misunderstand God and start down a road to de-creation ourselves. So here's the thesis for this morning: Reverend Bowen is wrong — Zephaniah and John do indeed have to do with each other.

John 3:16 is based on the underlying truth that, unless God steps in, unless God does something to change things, every one of us is going to perish. In fact, we're already perishing. The good news of John 3:16 is that God did step in, in Jesus Christ, so that everyone who believes in him, everyone bound up with him, will not perish but have everlasting life. But the underlying truth remains: apart from Jesus Christ, apart from belonging to the God of Israel and receiving his grace, there is only one end we can have, and that is the end of Zephaniah, that is perishing. That's what Zephaniah 1 is describing: an end apart from God.

Zephaniah lives at a time when Assyria is still running things in their usual, brutal way. It is a time when, in order for Judah to *get* along, they figure they have to *go* along. So, while they still follow the basic traditions of worshiping the Lord, they also bow to other gods. Their kings are walking around in Assyrian dress, the people are offering Assyrian sacrifices, and everyone's practicing Assyrian customs. And they figure that, because they still talk about God, because they've got some Old Testament version of John 3:16 rattling around in their memories, all of this will be fine with God. But they're wrong about that. They don't remember who they are; and that's what Zephaniah is saying:

> At that time I will search Jerusalem with lamps
> > and punish those who are complacent,
> > who are like wine left on its dregs,
> who think, "The Lord will do nothing,
> > either good or bad."

> (1:12, NIV)

It's John 3:16 again — you perish unless you take that salvation provided by God. And the people of Judah in Zephaniah's time have let go. They're paying some lip service, but they're sure that the Lord won't ever turn against them. And that's where they're wrong. And that's something *we* must remember, living in a world where getting along still means going along, where we've always got people to tell us that a little Christianity, a little worship, a little money, a little devotion, is more than enough. Complacency earns judgment. Listen to what Elizabeth Achtemeier says about these first words of Zephaniah:

> We Christians sometimes believe that the cross will always shield us
> from similar condemnation, but there is no automatic guarantee in
> the gospel of Christ against such death. Where the worship of his
> lordship becomes mixed with allegiance to other lords, where there

is belief that luck or the stars or the powers of this world ultimately control our destiny, where we therefore neglect the worship of the Lord and conform to the ways of society and water down his commands for convenience or ideological servitude, we too are confronted by a God who can say to us, "I will utterly sweep away everything from the face of the earth."[13]

Don't kid yourself about this. We in Western society have a remarkable ability to consider ourselves eternally secure no matter how divided our loyalties, how deep our grudges, how petty our complaints, how selfish our priorities. And so we take offense at anybody like Zephaniah who implies that it may not be that way at all. "I will stretch out my hand against . . . those who bow down and swear by the Lord, and who also swear by Molech" (1:4-5, NIV). Zephaniah sees an end to such two-faced faith, even if it means throwing all of creation into reverse.

But, like every prophet we've read and every author in the Scriptures, Zephaniah also sees a new creation where the old one used to be. Zephaniah sees life where there should be only death. Zephaniah sees a God who doesn't want anyone to perish. And that's the other way in which Reverend Bowen is wrong to say that John 3:16 doesn't have anything to do with Zephaniah. That's why, when we're reading chapter 1 about the end Zephaniah sees, we must remember to keep reading till the end of Zephaniah.

At the end of Zephaniah the Lord says to Jerusalem, his capital city which also has received his punishment:

> I will remove from your midst
>   your proudly exultant ones,
> and you shall no longer be haughty
>   in my holy mountain.
> For I will leave in the midst of you
>   a people humble and lowly.
> They shall seek refuge in the name of the Lord —
>   the remnant of Israel;
> they shall do no wrong
>   and utter no lies,
> nor shall a deceitful tongue
>   be found in their mouths.

13. Achtemeier, *Nahum–Malachi*, p. 65.

Then they will pasture and lie down,
    and no one shall make them afraid.

                                                                (3:11-13)

Then the Lord goes on to say,

Sing aloud, O daughter Zion;
    shout, O Israel!
Rejoice and exult with all your heart,
    O daughter Jerusalem!
The Lord has taken away the judgments against you,
    he has turned away your enemies.

                                                                (vv. 14-15)

For those who humbly believe, who trust in the name of the Lord, who look to God for salvation, there is no perishing at all. They will remain. For them there is only life. On that John and Zephaniah entirely agree.

The whole earth deserves God's judgment, but that's not his will. So for the humble ones who bow before him, the judgment of Zephaniah is removed by the God who doesn't wish to sweep everything away but to give everything life. And what life it is! The day Zephaniah sees is a day when God's people will be in full celebration: "Rejoice," he says, "exult with all your heart!" But more amazing still, in Zephaniah's picture the Lord is rejoicing, too, right along with everybody else. "The Lord, your God, is in your midst," says Zephaniah, "he will rejoice over you with gladness . . . he will exult over you with loud singing" (v. 17). What God has waiting for those who trust in him is nothing less than the most outrageous celebration you can imagine. And he will be in the middle of it, not judging or punishing or even saving anymore — just celebrating. The Lord, says Zephaniah, will be the one at the piano.

Life, celebration, joy — that's the goal. That's the end Zephaniah really has in mind. But if you want to be proud, if you want to go your own way, then you can have another end. C. S. Lewis said that there are really only two kinds of people in the world when you really come down to it: those who say to God, "Your will be done," and those to whom God says, "All right already — your will be done." But make no mistake — God's will is the one that leads to the celebration.

In his comments on Jesus' parable of the virgins waiting for the bridegroom, Robert Farrar Capon, in his inimitable, startling way, reminds us what we're waiting for:

"Watch therefore," Jesus says at the end of the parable, "for you know neither the day nor the hour." When all is said and done — when we have scared ourselves silly with the now-or-never urgency of faith and the once-and-always finality of judgment — we need to take a deep breath and let it out with a laugh. Because what we are watching for is a party. And that party is not just down the street making up its mind when to come to us. It is already hiding in our basement, banging on our steam pipes, and laughing its way up our cellar stairs. The unknown day and hour of its finally bursting into the kitchen and roistering its way through the whole house is not dreadful; it is all part of the divine lark of grace. God is not our mother-in-law, coming to see whether her wedding-present china has been chipped. He is a wonderful old Uncle with a salami under one arm and a bottle of wine under the other. We do indeed need to watch for him; but only because it would be such a pity to miss all the fun.[14]

That's the day of the Lord for us who rest in him, for us who humbly wait for our salvation. And it's not something we can take lightly or mix in with other devotions or just assume because we call ourselves Christians. It's far too serious a matter for that; after all, God gave up his only Son. But he gave him up for *life*. And everyone who trusts in him will have that life. Everyone who trusts in him has that kind of party to look forward to. Everyone who trusts in him knows that that is God's will, to be right there in the middle of it all — celebrating — because he so loves the world, that he wants it to live, forever.

The Word of the Lord, according to Zephaniah. Thanks be to God.

14. Robert Farrar Capon, *Kingdom, Grace, Judgment: Paradox, Outrage, and Vindication in the Parables of Jesus* (Grand Rapids: Eerdmans, 2002), p. 501.

Choosing Jerusalem

Text: Zechariah 1:1-6; 2:1-13

The Lord was very angry with your ancestors. Therefore say to them, Thus says the Lord of hosts: Return to me, says the Lord of hosts, and I will return to you, says the Lord of hosts. Do not be like your ancestors, to whom the former prophets proclaimed, "Thus says the Lord of hosts, Return from your evil ways and from your evil deeds." But they did not hear or heed me, says the Lord. Your ancestors, where are they? And the prophets, do they live forever? But my words and my statutes, which I commanded my servants the prophets, did they not overtake your ancestors? So they repented and said, "The Lord of hosts has dealt with us according to our ways and deeds, just as he planned to do."

Zechariah 1:2-6

Mark Helprin's novel *A Soldier of the Great War* is, more than anything else, about the change, the damage, that the First World War brought to one man's life — but not only his life. The story is just as much about the war's effect on his vision, his being, his soul. That man, Alessandro Giuliani, is dragged into and through and around the war for most of its duration. Usually he's a soldier, but often he's a victim and sometimes merely an observer. There's one scene, in Munich near the end of the war, in which Alessandro experiences regular, everyday, civilian life again. For the first time in years his movements and responses are not controlled by a commander or an enemy or a bullet.

In Munich Alessandro is mesmerized by peace, by its form, its color. Even though he's filled with hunger and cold, he walks the streets for hours. He watches the city. He watches the faces of the women and children, and the old — the ones he knows stayed behind, the ones who weren't in war. He looks at them, because their faces still have the look of comfort, a look that's possible for them, says Helprin, because they have not encountered the blackness that devoured so many lives and souls.[15] Surely they've talked about the war, they're aware of the war, perhaps they've even

---

15. Mark Helprin, *A Soldier of the Great War* (San Diego: Harcourt Brace Jovanovich, 1991), p. 601.

seen something of the war. But not *knowing* the war, not living what Alessandro has lived and seeing what he has seen, has left them so far from him now, made them such different people, that he and they can never really be the same again. That's what wars and persecutions and genocides do. The ones they don't kill they change forever.

Just like exiles. So, if we're going to hear the message of Zechariah — and Malachi, for that matter — we must think about that, we must understand that. We must understand that talking about exile, being aware of exile, seeing pictures of exile — all of that has little to do with *living* an exile. Nothing else is the same.

Some of you know that, and so you relate to Zechariah in a way that I cannot. I'm thinking of those of you who lived through the Second World War in Holland. You know what it's like to see your homeland overrun by strangers, to lose your freedom and your dignity and your possessions. You know what that's like, some of you, all too well. Perhaps still today you have some of the same feeling Alessandro Giuliani had on the streets of Munich — that the rest of us have no idea what life can turn into, how bad it can get. I'm sure for many of you that was a faith-shaking event, an event that at times made you wonder about the purpose of God and the love of God and the power of God. And so now think about these Jews who lived through the exile to Babylon and how their lives were changed and how their faith was shaken.

Their land was overrun; their freedom and dignity and possessions were destroyed. And their faith was not just shaken but voided; it was nullified. Psalm 137, those piercing words of recent exiles, puts it so clearly:

> By the rivers of Babylon —
>   there we sat down and there we wept
>   when we remembered Zion.
> On the willows there
>   we hung our harps.
> For there our captors
>   asked us for songs,
> and our tormentors asked for mirth, saying,
>   "Sing us one of the songs of Zion!"
> How could we sing the Lord's song
>   in a foreign land?

Without the temple, without Mt. Zion, without Jerusalem these people have no songs to sing, no place to worship, no way to God. You kill Jerusalem, you nullify their faith. Now these survivors of the exile, who haven't seen their temple in seventy years, are coming back from Babylon, and it's understandable that they have a different look on their faces, that they're not the same people they used to be. The ones exiles don't kill they change forever.

So that's where we are at the beginning of the prophecy of Zechariah. It's 520 B.C. Seventy years have passed since Nebuchadnezzar came through and destroyed everything. Now Persia has taken over the world, and a more merciful regime has allowed a few Jews to go home. But the city they've come home to, the city of David, looks like a ghost town, or a battle zone. They're back, but they're changed. And they're wondering about their God; they're wondering about his purpose and they're wondering about his love and they're certainly wondering about his power. Where was he when Jerusalem went up in flames?

And so, in the eighth month of the second year of the reign of Darius the Persian, the word of the Lord came to Zechariah. And the message that Zechariah delivered from the Lord to these returned exiles comes in two parts, though the second is the big one, the main one, the one they need to hear today. But to get there, they need to hear the first part; they need to get something straight and never forget it. And this is it: the exile was God's idea.

That's the first thing Zechariah has to say to his people:

The Lord was very angry with your ancestors. . . . Return to me, says the Lord of hosts, and I will return to you, says the Lord of hosts. Do not be like your ancestors, to whom the former prophets proclaimed, "Thus says the Lord of hosts, Return from your evil ways and from your evil deeds." But they did not hear or heed me, says the Lord. Your ancestors, where are they? And the prophets, do they live forever? But my words and my statutes, which I commanded my servants the prophets, did they not overtake your ancestors?

When my word and your ancestors faced off, it was my word that lasted — that's the first thing God says through Zechariah. And how important that is for them to know. These people may look around at the crumbled buildings and overgrown streets and think that it happened because God was too weak to prevent it, that God lost. But God tells them, It happened because I ordained it. It happened because your mothers and fathers wouldn't listen, wouldn't walk with me, wouldn't live like my children. The rubble around Jerusalem isn't evidence that I failed or that I've been somewhere else; the rubble, the destruction, the weeds are evidence that I've been at work. They're evidence that I was here and I responded when my people kept turning away. The exile was my doing.

Those can't be easy words to hear when you're suffering, to learn that the suffering was from God, a response to your sin. And they're not easy words for us when we consider that God's activity still may include such response to sin. Just as God was calling Judah to walk in his ways, to serve him lovingly, to be his people — so he calls us. And when we turn away from him for gods we prefer and lives we can run, it's foolish to think that he cannot or will not respond, that we never face judgment, that our suffering never arises from our own disobedience. "So they repented. . . ."

But that's not all Zechariah has to say. In fact, that's only the preliminary prophecy, the introduction. First he has to make sure these folks understand that God hasn't gone anywhere for the last seventy years, that their exile has been part of his purpose, that the earth still belongs to him. They must know that what God sets out to do, he does, and nothing will get in his way. And then they must hear the *main* point of the prophecy, the real message of Zechariah.

And that message comes in the form of visions and angels, eight visions to describe what God is going to do. We read the third one in chapter 2. But all of the visions have the same message; they all describe the same idea, just from different perspectives. The first vision describes it this way: "Thus says the Lord of hosts: My cities shall again overflow with prosperity; the Lord will again comfort Zion and again choose Jerusalem" (1:17). That is the main thing Zechariah has to say to these former exiles, these worn-down, empty-handed, broken-hearted, homeless people. He says it again at the end of chapter 2, verse 12, and this time he adds, "Be silent, all people, before the Lord; for he has roused himself from his holy dwelling." The Lord has roused himself. God is out to do something. And what he's out to do is restore their home. "My cities shall again overflow with prosperity; the Lord will again comfort Zion and again choose Jerusalem."

That's the news. That's the message. God will again choose Jerusalem — in spite of the past, in spite of the judgment he levied there, in spite of the shambles the place has become. God wants it. The Lord will rebuild it. And that, of course, is reason for celebration, that gives hope to these desperate exiles. Seventy years and two world dynasties later, God is still working out his plan, and Jerusalem — even torn up and run over — is at the center of it.

And that takes us to the vision we read in chapter 2. Zechariah sees a man with a measuring line in his hand. He's off to measure Jerusalem. He wants to make sure they get everything right the second time around — Jerusalem put back together just the way it was, just the way it's supposed to be. He's heard the good news that God will again choose Jerusalem, and now he's off to get the numbers, so the construction crews don't make the wall too narrow or put the temple in the wrong spot.

But before he can line up his ruler the angel tells Zechariah, Run! Catch him. Tell him we don't need his numbers, because the new Jerusalem isn't going to be like the old one. The new Jerusalem is going to be a city without walls, because if it had walls it would be too small, it wouldn't be able to hold all the people and all the animals living there. And don't worry, even though the new city won't have a wall, it'll be protected. The Lord himself will guard it. And the Lord himself will be the glory within it.

These former exiles standing around Zechariah in a rusted, old, run-down city need to know that God will choose Jerusalem again. And the new version will be nothing like the old one. No empire, no army, no enemy will ever be a threat to her, will ever step inside her. And the city will be full, not with a few refugees, but with the whole world. That's the good news of Zechariah. That's the good news of his visions. It's really good news when you've just gotten home from exile. And it's really good news still today.

I believe it's true that, when we turn away from God, it is always a dead end we turn toward, a painful end; and so our suffering may even be his judgment. That's true. But it's also true — and this is the message of Zechariah — that, even though God has nearly destroyed Jerusalem in judgment, he will choose it again; he is determined to do so. He has roused himself to do this. "Return to me, says the Lord of hosts, and I will return to you."

We're not all survivors of war like Alessandro Giuliani. But we are all bearers of pain, secret pain, pain that has changed the expression on our faces, pain that can make us feel different from everyone else. Here's the good news of Zechariah: the Lord Almighty has a new place for every one of us marred by exile or war or something else, something similarly devastating — even if it was suffering we brought on ourselves. God will choose Jerusalem again, he will choose us again, in spite of the past, in spite of the judgment he levied, in spite of the shambles we've become.

He's got a place where he will bring every kind of person, every kind of sinner, to live in the presence of his glory. He will choose Jerusalem again, and the new one will be nothing like the old. Here there will be no enemies, no sin or war or weakness; there will be no one who does not bow before the Lord and bring their lives to him. And that leaves only one question: Will we return to him? Will *we* choose Jerusalem? It would be a shame to be left out.

The Lord has roused himself to do this thing. This is the purpose he has decreed. And he will accomplish it, no matter what his effort, no matter what his cost, no matter what his suffering. In the name of Jesus Christ, Amen.

God's Lasting Burden

Text: Malachi 1:1-5; 4

See, the day is coming, burning like an oven, when all the arrogant and all evildoers will be stubble; the day that comes shall burn them up, says the Lord of hosts, so that it will leave them neither root nor branch. But for you who revere my name the sun of righteousness shall rise, with healing in its wings. You shall go out leaping like calves from the stall. And you shall tread down the wicked, for they will be ashes under the soles of your feet, on the day when I act, says the Lord of hosts.

Malachi 4:1-3

Love is not a feeling, says psychiatrist M. Scott Peck in *The Road Less Traveled*. Love is not a feeling, it's an action, an activity, a decision. So, says Peck, "an alcoholic man, whose wife and children are desperately in need of his attention at that very moment, may be sitting in a bar with tears in his eyes, telling the bartender, 'I really love my family.' People who neglect their children in the grossest of ways more often than not will consider themselves the most loving of parents."[16] That's the problem when we confuse love with the *feeling* of love. It's easy to proclaim our love in what

16. M. Scott Peck, *The Road Less Traveled* (New York: Simon and Schuster, 1978), pp. 119-20.

we feel; it takes work, it takes attentiveness, it takes pain to profess our love in what we do.

And now, as we come to the last prophet in the book of the twelve, to the very end of the Old Testament, we see that the people of Judah couldn't agree more. "How have you loved us?" they have been asking God. How have you loved us? What is there to show for your love? An exile? Poverty? It's been sixty years since we came back, since we rebuilt your temple, since Zechariah prophesied about a brand-new Jerusalem, and we've seen none of it. And we've seen none of *you*. All we've seen is our lives run by Persians and our God nowhere to be found.

The relationship between God and his people had always rested on a covenant in which God promised to guard and bless Israel and Israel promised to count on him and follow him and live with him. But now, as Elizabeth Achtemeier puts it,

> Israel in Malachi's time had grown tired of waiting and obeying and loving because nothing — apparently nothing at all — was happening in her world. . . . Nothing faced Israel but the "dailiness of life," obeying God's commandments in daily relations with neighbors and friends; spending money to pay tithes for the support of the priests; giving up prized lambs and calves to be burnt on the altar; learning religious traditions that seemed as distant as the God they portrayed; praying prayers that disappeared, unanswered, into the blue. God apparently was doing nothing at all in Judah's life, and all his promises for the future seemed hollow mockeries of her service to him.[17]

God apparently was doing nothing, and for these people, doing nothing had nothing to do with love.

And that's where we are at the beginning of Malachi. A charge has been laid against the Lord, and the charge is that he has not loved his people, not *really* loved them, not paid attention to them and cared for them and given himself to them. And as proof, the people of Israel cited the people of Edom. The people of Edom come from Esau, the brother of Israel's father Jacob. And the Lord chose Jacob over Esau, according to the story that these people have heard for so long. But it was the descendants of Jacob who were carried off to Babylon, not the descendants of Esau. Edom actually made out like bandits in the deal; they worked as Babylon's

17. Achtemeier, *Nahum–Malachi,* p. 175.

informants, spied on Israel, helped the invaders, cut off escape routes, and ransacked Jerusalem after everything was said and done. So, if Jacob is the one God chose, the one God loves, why is Edom prospering, why has Edom become a world player, why has Edom been blessed, when they sold themselves to the Babylonians, when they betrayed the people of Israel, when they have nothing to do with the Lord God Almighty? Edom thrives, Judah languishes. The Lord has not kept his word. That is the charge.

So now, before we close the book of the twelve, Malachi gives us God's response. "An Oracle" — that's the first word, the description of what will follow. But the word *oracle* also means "burden." And when that word turns up in situations like this one — before a prophecy — it's almost always followed, as it is in Nahum, for instance, by a strong word of judgment. And that makes sense. When there is an announcement of judgment to be made, it's not simply a proclamation; it's also a burden. It weighs on God's heart to judge and punish and condemn.

But Malachi isn't a prophecy of judgment, not in that sense. In Malachi the burden on the heart of God is something else. "A burden: The word of the Lord to Israel by Malachi. I have loved you, says the Lord." That's the response to Israel's charge: I have loved you, and I love you still — that's the sense of that verb: past and present. And in fact that love for you is not just a feeling, God says, it's not just a statement or a promise; that love for you is a burden. I've waited for you as you sold yourself to other gods, and I pleaded with you to turn back to me as you caroused in sin, and I wept over you even as I opened your gates to the Babylonians. Don't tell me I don't love you — I have loved you and I still love you, and that love is a burden I bear. Probably many of us, certainly many of us parents, know the way love, *real* love, can qualify as a burden.

And then the Lord goes on to address their complaint. After all, saying he loves them is fine, but it's still just words. So you think I love Edom, because they got away with some things, because I let them have a role in your exile? It is not so. I am with Jacob, I am against Esau — that has not changed. And that is already being displayed. Edom has been dismantled, and they will not return. And one of these days you will see it, and you will know that I am the Lord of *all* the earth. I have loved you, and I love you still.

That's the answer to Israel's charge, and that's the meaning of those difficult words that God has loved Jacob and hated Esau. It's not an emotional statement; it's not a doctrinal statement; it's a historical statement — it's a statement of where God has been, who he is with, where he will be.

Edom broke her covenant, Edom violated God's people, and God will not merely sit and watch. You think Edom is first, that Edom has prospered? It is not so.

You are the ones I sought as my people, says the Lord. You are the ones I disciplined in Babylon. You are the ones I brought back home, in spite of your sin, to rebuild your temple, to renew your sacrifices, to walk again with me. You are the ones I have restored, the ones I have forgiven, the ones I have loved. And the evidence of that is that you are home again, with a rebuilt Jerusalem and a new temple. Know it: I have loved you, and I love you still.

But of course Malachi has a long way to go from here, and the Lord is not done speaking to his people. He has answered their charge, but now he has charges of his own. I have loved you, he says, but have you loved me? Your priests are not interested in my word; they're sloppy with my sacrifices; they bring animals before me that are diseased. Am I not worthy of the best you have to offer? Am I not the King of nations?

What about your end of the covenant? What about your keeping faith with me? You put away the wife of your youth because you desire another; you marry pagan women: "I hate divorce" (2:16). "Will anyone rob God? Yet you are robbing me . . . in your tithes and offerings!" (3:8).

Let's think about that last comment for a moment: "You are robbing me in your tithes and offerings!" This may seem like such an obvious topic because we're behind in our budget again, but, you know, I'm not really that interested, from a preaching perspective, in whether we make our budget. I'd like to know that we take seriously the commitments we make at the beginning of each year, more seriously than I think we do, but that doesn't really have to do with this issue of tithes and offerings.

Tithing, of course, is the idea of giving ten percent to the church. You might argue that that's Old Testament law and we're not bound by it anymore. But what we are bound by — at least, what our love for our God should be driving us to — is the principle that we give generously, that we give regularly, and that we give off the top, from the very best that we have. And that is where I have a very real interest as a preacher, because there are too many — in this very room — not giving in those ways, not giving in amounts that show our love. I am direly disappointed at the number of people in a congregation like this one who give far less than ten percent. That hardly seems like firstfruits giving to me. We owe our God our best. Love takes action. "Will anyone rob God? Yet you are robbing me! But you say, 'How are we robbing you?' In your tithes and offerings!"

As Malachi sees it, the question isn't whether God will be faithful, even though that's where he begins. The real question is whether his people will be faithful, whether we will be faithful, whether we will trust his love and keep waiting and watching and obeying until that day of the Lord. If we don't, if we don't believe him, if we don't give him his right place and count on him to do what he says, then we will not endure. "See, the day is coming," we read in the last chapter of the Old Testament, "burning like an oven, when all the arrogant and all evildoers will be stubble; the day that comes shall burn them up . . . so that it will leave them neither root nor branch. But for you who revere my name the sun of righteousness shall rise, with healing in its wings. You shall go out leaping like calves from the stall" (4:1-2). The Lord loves his people. The Lord will provide a new and perfect Jerusalem. Whether we're there depends on whether we think he and that love are real. Not all of those who say "Lord, Lord" now will be with him at the end. Malachi wants his people to know that.

But that's not his last word. His last word is a reminder of where he began: "A burden from the Lord: I have loved you and I love you still." This time he says it this way: "Lo, I will send you the prophet Elijah before the great and terrible day of the Lord comes. He will turn the hearts of parents to their children and the hearts of children to their parents, so that I will not come and strike the land with a curse" (4:5-6).

Thus ends the Old Testament. The first time I read these words about striking with a curse I was troubled. I wanted the last words before the testimony to the incarnation of Jesus Christ to be powerful and hopeful and grace-filled all at once. These didn't satisfy me. They didn't satisfy some others, either. Both the Greek translation and the Hebrew tradition have put some of the earlier verses in Malachi at the end. But that's not necessary.

Scott Peck is right: love isn't a feeling; it's action, it's commitment, it's attention. And on every page of his scroll, Malachi reminds us that, however unlovable Israel was, despite how little at times God must have *felt* like loving Israel, he always did. "I have loved you and I love you still" — but not through sentimental language or simple emotion. God's love is love that matters, love that shows up, love that is attentive. And Malachi keeps reminding us of that. As God rebukes Israel's priests and peruses Israel's marriage licenses and decries Israel's greed, Malachi reminds us that God is attentive to his people, always watching over them, always wanting them to walk more closely with him.

So, even after sending them off to exile and bringing them back home and sending them prophets and warning them of the day of the Lord, even then he has more to do, more attention to pay: he says he will send the prophet Elijah to turn their hearts back where they should be, so that they will live, so that he will not come and strike the land with a curse. The Old Testament doesn't close with judgment; it closes with the *threat* of judgment. It closes with a God who loves his people sending them one more prophet to avoid a curse forever. That man would be John the Baptist. But, of course, God didn't stop even there; God's burden of love spurred him to send one more, not a prophet this time but a Son — a Son who would bear the curse himself. Love isn't a feeling. It's a decision; it's action. This God has decided; this God has acted. This God has loved.

The Book of Sirach, in the Apocrypha, says: "May the bones of the twelve prophets send forth new life from where they lie, for they comforted the people of Jacob and delivered them with confident hope." Those words may at first sound like a strange way of describing these prophets: "for they comforted the people of Jacob and delivered them with confident hope." After all, these twelve are known more for talking about judgment. But I hope we who have read them have seen that hope here, have seen that even those severe words are words of a God who is attentive to his people, a God who is committed to their having life and having it abundantly. They're the words of a God burdened by a promise he is determined to keep: "I have loved you and I love you still."

I hope we know that God better for having heard of him through these prophets. And I hope that right now, even if you do not see his kingdom coming or his attention directed to your life, even if he's doing absolutely nothing as far as you can tell, I hope you will hear these words, "I have loved you and I love you still," and believe them. Believe them and hold on to them and live through them and rest in them. Because the love of this God is not a feeling, it is not a whim; it is a decision, it is an oath by the Lord Almighty that you will be restored: "For you who revere my name the sun of righteousness shall rise, with healing in its wings. You shall go out leaping like calves from the stall." The Word of God according to Malachi, and Hosea and Joel and Nahum and Micah and Jonah and Amos and Obadiah and Zechariah and Haggai and Habakkuk and Zephaniah — the twelve prophets who comforted the people of Jacob and delivered them with confident hope.

Vegetarians in Babylon

Text: Daniel 1

The king assigned them a daily portion of the royal rations of food and wine. They were to be educated for three years, so that at the end of that time they could be stationed in the king's court. . . . But Daniel resolved that he would not defile himself with the royal rations of food and wine; so he asked the palace master to allow him not to defile himself. Now God allowed Daniel to receive favor and compassion from the palace master. The palace master said to Daniel, "I am afraid of my lord the king; he has appointed your food and your drink. If he should see you in poorer condition than the other young men of your own age, you would endanger my head with the king." Then Daniel asked the guard whom the palace master had appointed over Daniel, Hananiah, Mishael, and Azariah: "Please test your servants for ten days. Let us be given vegetables to eat and water to drink. . . ."

Daniel 1:5, 8-12

I used to have a friend in the army reserve, a very clear-minded person, very black-and-white on the issues — political issues, biblical issues. He saw only one way to do things. Yet I remember him telling me that strict biblical ideas just don't work in the army. In the army — at least in his part of it — the foulest language and debasing other human beings are part of the process, part of the social structure, part of the way that world works. That's the way he has to operate, because, if he were to ignore those things, he couldn't hope to survive.

He's got a point, of course; at least it's one we hear often enough: "I wish it were different, but the only way to operate in my job is to put it first in my life or to fudge on some of the numbers or to follow orders, no matter what I may think of them. There's no other way I can make it." The idea is that the principles of the Christian faith, those things that mark us as the people of God, are fine for Sundays, for dealing with each other, for charitable causes, but the rest of the time we have to survive at work, we have to survive in school, we have to survive in a world that has its own set of rules that have little to do with Sunday. If we ignore those things, we can't hope to make it. You see, the truth is, if you're in Jerusalem, you can do it God's way, but we don't live in Jerusalem.

Neither does Daniel, not anymore. You see, the book of Daniel — at least chapters 1-6 — is about living away from Jerusalem, living under somebody else's control, somebody with another set of rules. The book of Daniel is about living in Babylon. And Babylon is not the place for a good Jewish boy to be, because in Babylon they have a different kind of king and a different way of life and a different god. Daniel and his friends aren't in Jerusalem anymore.

But it's worse than that. Not only has Nebuchadnezzar king of Babylon besieged Jerusalem, and conquered Jehoiakim king of Judah, and made off with the best and brightest young Israelites, but he has also gone into the temple of the God of Abraham and Isaac and Jacob and helped himself to whatever he liked. He looted the place. Forget defeating Babylon — the Lord, it seems, isn't even running *Jerusalem* anymore. That's how it looks if you've watched it all happen, if you've watched Nebuchadnezzar thumb his nose at the God of the Jews. So, if you want to survive, it seems, there's only one way to play it, and that's Nebuchadnezzar's way, that's Babylon's way. There's no such thing as Jerusalem anymore. That's how it feels, and that's what it looks like.

And it couldn't look more that way than it does for Daniel and his friends, whose names are no longer Hananiah and Mishael and Azariah, but Shadrach, Meshach, and Abednego. They're so far from Jerusalem now that even the church remembers them as Babylonians. The four of them are brought to Babylon on full scholarship: room and board, tuition, physical fitness training — all of it on Nebuchadnezzar's tab. His plan is to take the best and the brightest from the nations that he conquers and then turn them into men he can use, men to serve on his cabinet, men to advise him, men to further the cause of Babylon. That's what these four Jewish boys are brought here to do.

And the first thing to go is the names. If you're going to live in Babylon, you've got to have a name Babylonians can pronounce. More than that, you've got to have a name Babylonians can understand. So Daniel, which means "God is my judge," is out, while Belteshazzar, which is a prayer to the god of Babylon, is in. Hananiah, which means "The Lord shows grace," is out, while Shadrach, which praises the moon-god of Nebuchadnezzar, is in. You see, in Babylon everything's different, and so the names must be different, too.

Daniel apparently doesn't care what they call him. He accepts the name change, just like Joseph accepted it in Egypt, and Esther accepted it in Persia. Apparently a name is nothing to lose your head over. Maybe that's because you can call him whatever you want, but he'll still be Daniel, and God will still be his judge. Anyway, the name change goes smoothly enough. And I guess so does the scholarship. We don't hear anything about Daniel refusing to go to class or demanding prayer in school or something; he goes along with that part. He accepts Nebuchadnezzar's free ride; he takes part in the training. So this far, through verse 7, living in Babylon isn't a big problem for Daniel. It's the diet that gets in the way. Now Daniel draws the line; now Daniel turns into a vegetarian.

"But Daniel resolved that he would not defile himself with the royal rations of food and wine. . . ." Daniel can live in Babylon, but he can't eat from Nebuchadnezzar's butcher. He can't take the food and wine from Nebuchadnezzar's table. So Daniel asks the chief steward or the dean of students or somebody for permission to go the vegetable route, to knock the fat out of his diet, to break the rules of Babylon. But that's a big request, because this guy's got his own orders to follow, his own set of rules to worry about. In Babylon it's not only faithful Jews who risk losing their heads. Those lions they have there are equal-opportunity devourers. So Daniel works around him and proposes a test to his guard. Give us ten days and we'll see what happens. If we're not holding our own with the other freshmen, you can change your mind. Just give us a chance, says Daniel. See if we can do it our way. Let's hit the salad bar.

And of course the whole thing turns out to be a smashing success. At the end of the ten days Daniel and Hananiah and Mishael and Azariah are as fit as fiddles. They look great; as a matter of fact, they look better than everybody else. And not only do they look better, but they train better, too. They're smarter, they're quicker, they're healthier, they're more mature than all the other students Nebuchadnezzar has collected — ten times better, in fact, than anybody else the king has in his entire empire. Daniel not only survives in Babylon; he turns out to be class valedictorian.

It's not a bad story. Daniel remains obedient in the foreign land with its foreign rules and its other gods, and he ends up a success anyway. Daniel refuses to defile himself at the risk of his own life, and in the end he goes right to the top of the class. Daniel is faithful to God even a long way from Jerusalem, and so Daniel is protected and honored and blessed beyond anyone's expectations.

And I wish it were always that simple. I wish that at the beginning of this church year I could promise you the same, but I can't. The temptation here is to say, Dare to be a Daniel, dare to stand out from the crowd, dare to keep your faith in a foreign environment, and God will bless you, too. You too will be healthy and wealthy and wise. You too will make it to the top. You too will survive Babylon. Just be faithful.

That's the temptation, because if it's simple like that, preaching is easier and faith is easier and life is easier. The problem is that we know better. The problem is that there were faithful people in Auschwitz and the gas chamber strangled them like it did the others. And our friend Linda Doezema was faithful, but cancer still devoured her body. The truth is that the world's history is littered with stories of faithful people who lost their savings or their loved ones or their lives. It might be nice to go home today telling ourselves that, if we just obey like Daniel and his friends, we'll be fine, our problems will be over, we'll surpass all of our peers because God will be with us. It might be nice to go home that way, but it would be wrong. Babylon is always a dangerous place for people who believe in something else.

So we can't count on Daniel's results. But if we're from the same people as Daniel, if we also belong in Jerusalem, then we can count on what Daniel counted on. We can count on the one thing that does not change from Jerusalem to Babylon, from good times to bad, from victory to exile. And that is the presence of our God. It's true that, if you're standing in downtown Jerusalem on that day Nebuchadnezzar comes marching through town, things don't exactly look like God's behind them. When the king of Babylon walks into the temple of the Lord and makes off with sacred objects, it looks like the Lord's having a bad day, like he's over-matched, out of control. But that's only how it looks. And that's why we read the book of Daniel. The book of Daniel says to the rest of us that appearances aren't everything; image is nothing. The book of Daniel says to the rest of us that the Lord's temple may be profaned and his city overrun and his people in exile, but he remains the Lord of heaven and earth, the Lord of Jerusalem and Babylon. It's the Lord who delivered Jehoiakim king of Judah into Nebuchadnezzar's hand; it's the Lord who moved the heart of the guard to let Daniel break the rules; it's the Lord who gave knowledge and understanding to these four young men.

My friend is right, of course he's right: there's a different set of rules in many of the places that we find ourselves each week. And in those places, whether it's the military or an accounting firm or junior high school, it can seem like the only way to survive is to play it the way everybody else does. It's dangerous in Babylon. But here's the good news this morning: you've been set free from that. You've been set free from the Nebuchadnezzars of the world, from those who run things according to some other god; you've been set free, because your life isn't in their hands, anyway, it's in the Lord's. Even in Babylon, the Lord is God; even in Babylon, the Lord is with his people.

So the question for Daniel, and the question for us, is: Are we going to be his people? Are we going to trust in him or in the ways of Babylon?

There's some debate as to why Daniel draws the line at the diet instead of the other stuff. What is it about Nebuchadnezzar's cooking that Daniel can't take? I think the answer is in chapter 11. There it says that those who eat from the king's table become partners with him, they are his allies, his loyal supporters. If Daniel eats Nebuchadnezzar's food, he becomes Nebuchadnezzar's man, he becomes part of Nebuchadnezzar's kingdom, he belongs to Babylon. But Daniel knows that the way to survive in Babylon isn't to be partners with Nebuchadnezzar; it's to remain part of the people of God, even if that means doing something that puts him in great danger, even if it means doing something that costs him his life. Daniel knows that as long as he belongs to the Lord, he's in good hands. We find out over and over again in this book that he's right about that.

Much of the world in which we operate, especially the world in which most of *you* operate, is a foreign, dangerous place, a land of exile, with all kinds of strange gods; and the temptation is, when in Babylon, do as the Babylonians do. That's what survival seems to demand. But as long as we remain who we are, as long as we belong to the God of Abraham and Isaac and Jacob, the God of Daniel, survival isn't our concern, no matter how far we are from Jerusalem. God's people always have a bright future. And, believe me, it has nothing to do with a scholarship from Nebuchadnezzar.

"And Daniel continued there until the first year of King Cyrus" — this is the last sentence of the first chapter. But it's a strange sentence, because it jumps ahead seventy years; it tells the end of the entire story. It tells us that Daniel will outlast the exile. He'll be there when a new king will come to power and the Jews will go home. That's why it's so important, because that's how it is: God's people will outlast Nebuchadnezzar; they will survive the pretenders to the throne. We're vegetarians in Babylon, but one day we will feast at the table of the real King. Until then, we have this bread and wine, and we remember that this world and its menu don't rule us. We have this bread and wine, and we remember that one day we will live only in Jerusalem, we will live free from danger, we will dine forever at the table of the King of kings. In the name of Jesus Christ, Amen.

Found in the Cosmos

Text: Daniel 2

In the second year of Nebuchadnezzar's reign, Nebuchadnezzar dreamed such dreams that his spirit was troubled and his sleep left him. So the king commanded that the magicians, the enchanters, the sorcerers, and the Chaldeans be summoned to tell the king his dreams. When they came in and stood before the king, he said to them, "I have had such a dream that my spirit is troubled by the desire to understand it." . . . So Daniel went in and requested that the king give him time and he would tell the king the interpretation. Then Daniel went to his home and informed his companions, Hananiah, Mishael, and Azariah, and told them to seek mercy from the God of heaven concerning this mystery, so that Daniel and his companions with the rest of the wise men of Babylon might not perish. Then the mystery was revealed to Daniel in a vision of the night, and Daniel blessed the God of heaven.

Daniel 2:1-3, 16-19

Mother Teresa possessed a wisdom, a biblical wisdom. It showed in her choices and in her observations. She noted once that some Westerners she met — wealthy types from Europe and America — actually seemed to her sad and poor, poorer even than her Calcutta poor, who of course are the poorest of the poor. Yet these others — these modern, healthy, educated, all-around well-off folks — says Mother Teresa, seem in some deeper sense to be missing something, to be lost.

Walker Percy, in his book *Lost in the Cosmos,* wonders how that can be. How can it be that, in spite of our advancements in medicine and science and technology, in spite of the ways in which life is so comfortable today, in spite of increases in knowledge that were unimaginable not long ago, we modern people are not a very happy lot? In fact, the more we do and know the less happy we seem to be, certainly the less settled we are. So, as we live better, we also take our own lives more, much more, than twenty years ago; and, as relational tools and experts abound, divorce is more common than ever before; and, as we *have* more and *do* more and *know* more to satisfy us, to make our lives complete, we also display signs of depression more than all other medical symptoms combined. Percy has reflected on these things and concludes that we modern people, as much as we have conquered the world around us, as much as we have explored the solar system, as much as we have come to comprehend galaxies and electrons alike, are still a long way from understanding ourselves. In fact, the closer we get to understanding everything else, the less we understand us. After all of the other mysteries of the universe have been solved, the mystery of *me* still remains. So, says Percy, the modern, educated, all-around well-off person is lost in the very cosmos she has mastered.

Walker Percy, meet King Nebuchadnezzar, a man ahead of his time. Nebuchadnezzar is ahead of his time because he has convenience and comfort and opportunity like nobody else in the ancient world can imagine. Wealth, respect, power, knowledge are all at his fingertips; the world itself is in his hands. Nebuchadnezzar's not just a king; he's an emperor. He's created one empire out of all the countries of the world. He's strolled through capital cities and made them his. He helps himself to anything he likes. It's not just Babylon this man runs, it's the whole map, and everybody on it. Nebuchadnezzar defines having it all.

But Nebuchadnezzar's a man ahead of his time in another way, too — in the Mother Teresa and Walker Percy way. Because all that he has isn't enough. This king of kings has a problem. There's a part of life that he can't control, a mystery that he can't solve: a dream. Nebuchadnezzar has turned insomniac because a dream is haunting him, and he has to find out what it means, he has to get some rest. Nebuchadnezzar, the ruler of the world, can't control his own sleep. He's lost in a cosmos that he owns.

But Nebuchadnezzar is not a man without options. After all, he has the entire Babylonian kingdom at his disposal, on hand to solve his every problem. So he summons every expert, every Ph.D., every talk-show host and psychic friend — all to help him get back to sleep, to put this dream to bed, to help him solve the mystery. But, since Nebuchadnezzar's been so unsettled lately, he's also become a little suspicious of the pat answers. He's wondering if he isn't wasting that $2.95 a minute on Dionne Warwick's palm-reader. Maybe all these experts don't really know what they're talking about; maybe they don't have the answers any more than he does. So Nebuchadnezzar adds a little twist to the usual procedure. Don't just take my credit card and hand me some all-purpose interpretation; tell me the dream, too. Then I'll know you're on the up-and-up, then I'll know that what you say is true. And by the way, if you can't tell me, I'm going to convict each of you of fraud and cut you into little pieces. Nebuchadnezzar may be lost in the cosmos, but he's still king of Babylon.

Well, this is where some serious flustering begins. First, these sooth-sayers try to keep him talking, pretend they didn't hear this business about telling him the dream as well as its meaning. When that doesn't work, they let him know that such a request is way beyond any sorcerer's job descrip-tion: "Mighty Ruler, you must have hit your head on the side of the throne again. There is not a person on earth who can do what the king asks. No one can reveal it to the king except the gods, and they do not live among human beings." When you come right down to it, even the magicians and sorcerers and enchanters are lost in the cosmos. It's out of their control, too; peace has to come from somewhere else. And now Nebuchadnezzar re-alizes it, too, and he's had enough of artificial, tell-me-what-I-want-to-hear wisdom. All of them to death row, he says. Every wise man in the place, ev-ery expert, every advisor — all the knowledge and the wisdom and the magic in the world can't help Nebuchadnezzar find a place in the cosmos and a good night's sleep.

Fortunately for Nebuchadnezzar, along the way of conquering the world and becoming the master of his universe, he picked up a few people who aren't lost. *Un*fortunately, he's about to execute them with all of the other advisors. But Daniel gets to him before execution day and makes a last request: "Let me have a shot at your dream. There's a different way of going about this, king; you may have your answer yet." Daniel isn't a sor-cerer or a magician or anything — he knows *he* can't do what Nebuchad-nezzar asks — but he also knows that there is one who can. So he and Hananiah and Mishael and Azariah go to their Babylonian home and pray to the God of Israel.

And there is the verification Nebuchadnezzar's looking for: Daniel learns the dream. It's a dream about kingdoms, says Daniel. It's a dream about a statue. A huge, amazing statue, with a gold head and silver chest and bronze mid-section and iron legs and feet of iron and of clay. But there came a stone that was not from human hands and it struck the statue on its feet, and the whole thing came tumbling down: the gold and the silver and the bronze and the iron and the clay, all of it destroyed, all of it turned to dust. But the rock became a mountain and filled the whole earth.

The metals are kingdoms, mighty one. The head of gold is you. You have all dominion and power and glory, just as you think you do. You are the king of kings, the ruler of the earth, because God has made you so. And after you will come another and after that another and still another, but then, one day, the God of heaven will have enough of kings and kingdoms and empires. One day the God of heaven will establish a different kingdom, a new kingdom, an eternal kingdom that will not pass away. And it will destroy all the ones that have come before it. It will fill the entire earth. And it will last forever. That's your answer, Nebuchadnezzar. That's your dream.

And now comes the most surprising part of this story: Nebuchadnezzar's response to Daniel. After all, this isn't great news that Nebuchadnezzar has just received. Daniel has told him, "You are the master of the universe, you are the king of kings, but that's because God has made it so. It's not *your* greatness that has allowed you to rule any more than it's *my* greatness that has allowed me to interpret. And one day it's all going to end. One day God will change formats; he's not going to use the empire method anymore. And everything you have — even you, the head of gold — will come crashing down and will be no more. And *then* there will be the kingdom that will last forever. But it won't be yours.

I probably don't need to tell you that a sitting world emperor usually doesn't stand for such talk. After all, Nebuchadnezzar's not just a king, he's a god there in Babylon. You'd expect him to be furious, to refuse even to consider the mortality of his power; you'd expect Daniel to be in the lions' den this time for sure. But that's not what happens. Instead, there's Nebuchadnezzar on his knees before Daniel, humbling himself before this Jewish servant he picked up on his trip to Jerusalem. He says, "Truly, your God is God of gods and Lord of kings and a revealer of mysteries, for you have been able to reveal this mystery!" (2:47).

Nebuchadnezzar's just been told that he doesn't own the world — or if he does, it's only because God gave it to him. And, more than that, he's been told that his kingdom isn't the last one, not even the best one, and that one day it's going to crumble like every human empire. And his response is to prostrate himself before Daniel and Daniel's God. Now Nebuchadnezzar is settled; now the mystery has been revealed; now Nebuchadnezzar can go to sleep.

Last week, when we began discussing Daniel, I said that this book is about life away from Jerusalem, life away from the temple; it's about life in Babylon. And Babylon, I said, is a dangerous place for people of God. That's true. But, you know something? There's a way in which Babylon is a far more dangerous place for Babylonians. There's a way in which Babylon is far more dangerous to Nebuchadnezzar than it is to Daniel. As uncertain as life may be in exile, as lost as he may be on the streets of Babylon, Daniel is always at home in the cosmos. He knows his place. Nebuchadnezzar doesn't have that luxury.

Nebuchadnezzar can have the world in his hands, but it doesn't give him a good night's sleep. He can't look into the future and know his place. He can't escape the mortality of his life and his kingdom. And having everything the world has to offer only makes that more clear to him. Owning the whole world still hasn't brought him peace.

Daniel's words may diminish Nebuchadnezzar in terms of his pretending to be a god or his hope that his kingdom will go on forever, but, even so, Daniel's words are good news, because they reveal the mystery; they tell him who he is and where he's going; they show him his place. And if you want to get to sleep, you don't need to own the cosmos, you just need to know your place in it. You need to know who you are. You need to understand the mystery.

Walker Percy says we know more and more about the cosmos and less and less about ourselves. He's probably right, because the mystery of who we are doesn't lie in having more or knowing more or accomplishing more. The book of Daniel tells us that: no wise man, no enchanter, no diviner can explain the mystery the king has asked about, but there is a God in heaven who reveals mysteries. He's the one who can tell us about ourselves.

We are a well-off people, a people that define knowledge and convenience, that have *made it* in so many ways. But those things can't tell us who we are and where we're going and what our place is any more than Nebuchadnezzar's sorcerers could tell him his dream. We can recognize the Milky Way and still not recognize ourselves. We can map out Mars and still be lost in the cosmos. Remember, Nebuchadnezzar couldn't find rest in a world that he owned. As long as we try to find rest, to find our place, in what we know or make, in how much comfort or power or security or convenience we have, we'll be lost, too, lost completely. And the danger is that, the more we have and know, the more we're tempted to believe that's where the answers are.

But if we see, like Daniel, that wisdom and power are God's, that he changes times and seasons, that he is "immortal, invisible, God only wise," if we look for the eternal kingdom that will shatter all the pretenders that went before it, if we wait upon the God in heaven who reveals mysteries, then we, like Daniel, will sleep well, we'll be at rest, even a long way from Jerusalem, even in exile, even in a danger-filled, idol-ridden place like Babylon.

It's funny: the folks who know the least in this story — that gaggle of sorcerers and magicians and astrologers — come so close to getting it right. When Nebuchadnezzar wants them to tell him what he has dreamed, they say, "There is no one on earth who can reveal what the king demands . . . no one can reveal it to the king except the gods, whose dwelling is not with mortals." It's the one God they don't know who happens to do that very thing. That God does reveal mysteries to his people, like Daniel. That God has a Word for troubled souls like Nebuchadnezzar. And that Word became flesh, and for a little while God did indeed dwell with mortals, so that *his* kingdom would come, so that you and I and Nebuchadnezzar would have a place in it, so that wherever we are, we are not lost but found, anywhere in the cosmos. In the name of Jesus Christ, Amen.

But If Not

Text: Daniel 3

"Now if you are ready when you hear the sound of the horn, pipe, lyre, trigon, harp, drum and entire musical ensemble to fall down and worship the statue that I have made, well and good. But if you do not worship, you shall immediately be thrown into a furnace of blazing fire, and who is the god that will deliver you out of my hands?" Shadrach, Meshach, and Abednego answered the king, "O Nebuchadnezzar, we have no need to present a defense to you in this matter. If our God whom we serve is able to deliver us from the furnace of blazing fire and out of your hand, O king, let him deliver us. But if not, be it known to you, O king, that we will not serve your gods and we will not worship the golden statue that you have set up."

Daniel 3:15-18

When the story of Daniel was published for the first time, when it was put together and told as we have it here, it wasn't Nebuchadnezzar the Jewish people had on their minds. He was long gone. When this book first came to print, there was another ruler in the headlines. His name was Antiochus IV — Antiochus *Epiphanes*. He added that second name himself; it means "God manifest, God in person," which tells you something about his disposition.

Antiochus ruled about two hundred years before the birth of Christ. He was at the end of a dynasty that was dying, that was being pressed on all sides, especially by Rome. And he thought it would help keep his kingdom together if he made all its different peoples alike. So he did that; he tried to make them all Greek — Greek-speaking, Greek-acting, Greek-believing. But Antiochus was also short on cash, so he'd rummage through his subjects' towns, looking for something he could pawn. Antiochus was desperate, and he was angry. But none of that mattered to the residents of Jerusalem; what mattered to them is what Antiochus did to their city and to their temple and to their faith.

He did some of the usual stuff: he set up worship to other gods, he took valuable possessions from the temple of the Lord, he broke promises. But he also did more. Antiochus set out to take away anything that was particularly Jewish about the Jews. And that, he soon realized, meant taking away their religion. In the year 167 B.C., when the citizens of Jerusalem weren't responding to his ideas so well, the king who called himself god sent a large army to their city. They seemed peaceful, but they turned on the people, enslaving some, butchering many. Before they left, they looted the place and tore down its walls.

And then Antiochus took over the temple. Sacrifices were suspended, observance of the Sabbath was outlawed, and religious feasts were prohibited. Copies of the law were ordered destroyed; the circumcision of children was forbidden. Antiochus took away the marks of the Jewish faith; he took away what it meant to be a Jew. For those who disobeyed, the punishment was death. Finally, in December, he turned the temple of the Lord into a Greek shrine. The altar was used for sacrifices to Zeus; the flesh of pigs was offered on it. In the words of Daniel, it was an "abomination of desolation." The Jews rebelled. Palestine became a war zone. And Antiochus became even more brutal.

We've read three chapters of the book of Daniel now, three chapters of neat and clean reward-for-righteousness. We've seen Daniel and his friends Hananiah, Mishael, and Azariah — who in Babylon are Shadrach, Meshach, and Abednego — stand up for their convictions and put their trust in God as the one who will answer their prayers; we've seen them put their lives in grave danger; and each time we've seen things work out perfectly, smooth as silk. Not only do they get to live, but they look healthier than all the pagans, they reveal the meanings of dreams, they come out burn-free after a trip through Nebuchadnezzar's incinerator. It's all so simple: have faith and the vegetable diet will be no problem; pray to God and he'll answer that very night; worship only the Lord and you will survive 10,000 degree heat. It always goes according to plan.

In fact, everything goes so smoothly that it's a little hard to take Shadrach, Meshach, and Abednego seriously when they tell Nebuchadnezzar in verses 17 and 18: "If our God whom we serve is able to deliver us from the furnace of blazing fire and out of your hand, O king, let him deliver us. But if not, be it known to you, O king, that we will not serve your gods and we will not worship the golden statue that you have set up." *But if not?* And what are the odds of that? What are the odds that this God, who's always there for Daniel and his friends at the first sign of trouble, won't be there this time? Do they really think that maybe he *won't* rescue them, that he'll let them die in the furnace? How could they, the way this book's been going? This whole set of stories just seems too good to be true, certainly too good to be real. We know better.

That is why it's important for you and me, when we read the stories of Daniel, to know the story of Antiochus Epiphanes, too. It's important for us to know that the person telling us these things about Daniel is living during the time of Antiochus. The writer of this book has seen faithful Jewish people die when they refused to violate their faith. He has seen mothers who circumcised their children put to death with their families. He has seen young men executed for refusing to touch unclean food or defend themselves on the Sabbath or bow before the gods of Antiochus. The person who is telling us the stories of Daniel knows all too well that it isn't so smooth, that God isn't at our beck and call, that we don't know if he will rescue us from the furnaces of evil or not.

As you read through the book of Daniel you could really get confused about now. After all, at the end of the last chapter, we read about Nebuchadnezzar bowing before Daniel and acknowledging Daniel's God as the God of gods and the King of kings. But now, at the very beginning of chapter 3, we find out that the guy spent his summer building the largest statue anybody's ever seen. And he's come up with the idea that, whenever anybody on the face of the earth hears the royal orchestra strike up "76 Trombones," they're to fall down and worship this statue. And if they don't do it every time they hear the music, as soon as they hear the music, they'll be thrown into a blazing furnace. That hardly sounds like the king we knew at the end of chapter 2, the man who wants to make Daniel palace chaplain.

That's an interesting observation. But it's really not all that important. It would be if the book of Daniel were a biography of King Nebuchadnezzar or a detailed analysis of the Babylonian conquest of the Jews, but it's not. It's not a biography or an analysis at all. It's a message. The book of Daniel is a message to a bunch of people living in Jerusalem who are under all kinds of pressure to give in, to compromise their faith. Daniel is a message to people who have seen their temple defiled and their city ruined and who face death at every turn. These stories are for them. They're a word from God for people whose lives are being threatened and destroyed and taken away by Antiochus Epiphanes.

You see, like Antiochus, Nebuchadnezzar is also a god-pretender. The world is in his hands. If he builds a statue, you admire it. If he says bow, you say, How low? But in spite of all his power, and in the midst of all his satraps, prefects, governors, counselors, treasurers, justices, and magistrates, there are three powerless Jewish young men — who couldn't even keep their own names — who will not worship his statue. And the first hearers of Daniel know what that means. It means somebody's going to die. And they're right.

Some grumblers come along and tell the king, "There are some Jews who pay no attention to you, O king." And Nebuchadnezzar is furious. If there's one thing an emperor can't stand, it's when somebody doesn't pay any attention to him. "Is it true?" he asks these three young men. "Do you really dare such a thing? Well, look fellas, let's not have anybody say I'm not reasonable about this. The next time you hear the band strike up a tune, hit the ground, and we'll be square. But if you don't, it's the oven for you. *And who is the god that will deliver you out of my hands?*" For Nebuchadnezzar there is no such god. For Nebuchadnezzar the furnace always has the last word. For Nebuchadnezzar the furnace settles all bets. For Nebuchadnezzar you serve only a god who saves you *today,* and today the god who will save you from the furnace is that statue he built. For Nebuchadnezzar you worship what works. But not for these three; these three see things differently.

As far as Shadrach, Meshach, and Abednego are concerned, you don't change gods like you change shirts. Their God is a god you serve to the end, because he's the God of heaven and earth and all things in between. So they give Nebuchadnezzar the only answer they have: "If our God whom we serve is able to deliver us from the furnace of blazing fire and out of your hand, O king, let him deliver us. But if not, be it known to you, O king, that we will not serve your gods and we will not worship the golden statue that you have set up." Whatever the future holds, this is their God, the God who they know is faithful to them whether or not he saves them today. Whether Nebuchadnezzar's oven is working or not, Shadrach, Meshach, and Abednego serve only one God, the God of Israel, the God of the world, the God of the furnace. They don't want to die, but if living means changing gods, then living isn't worth the price.

I don't know who that fourth person is that Nebuchadnezzar spots walking around in there, but I know what he means, what he stands for: he stands for the presence of the Lord. And he'd be there whether or not the flames do their job that day. The God of Daniel, the God of Shadrach, Meshach, and Abednego, the God of the Jews, is with his people in the fire, even if he does not save them. The God of the Jews is with his people in Babylon, and he is with his people in the days of Antiochus, days of suffering and persecution and death. He is the God of heaven and earth, the God of the furnace and the flame, the God who is out to save, the only God to serve.

It's kind of funny: by the end of the story Nebuchadnezzar's back on the side of the Lord, and that wonderful statue is shoved in the back of his garage somewhere, forgotten. Persecution and blasphemy and idols will come and go, but at the end of the day, even the king behind it all has only one God worth worshiping, and that is the God of Shadrach, Meshach, and Abednego. That's what they know all along. Even if he doesn't rescue them, trading in the Lord of heaven for a god somebody built is never an option, even if it would let you live a little longer.

You may be familiar with Alexander Solzhenitsyn's classic, *One Day in the Life of Ivan Denisovich*. It's a novella about a day in the life of a man who has been in one of Josef Stalin's work camps for eight years. It's an account of pain and hunger and fear, where men have lost nearly all control, a place where survival is the focus of every minute of the day. Well, in this joyless environment where self-preservation is all anyone thinks about, there is one prisoner who is different from the rest, a man who possesses a certain contentment, even there, and so he stands out as generous and kind toward the other inmates. He's Alyosha the Baptist, that's what they call him. He's an honest, faithful, quiet Christian, who has peace there, even though his life in that miserable prison camp is no more secure than anyone else's.

Before they go to sleep, Ivan Denisovich tells Alyosha the Baptist that his faith is a waste of time, that prayers are just like their appeals to the camp office — they're either ignored or come back rejected. Alyosha prays, but what has it gotten him? He has no more food, he is not being set free, his status is no better than anyone else's. But then Alyosha explains that that's not why he prays — to have more food or to be released. He prays for things of the spirit; he prays that the Lord Jesus will remove the scum of anger from his heart. Alyosha the Baptist knows that being free, surviving — those aren't the vital things in life. What matters is that he is owned by the God who owns the world, even if he doesn't rescue him today.

The God of Alyosha and the God of Shadrach and Meshach and Abednego is also the God of Josef Stalin and Antiochus Epiphanes and King Nebuchadnezzar, no matter what they happen to think. He is the God of their statues and the God of their satraps and prefects and governors. And he is the God of their furnaces. So we stick with him whether we survive the heat or not. Unlike the outcome in Daniel 3, the furnaces we find ourselves in often work very well and provide a good deal of suffering and pain, and there may be times when we could take the suffering away by worshiping something else, like money or work or family. But we stick with the God of Daniel anyway, not because he will save us from every terrible threat, but because he is the God of every furnace and every king. And he is our God, too, the God of truth and justice and love. Whether or not he saves *today,* he will always be the God of our salvation. In the name of Jesus Christ, Amen.

Better Off with the Lions

Text: Daniel 6

When the king heard the charge, he was very much distressed. He was determined to save Daniel, and until the sun went down he made every effort to rescue him. Then the conspirators came to the king and said to him, "Know, O king, that it is the law of the Medes and Persians that no interdict or ordinance that the king establishes can be changed." Then the king gave the command, and Daniel was brought and thrown into the den of lions. The king said to Daniel, "May your God, whom you faithfully serve, deliver you!" A stone was brought and laid on the mouth of the den, and the king sealed it with his own signet and with the signet of his lords, so that nothing might be changed concerning Daniel. Then the king went to his

*palace and spent the night fasting; no food was brought to him, and sleep
fled from him.*

Daniel 6:14-18

By this point in the book of Daniel there's one question begging to be answered, and that is: Are these kings ever going to get some sleep? It began
with Nebuchadnezzar's nightmares in chapter 2, but now this emperor insomnia has been going on for over sixty years. Nebuchadnezzar is haunted
by dreams that mean something he can't figure out. Just when he gets the
one about the gigantic statue all settled, two chapters later he's got the
world's biggest tree turning into a human being and living like an animal.
Then, of course, it was Belshazzar's turn, though not a dream this time —
if only it were a dream! Belshazzar is terrorized by a disconnected limb
that crashes his party, some floating hand that writes his obituary on the
wall. Fortunately, in all those instances, Nebuchadnezzar and Belshazzar
have Daniel to call upon; they have Daniel to decode God's messages and
get them back to sleep. That's why, I must admit, I feel sorry for King Darius.

What's keeping Darius pacing the floor all night isn't a dream to interpret or a message to decode; it's not just a matter of getting Daniel over
to the palace for some answers. Darius's problem is that Daniel can't
come to the palace; what's keeping him up is that Daniel, his advisor, his
friend, is sealed up with a bunch of lions, and there's not one thing that
Darius the king can do about it. If only somebody had just written on his
wall.

So I feel sorry for Darius, because he suffers from the same sort of
restlessness that Nebuchadnezzar and Belshazzar took to bed with them.
He's finding out the same thing that they found out: even the most powerful man in the world can't guarantee his own soul's peace. So he feels
their pain; but unlike Nebuchadnezzar and Belshazzar, Darius the Mede
doesn't have Daniel to help him get some sleep, because Daniel is indis-
posed at the moment. And the plan is that he won't be coming back.

Darius must be kicking himself that he ever got into this mess. He
would be snoozing in his bed right now if he hadn't let that idea about everybody worshiping him go to his head. But that's what happened. The
king was duped. He bought all that flattery about being somebody to
worship; he believed those scheming officials who suggested that a great
way to kick off this new religion of Darius would be by royal decree.
"Make a law. Suspend the bill of rights for a few days. Let the people practice worshiping just Darius; after all, there's nobody more important,

more powerful, more god-like than you, Darius, right?" Well, who can argue with words like that? A law it is: for thirty days anyone who prays to anything but Darius shall be thrown into the lions' den. "And just to make sure everything's official, Darius, we'd better have it notarized. What do you know, Kareem here happens to be a notary public. Do you have your driver's license, Darius? Okay, it's all set; everything's legal: you're a god."

It all seems so ridiculous now. It all seems such an obvious set-up — first of the king, but really of course of Daniel. But with that law the schemers and the flatterers have everything they need: they know Daniel well enough to know that no decree of the king, notarized or not, is going to keep him from praying to his God. They know Daniel well enough to know that all they have to do is wait and watch, and he'll be visiting with lions in no time.

And, of course, they're right about that. Daniel doesn't organize a protest or anything, he doesn't try to overthrow the government and take its power, he just goes on doing what he always does — he prays in the direction of Jerusalem, he prays to the Lord. And praying to the Lord is now a violation of Code 647-23b. "King, what's the penalty for that one, again? The lions' den. Oh, yeah. Well, Daniel just broke your law — we'll go pick him up."

And that's why Darius is counting sheep tonight. Because his law was broken by somebody he likes, somebody he needs. When the king heard that it was Daniel in custody, he got a lump in his throat and a pit in his stomach. When the king saw Daniel in handcuffs and heard those roars a few feet away, he had only one thing on his mind: he was determined to save Daniel, and he wasn't going to sleep until he pulled it off.

Now I find that to be a pretty encouraging sign. Daniel's under arrest, but he's got himself some fine representation. Actually, he's got more than that: Daniel has the politicians on the case. No, even that doesn't do justice to what Daniel has going for him at this moment, because what Daniel really has on his side, "determined to save him," is none other than the ruler of the entire world. Not just a governor who can pardon or a king who can set free, but the emperor over every nation around, the man that runs the world, the man all people everywhere are worshiping. That man is spending his entire day trying to commute Daniel's death sentence, trying to keep him alive, trying to save him.

But he can't do it. "Remember, O king," Daniel's enemies say, "that according to the law of the Medes and Persians no decree or edict the king issues can be changed." Darius may rule, but he'd better not try to break one. He can turn entire countries into slaves and move whole nations around like game pieces, but he'd better not try to repeal a law of the Medes and Persians. The law submits to no man. So the most powerful person in the world, Daniel's loyal supporter, who can have anything he wants, can't have this — and he ends up fidgeting and pacing and worrying outside, while Daniel gets served up like meow mix. That's why I feel sorry for Darius, because life really is harder *outside* the lions' den.

Have you noticed? It's outside the lions' den, outside the furnace, outside the lives of Daniel and Mishael and Azariah and Hananiah that nobody can get to sleep. The insomnia, the restlessness, the anxiety — they're not with the lions; they're in the palace. It's the emperors who aren't able to sleep. You're really better off with the lions.

Do you know who's *not* spending the night with those lions? It's all the people who have been worshiping Darius. Every person outside the lions' den is somebody who's been spending this whole month worshiping nothing else but Darius, putting their faith only in Darius, finding hope only in the power of Darius. And you know what? Darius can't save. Even when he's determined to save, even when he's staying up all night in order to save, even when he has nothing else on his mind but to save, Darius cannot save. That's why he can't sleep, because he may rule the kingdom, but the laws of the Medes and Persians rule him.

Daniel had a decision to make when that law was pronounced: he could give up God for February, or he could go on worshiping him like he always has. So he insists on obeying God rather than human beings, and his enemies use that to hurt him, to have him executed. But what option did he have? Falling down to Darius sure doesn't guarantee anything. Darius can't save, even when he's determined to do it. But Daniel's God can save even when the plan against him goes like clockwork. Outside the lions' den you may be alive, but you have nothing to count on: the god you worship is biting his nails and pacing the floor, unable to help, because it's the law that rules all things. And even the most powerful man in the world can't break the law. That would take somebody with some real power.

Life is harder outside the lions' den because, no matter who you have on your side, no matter how determined they are to save, they're subject to the laws that run the world. You see, you can make people worship you, but that still doesn't make you a god. And that's the problem with Darius. If he were worthy of the worship, he'd be able to save, law or no law. If he were worthy of the worship, he'd be fast asleep and Daniel would be alive and well.

It's so easy to be confused by these stories and to teach some really bad things because of it. It's easy to think from these stories — whether you're in chapter 1 when Daniel won't eat Nebuchadnezzar's food or chapter 3 when the boys end up in Nebuchadnezzar's furnace or here in chapter 6 with the lions — that the good news here is that if you're only faithful enough, God will save you from every trouble, every threat, every danger. But that's not it. The good news here isn't that God will save you from a speeding bullet, as long as you're obedient. The good news is that, when this God determines to save, he can do it, and the law of the land won't stop him. Daniel had a choice between worshiping a king whose power was limited, whose power was human, whose power was on loan, and worshiping the Lord God of Israel, whose power stretches across the world, even into Babylon, even into the mouths of lions. And the law that says in Babylon the king runs the show, and the law that says hungry lions always eat human beings, none of those ever get in his way, not when God is determined to save.

In a sense Daniel chose to be with those lions — the law was perfectly clear. But it was a wise choice, because at the same time Daniel chose to remain with God. Inside the lions' den there may be danger, but that's also where the living God is. Outside the lions' den there is only a god who worries himself sick; outside the lions' den you're on your own. Daniel *is* courageous and faithful and honorable, that's all true; but he's also wise. He knows that life is found with the Lord. Even if it means hanging out with lions, it's still a whole lot safer than clinging to Darius.

At the start of our study of Daniel I said that it's one thing to worship God in Jerusalem, where everybody sings hymns and says prayers and reads the Bible; it's another thing altogether to worship God in Babylon. That's true. And in our lives we're more often in Babylon than in Jerusalem, I think. And there it seems so much safer, so much easier, to set God aside for a while in order to be more successful or close with your family or popular or wealthy. And choosing God in those situations brings a price; it costs you success or closeness or popularity or safety. It brings danger. It'd be so much easier just to give up God for a month.

But that's not right, and it's never necessary, and it's certainly not wise — because, whether it seems like it or not, whether those lions feel hungry or not, the God we serve is the God who saves. And no law can stop him — not the law of the Medes and Persians, not the law of nature, not the law of life and death.

Jesus Christ was sealed up with a stone once, too. In his case, of course, it wasn't a den but a tomb. No angel from God prevented his death, because the God of Daniel was determined to save — not Jesus but us. And the law of death and sin would not stand in his way. That's our

God — a God who cares that much, a God that determined to save, a God who does save. That never changes, no matter what the lions we meet end up doing.

The book of Daniel is about choices and appearances and sovereignty. It's about the fact that, no matter how it appears, it is the Lord who is to be worshiped and not the emperor. It is about the fact that the decision to be faithful to him, no matter where it leads you, is always the right one. The book of Daniel is about the fact that you survive in Babylon by worshiping the God of Israel, even if it sends you to the lions, because your God is the only one who can save — just ask Darius.

It's funny: almost seventy years have gone by in these six chapters. Daniel's gone from sixteen to eighty-five. But we don't hear that. We don't hear about the end of his life. What we keep hearing is that Daniel made it again; Daniel prospered during the reign of Darius the Mede and went on to live in the time of Cyrus the Persian. It seems that emperors come and emperors go; but, in spite of all the danger in Babylon, Daniel keeps on living. And maybe that's just the point. Daniel *will* keep on living, whether or not the lions open their mouths, because he is with the Lord, and where the Lord is, there is life. There is the God who saves.

SERMONS FROM THE BOOK OF REVELATION

— THIRTIETH SUNDAY IN ORDINARY TIME —

Advent in Smyrna

Text: Revelation 2:8-11

"And to the angel of the church in Smyrna write: These are the words of the first and the last, who was dead and came to life:
"I know your affliction and your poverty, even though you are rich. I

know the slander on the part of those who say that they are Jews and are not, but are a synagogue of Satan. Do not fear what you are about to suffer. Beware, the devil is about to throw some of you into prison so that you may be tested, and for ten days you will have affliction. Be faithful unto death, and I will give you the crown of life. Let anyone who has an ear listen to what the Spirit is saying to the churches. Whoever conquers will not be harmed by the second death."

Revelation 2:8-11

It makes sense that Advent is four weeks and Christmas only one or two days, because Advent is more real than Christmas. Advent has more to do with what real life is like. So, this side of heaven, we must spend as much time in Advent as possible. We must learn to wait.

I've mentioned Kathleen Norris to you before. She's the poet who moved from New York City to the western edge of North Dakota to live in her late grandmother's house. That's where she wrote *Dakota,* a book about the different way culture and relationships and life itself operate in that rugged, rural land. At one point she talks about her experiences preaching; since reserve preachers are hard to come by in that area, and since she was raised a Presbyterian and trained as a writer, Norris is often asked to preach at the churches within a few hours of her home. One thing she says gets to the heart of the season of Advent: it's the difference that she notices between the worship in the rural, country congregation and the worship in the church in town. In the country, she says, folks know what Advent is about and are able to appreciate it. In the city Advent doesn't have much meaning; they just want to get on with Christmas.

The experience of country living has taught that rural church something important, Norris believes. Country people know that life is hard, that you have to prepare for its joys. You have to work hard in the spring if you expect something good in the fall, and in the meantime the land and the weather and the varmints can be brutal. Country people know the real world; they know its pain and its danger and its power. In the country they know how to wait.

And that is a lot like the church in Smyrna. One thing you have to say about this church is that it knows the real world; it knows its pain and its danger and its power. It knows that life is hard and that faith is hard. This church knows how to wait.

So this text is a difficult one, because waiting is difficult, especially when it's Messiah-waiting that you're doing. And this text this morning is difficult, because it's honest about what happens while we wait. This is a real-world text. And it's an important one for us city people, because Christmas is never far away for us; it's at our fingertips, and it's not hard to skip over Advent, to leave the real world, and go right to December 25. But in creating Advent the church has said that it's important that we not do that; it's important that we take our time getting to Bethlehem. The church has said that it's important for us to pause and consider and prepare and work while we're waiting for our Messiah. And there is no better way to do that, I am quite sure, than by considering what the church of Smyrna is doing while it waits for our Messiah. Because, for this church, every week is a week of waiting; for this church every week belongs to Advent.

You see, in Smyrna, to be a Christian just about *means* to wait — to wait to be prosperous, to wait to be respected, to wait to be safe. In Smyrna Christians are discriminated against, and they're not paid well, and they're pretty much despised. In Smyrna there is a large Jewish community, and there is great tension between the Jewish believers and the Christian believers, most of whom of course used to be Jewish. And the Jews in Smyrna are using their influence and their presence to hurt the Christians. They do that best by pointing out to the Roman authorities that this group of people, this church, is not a Jewish congregation. They work hard to make it very clear who is a "real" Jew and who is not. And that is very important, because Jewish people have privileges in the Roman empire. They have a special place because years before they took the Roman side during a rebellion. So the Jews are allowed to keep their own religion and worship their own way. And they make it very clear that the Christians are not Jews and deserve no privileges, and that the Christians should be forced to do what everyone else does.

This is a problem for the Christians, because what everyone else does is worship the emperor. The Romans have a law that the emperor is a god. He is to be worshiped by everyone who lives in the empire. Now this isn't such a big deal — it doesn't involve spending two hours a week in the First Church of Nero or memorizing some emperor's catechism. What it mainly involves is little things, like having phrases about the divine emperor on your contracts, or paying a tax that goes to the emperor cult fund, or saying at the beginning of a town meeting "Our Lord and our God" when his name is announced. It is mostly little things that a person can do and not really believe. But if you don't do them, that's another story, because then you will die.

So this text is a difficult one because waiting for the Messiah means death in Smyrna. And it's not just about the death of individual Christians; it's about the death of a church as well, or at least the probability of it. This letter is written to a church that knows the real world, a church that is paying for its faith in blood and bruises and poverty and slander. This church knows that in Advent evil still has quite a say.

This is no Christmas card, this message from the Lord that we read in Revelation 2. This is an Advent card, because this is a card that says that faith is hard and life is hard and death comes — at least during Advent it does. This is a card that says the suffering the church has been going through isn't going to let up. Instead, the devil's going to turn up the heat, it says. He'll "throw some of you into prison, that you may be tested, and for ten days you will have affliction," it says.

Now that sounds like fairly good news for the Smyrnans. Ten days isn't so bad. At least it's temporary and relatively short. But the way it's written here doesn't mean that they'll be free after ten days, that they'll be let go and the persecution will be over. It means that, at the end of the ten days, they'll be in the arena where they'll be executed. The ten days only leads up to the real punishment. This is no Christmas card from our Lord; the message this church receives is that it's going to die.

But still, from Jesus' point of view, this congregation is rich. In spite of their poverty and suffering and persecution, in God's eyes they have it all, because they're obedient, because they will not compromise, because they heard their Lord say, "Take up your cross and follow me, even though I'm headed off to die," and they're doing it, because in the midst of all of their difficulties they're living like disciples. They are rich, because they know how to wait for the Messiah.

I don't believe that we always do. I think Kathleen Norris is right: in the city, where everything we want is so close to being ours, where self-help books claim they can get us anything we're after, where technology makes gratification immediate, we're not trained in waiting. We want to get on with Christmas.

And, as Norris points out, in many ways the city has come to the church, too. The church, in many places today, is not so interested in faithfully waiting as it is in prospering. The church is not so interested in faithfully waiting as it is in surviving. And so we hear people say, If the church is going to last, if the church is going to be here in fifty years, these are the changes it has to make. And often the church makes those changes, for that reason. And that is why the church today should spend more time in Advent than ever.

One thing is clear: survival is not the goal of the church in Smyrna. If they wanted to make sure their church will survive, they could do it. All it would take is a little lying, a little nodding along at the beginning of a meeting, a little pretending that they're not really worshiping something else. If the church wanted to survive, it wouldn't be very hard to pull off in first-century Smyrna. All it involves is a bit of compromise, a bit of self-deception, a bit of pretending not to know the man, as Peter put it in one of his lesser moments. But that's not what this congregation does. They will wait for Christmas, even if the waiting kills them. They choose death over denial, obedience over survival, the gospel over the world — and so, alive or not, the Smyrnan church is rich.

May we be that wealthy. I care a great deal about this congregation. But I don't know if it's going to last. We don't have a letter from the Lord telling us what's about to happen. But I do know this: death is never the worst option. The worst option would be dropping our cross and picking up something a little easier to carry. The worst option would be when we stop waiting for the Messiah and try to make the affliction of Advent go away, when we try to survive. We have different priorities.

Whatever choices or plans we make, we must remember what the Word of God says: our goal is not to survive; our goal is to be faithful. And sometimes, as in Smyrna, being faithful and surviving are two different things.

On the first Sunday of Advent it's the tradition of the church to remind itself that Jesus will return, that, just as the people of the Old Testament were waiting for him to come, so we are waiting for him to come back. On the first Sunday of Advent the church remembers that he is coming back, and, because he is coming back, no matter how long the wait, no matter how long this Advent season lasts, because he is coming back our lives are changed. Everything we do is done knowing that he is King and he is risen and he is coming back. That's how the Smyrnans lived — like they were waiting for him. And because of it our Lord called them rich.

When you read these words as John wrote them, verse 10 really stands out: "Do not fear what you are about to suffer," says the Lord. In spite of how poor they are, in spite of the persecution, in spite of the death that the devil is bringing their way, the message is, "Do not fear what you are about to suffer," because the one writing these words is "the First and the Last, who was dead and came to life" (v. 8). If that is true, then death cannot be the final enemy, either for the Christian or for the church. "Do not fear what you are about to suffer. . . . Be faithful unto death, and I will give you the crown of life."

I don't know if there will be a Rochester Christian Reformed Church fifty years from now. I don't even know if there will be a Christian Reformed denomination fifty years from now. And, as much as either of those deaths would sadden me, neither occurrence would say one word about how our Lord considers us or whether we will be with him or whether he will come again. "You are rich," he said to the poorest church around. "You are rich," he said to a church facing its own death. "Be faithful. And I will give you the crown of life." I don't know how long we'll be here, but I do know that when someone says, We must do such-and-such, we must make this compromise, or we will die, we should say, So what if we die? As long as it's still Advent, faithful people and faithful churches are going to die. And that's okay, if the crown of life is waiting on the other side.

Kathleen Norris writes that on the first Sunday in Advent "the lectionary reading was from the text in Isaiah that begins 'Comfort ye, comfort ye my people,' and reminds us that 'all flesh is grass.' I preached a sermon at Hope Church [in the country] that attempted to address the meaning of Advent in terms of the tangle of pain and joy we feel in preparing for birth and death. The town church had opted for no sermon that day. Instead we sang Christmas carols and listened to sentimental poems from *Ideals* magazine. That text from Isaiah was read aloud during the service, but its meaning was clouded by cheer. We were busy comforting ourselves and had no wish to be reminded of our mortality."[18]

That's too bad, because recognizing our mortality is what Advent is about. Advent reminds us that faith is hard, that obedience leads to a cross, that life comes through death, and that the waiting can kill you. But Advent also reminds us that, no matter what, the Savior will arrive, Christmas will come, God will be with us. Therefore, in no way is there anything to fear — in life or in death — not when we belong to Jesus Christ, the first and the last, who was dead himself but now is the Lord of life. Amen.

18. Norris, *Dakota*, p. 173.

So Much for Keeping Score

Text: Revelation 3:14-22

"And to the angel of the church in Laodicea write: The words of the Amen, the faithful and true witness, the origin of God's creation:

"I know your works; you are neither cold nor hot. So because you are lukewarm, and neither cold nor hot, I am about to spit you out of my mouth. For you say, 'I am rich, I have prospered, and I need nothing.' You do not realize that you are wretched, pitiable, poor, blind, and naked. Therefore I counsel you to buy from me gold refined by fire so that you may be rich; and white robes to clothe you and to keep the shame of your nakedness from being seen; and salve to anoint your eyes so that you may see. I reprove and discipline those whom I love. Be earnest, therefore, and repent. Listen! I am standing at the door, knocking; if you hear my voice and open the door, I will come in to you and eat with you, and you with me. To the one who conquers I will give a place with me on my throne, just as I myself conquered and sat down with my Father on his throne. Let anyone who has an ear listen to what the Spirit is saying to the churches."

Revelation 3:14-22

We love to keep score — except maybe us Cubs fans. But the rest of us, we love to keep score. We want to know that we're winning, that we're ahead of the pack, that we have the approval of the universe or (in the more Christian version) the blessing of God. And our score-keeping mania is evident in the fact that the two questions that matter most in our society are "How much do you weigh?" and "How much do you make?" We want numbers, facts, bottom lines to validate our worth.

And it's a challenge not to think in those terms. It's a challenge not to accept the standards of soda commercials and car magazines. It's a challenge *not* to keep score — even for Christians, even for the church.

And so we must hear what the Spirit says to the church of Laodicea. There are seven of these letters to churches in Revelation 2 and 3. I don't know if they were sent off separately or if these churches had to wait for the book to come out, but I do know that eventually the church of Laodicea heard these words and that they came as a surprise. The last thing this congregation would expect is a letter of anger and judgment from the Lord. This church looks at itself and says, "I am rich. I need nothing." This church looks around and sees only a high score, only signs of God's blessing. So this letter certainly came as a surprise. But it's not hard to understand.

It's easy to understand because it's been very carefully written. You see, the writer of this letter knows Laodicea, not just the church but the city, too. He knows that the city is sort of the Wall Street of the area and that people there have a lot of money. He knows that in Laodicea they don't think much of Rome, that this city is very proud of its independence, of standing on its own two feet. He knows that the place is well respected for its medical school and that they make a medication for the eyes that is said to heal some kinds of blindness. And he knows that they breed a type of sheep that produces a kind of wool that everybody in Asia is dying to wear. The writer of this letter knows that Laodicea is the commercial center of this part of the world, with banking and fashion and medicine all booming here. He knows that this town is brimming with success in every way. Well, almost every way.

John the author of Revelation also knows that Laodicea has a problem. And the problem is its water. It's the one thing Laodicea doesn't really have: good pure water. And that's funny because two cities nearby are actually famous for their water. Colossae, eleven miles east, has a stream so pure and refreshing that it's part of their religion. Hierapolis, a neighbor six miles north, has hot springs that are famous for healing aches and pains and illness. Those cities are known for their water, but not Laodicea. That's the one thing Laodiceans don't do well, one area they're not so proud of. But, in good Laodicean fashion, they tried to fix that. They built a long system of stone pipes to bring water into the city from some hot spring five miles away. And it worked, too.

The problem was that they couldn't use the water for what they most wanted — they couldn't drink it. The water was still pretty warm when it got to town, and it wasn't so pure to begin with, so if you drank it, it would make you vomit. In spite of all their efforts, the water was still a blot on Laodicea's record. The city had industry and professional achievement and all kinds of money, but its water was sour. And, if we know all that, we see what this letter from the Lord says to the church of Laodicea, and why it comes to mind when we're talking about keeping score.

The church in Laodicea has been doing just that. This is a church that has wealth and is proud of it. It's a church where important people go, where the surroundings are the best that money can buy, where all the numbers look great. This is a congregation that is rich in every way, just like its city.

That's why these words had to come as a surprise. From the Laodicean church's point of view, all the criteria have been met, all the scores are in, and all the ways that we measure success say that God has blessed this place; this is the best church around. But the letter from our Lord says something else: "I know your works; you are neither cold nor hot. I wish that you were either cold or hot. So, because you are lukewarm, and neither cold nor hot, I am about to spit you out of my mouth." This church has the idea that things are great — and from the outside they are — but the message of the Lord is, "You think you're just like your city's wealth and fashion and medicine, a big success, but you know what you're really like? The water. You're like the Laodicean water. You're not hot and healing like the springs of Hierapolis, and you're not cold and refreshing like the stream in Colossae. You're just lukewarm, you're good for nothing, you make me want to vomit."

John uses the characteristics of Laodicea the city to send a message to Laodicea the church. "You think you're rich, but you're not. Really you're poor, you're blind, you're naked. You people who have all the money and the wonder-drug for the eyes and the finest fashions, from my perspective you're poor and blind and naked. Your numbers may all look good, your scores may be high, but it's your deeds that I see. It's your hearts that I can read. It's your devotion to me that I care about. So I'm about to spit you out of my mouth."

It's not easy to stop keeping score. It's not easy to put down the worldly measurements of wealth and fame and charisma and instead let Jesus Christ be the standard. The church can be an easy target for the ways of the world. In his book *Beyond Doubt* Neal Plantinga retells an instance from the days leading up to the Reformation. It concerns Erasmus, a man who knew how to cut things down to size, and who was especially insightful when it came to the church.

You may remember that time in the third chapter of Acts when a lame beggar asks the apostle Peter for money and Peter replies, "Gold and silver have I none, but I give you what I have: in the name of Jesus Christ of Nazareth, walk." Well, it's said that the pope and Erasmus were standing one day outside the gates of the Vatican. A long line of horse-drawn carts creaked heavily past them, loaded with the annual income of the church, the church's share of the taxes from the nations. A regiment of soldiers with drawn swords and cocked crossbows guarded the parade of treasures. The pope then turned to Erasmus and said with satisfaction, "No longer can the Holy Church say, 'Gold and silver have I none.'" To which Erasmus answered quietly, "No. Neither can it now say to a cripple, 'Walk.'"[19]

You can't measure the presence of God with bank accounts and attendance reports. You can't measure churches by what suburb they're in or how successful the members are, or whether they're up on the latest innovations. You can't do it. You can't keep score with God. That's the message to the church of Laodicea: stop congratulating yourselves; stop looking at these other things and look again to your Lord, or he will spit you out.

We must hear the anger in our Lord's voice as he speaks to Laodicea's church because we live in a land much like theirs. We live in a land that loves to judge by how much money, and how much status, and how many people. We live in a land that prides itself on independence just like Laodicea did. And, in that type of land, it is always easy for the church to get caught up in the ways of the world, to care more about success than about faithfulness and more about independence than about obedience. We must refuse such things. We must refuse pursuing only ministries that will increase our income or bring in more members, as if we're here to turn a profit. We must refuse to worship those idols; we must worship Jesus. The world judges from the outside; Jesus judges the heart. We must not forget that. The names have changed, but the Laodicean sin lives on today, more than it has in other times. We live in a time when the church is often like the world. So the anger of our Lord must be heard.

But that's not the only message here. You see, wrapped up in this judgment, wrapped up in this rebuke from the Lord, is the gospel itself. The message to the church is this: stop looking around for your validation; stop saying, I am rich because of what I have or who I am or what others think. Those things don't matter. What matters is whether you are loved by Jesus Christ, whether you rely on him for comfort, whether he directs your life. And that's not judgment; that is good news.

Keeping score never works. It's always a losing battle. And the church needs to admit that. We need to admit that the more we rely on who we are and what we have, the more we fail and fall short. We're God's people not because of all that we've done but in spite of it. Probably every one of us here wants to say, See? See how I'm rich? See how I've earned it? See how I show that God has blessed me? I know I want to say that. I want to say, Boy, that sermon was good. Now I know I'm okay. But the problem is, there's always one more sermon coming up, and even if that one's good,

19. Cornelius Plantinga Jr., *Beyond Doubt*, rev. ed. (Grand Rapids: Eerdmans, 2002), p. 203.

there's always one more after that. I can't win. It doesn't work to keep score. Jesus' word to us is, You don't have to.

The judgment in these words tells us that we may not say that the Lord is with us because we have so much, the Lord is with this church because it's such a nice facility with so many people and so much money. We may not say that. The good news here is that we don't have to. It's not about that. It's not about what we've done on our own. It's entirely about whether we're turning to Jesus, whether we're getting from Jesus what really matters. And that is good news, because not one of us can pull it off the other way. We're all a little Laodicean. Behind all the things we use to show our success, to show that God is with us, there's something like bad water ruining everything. So the good news is, Stop keeping score. Stop thinking that the blessing of God is always so easy to figure out.

Recently we considered the letter to Smyrna, a city whose situation is very different from Laodicea's. Listen again to those words: "And to the angel of the church in Smyrna write: 'These are the words of the first and the last, who was dead and came to life: I know your affliction and your poverty, even though you are rich. . . . Do not fear what you are about to suffer. . . . Be faithful until death, and I will give you the crown of life.'"

It's a lie that faithful people don't suffer. It's a lie that you can tell where God is by where the people are, or the money, or the success. It's a lie that those whom God loves always prosper. The sign of our comfort is never the numbers that the world uses to keep score; it's never the diploma on the wall or the condo on the lake. The sign of our joy and our hope is a sign of shame in our world, the cross of Jesus Christ. The sign of our consolation is that he suffered like us and for us and so gave us life, in spite of all the ways we die ourselves every day.

Our world says, You're only as good as your income; you're only as good as your status; you're only as good as you are successful. But the letter to Laodicea says that success has nothing to do with it. Faithfulness is what counts. Repenting and meaning it is what counts. Losing your life for Jesus' sake is what counts. Hear the gospel in this letter of judgment. Hear the good news that Jesus Christ loves you in spite of your weight and in spite of your income and in spite of yourself. Hear him say, "Listen! I am standing at the door, knocking; if you hear my voice and open the door, I will come in to you and eat with you, and you with me." Open the door, receive his love, accept his salvation, and be set free from earning it and proving it and staying ahead of everybody else once and for all. It's time to put all of that down, time to let Christ dress us and open our eyes and make us rich, in this age and the one to come.

— THIRTY-SECOND SUNDAY IN ORDINARY TIME —

But Will the Buses Smell Better?

Text: Revelation 21:1-6

Then I saw a new heaven and a new earth; for the first heaven and the first earth had passed away, and the sea was no more. And I saw the holy city, the new Jerusalem, coming down out of heaven from God, prepared as a bride adorned for her husband. And I heard a loud voice from the throne saying,
"See, the home of God is among mortals.
He will dwell with them as their God;
they will be his peoples,
and God himself will be with them;
he will wipe every tear from their eyes.
Death will be no more;
mourning and crying and pain will be no more,
for the first things have passed away."
And the one who was seated on the throne said, "See, I am making all things new." Also he said, "Write this, for these words are trustworthy and true." Then he said to me, "It is done! I am the Alpha and the Omega, the beginning and the end. To the thirsty I will give water as a gift from the spring of the water of life."

Revelation 21:1-6

There's a moment in the movie *Field of Dreams* that I recalled this week. The film, of course, is the story of a Midwest farmer who builds a baseball diamond into his cornfield in the hope that Shoeless Joe Jackson, a star player from seventy years ago, will show up. Well, not surprisingly, Shoeless Joe — and, eventually, a lot of other ballplayers — does show up. They all come to the field of dreams, where they can play to their heart's content, where the game never stops, where the bodies remain youthful and alive. Well, at the end of the first day in which Joe has come to the man's field, just as he's about to go back into the corn stalks for the night, he turns and calls out to the farmer, "Is this heaven?" The farmer pauses for a second, a sort of sheepish smile comes to his face, and then, with some embarrassment, he calls back, "It's Iowa."

Fair enough, we say. We understand his embarrassment, because heaven is not Iowa — as I've pointed out to various friends from Pella and Sioux Center and Oskaloosa. Iowa may build a nice baseball field and grow some tasty corn and hold some fine churches, but, surely, heaven must be somewhere else.

I just didn't think it was here. Listen again to these words from Revelation 21: "Then I saw a new heaven and a new earth, for the first heaven and the first earth had passed away. . . . I saw the holy city, the new Jerusalem, coming down out of heaven from God, prepared as a bride adorned for her husband." The first heaven and earth passed away; the holy city came down from God, the new Jerusalem. Jerusalem? A city? Coming down? *This* is heaven? I say to John. And now he's the one with the sheepish grin: It's Toledo!

When I was growing up, and actually for some years after as well, I had a fairly singular idea about what all was included in the eternal dwelling-place we always referred to simply as heaven. First, it was up; it was somewhere else, somewhere beyond the senses, past the sky. And heaven was somewhere I would, if I was good, get to go to someday, somewhere I would float to or be transported to — I'm not sure how, but I was sure that I was the one doing the moving. Heaven was fixed somewhere out there. And things in heaven were completely different from things on earth. It wasn't just a place of joy, it wasn't just a perfect place, it wasn't just a place where all the movies are rated G and all the football games are played without penalties. Heaven was beyond football games and movies. Heaven was another world, a place of bliss. "Bliss" was a good word for heaven; it was a heavenly word: bliss was quiet and harp-like and almost sleepy. Maybe not sleepy — dreamy. Heaven was dreamy. But heaven was not a city. Heaven, I was very certain, was *not* Toledo.

But try telling that to John, the author of Revelation, because according to John, Toledo is about as close as we can get. Okay, not Toledo, Jerusalem. Like that's an improvement. Every time Jesus came near the place he broke down in tears because it was so broken down in sin. Sure, Jerusalem had its moments as the city of God, but it had more moments as the city of idols. As Eugene Peterson says,

This was the city that David captured from the pagan Jebusites and then dishonored with adultery and murder. This was the city that became infamous for its child sacrifices and unlawful sorceries.

This was the city that mocked the saintly integrity of Jeremiah and turned a deaf ear to the powerful preaching of Isaiah. This was the city twice destroyed in judgment, first by the God-directed armies of Babylon, later by the Christ-prophesied Roman soldiers under Titus, and between the destructions only shabbily rebuilt by Nehemiah.[20]

That's right, the model for heaven in Revelation 21 isn't Toledo. Toledo would make more sense.

But even using a better city as the model wouldn't make Revelation 21 fit that picture I was given of heaven. What happened to being located in the sky? What happened to souls floating off to eternal life with angels providing the background music? Where are the harps? Well, the truth is, those ideas most of us grew up with aren't really that close to the biblical ideas about heaven. The truth is that those of us who are left won't be flittering or flying anywhere. Instead, heaven will come down, and that's how glory will fill our souls. Amazingly, heaven will come down and glory will fill not only my soul and your soul, but Toledo's soul, Amsterdam's soul, Jerusalem's soul. "The one who was seated on the throne said, 'See, I am making all things new.'"

We've missed that idea, haven't we? We've missed the idea of newness. We've missed the idea that what's here could somehow get over there. In another place Eugene Peterson says that people today want to go to heaven like they want to go to Florida: they think the weather will be an improvement and the people decent. Heaven's an escape, heaven's a rest, heaven's a garden, a hillside, a cornfield — Iowa, maybe — but heaven's not Toledo, heaven's not a city. Cities have far too much earth in them. And we expect heaven to be anything but earthy.

And that's strange, because in the Bible you don't have heaven without earth. In the Bible they're a set; they always go together. In the beginning God created the heavens and the earth, says Genesis. At the end, I saw a new heaven and a new earth, says John. Heaven and earth make up creation. Together they are the work of God. You can't have one without the other, and you do wrong to think of one without the other. Many people think that this earth is all there is, that the best we can hope for is to control smog a little better and get the streets a little cleaner; they think that heaven is a healthy retirement with enough money to travel on and

20. Eugene H. Peterson, *Reversed Thunder: The Revelation of John and the Praying Imagination* (San Francisco: Harper & Row, 1988), pp. 174-75.

kids who know when to go home. But those folks are misguided. They're nearsighted. They can see only what's right in front of them. And so they're missing a large part of the world. They've lost their perspective.

But vision can go bad in the other direction as well, and we've got things just as out of whack when all we can see is heaven, when we concentrate our eyes on the future, on the spiritual, on the eternal — as if what's going on here isn't part of the future, and doesn't belong to the spiritual, and has no place in the eternal. When all that matters is getting ourselves to heaven, when all that matters is what's going on in heaven, then that vision needs correcting as well. That vision needs to be re-set by the Scriptures, too. And we in the church need to remember that, because we're more likely to err in this direction. We run the risk of looking past this world and on to that. We run the risk of spiritualizing and fantasizing and falsifying heaven.

And, sad to say, some Christian authors are not helping us in that regard. Some Christian writers are telling us a lot about spiritual warfare, and they're saying that spiritual warfare is a warfare you cannot see, that it goes on above the clouds or at least beyond our sight, that it belongs in heaven. They miss the idea that this is the lot God is building on. They miss the idea that spiritual battles are not invisible battles or faraway battles but battles that occur right here every day. You want to be part of spiritual warfare? Volunteer at a homeless shelter; tutor an inner-city child; put out a forest fire. It may not be spectacular and it may not include glamorous descriptions of demons and angels, but those are things that belong to the heaven of the Scriptures. Those are the things that will matter in the new Jerusalem. The next time somebody says that the real battle is taking place between angels and demons above our heads, or that heaven is really somewhere very different from here, you tell them you've been reading another author who describes it a little differently.

"Then I saw a new heaven and a new earth," says John. You can't have one without the other. When we stop seeing heaven in Toledo, we stop seeing heaven at all. But it's in just those places that we need to see heaven. It's in just the old faithless city of Jerusalem that we need to see things to come. We need to hear and remember that God is going to take the failures and corruption and worn-out parts from the past and turn them into a city fit for his kingdom, a city fit for his dwelling-place, a city in which he has made all things new. Failure doesn't count you out of this town.

Listen to Frederick Buechner's description of the new Jerusalem:

Everything is gone that ever made Jerusalem, like all cities, torn apart, dangerous, heartbreaking, seamy. You walk the streets in peace now. Small children play unattended in the parks. No stranger goes by whom you can't imagine a fast friend. The city has become what those who loved it always dreamed and what in their dreams she always was. The *new* Jerusalem. That seems to be the secret of heaven. The new Chicago, Leningrad, Hiroshima, Beirut. The new bus driver, hot-dog man, seamstress, hairdresser. The new you, me, everybody.[21]

That's what's going on, that's the reason to celebrate — not because we're taking the 5:40 train to heaven, but because heaven is on its way here. What we see before us will form the stuff out of which the eternal city of God is made. Jerusalem, that alternately glorifying and blaspheming city, is the future home of God, right in our neighborhood. That is something to celebrate. The stuff out of which heaven will come is right before our eyes. So see it! God is making all things new.

Heaven isn't going to Florida. It's not the weekend getaway that never makes you get back. Heaven is everything around us made new, made holy, made right. Heaven is Toledo, but not Toledo right now. It's Toledo with God at the center, Toledo in which every Toledo-er will worship the Lord, and God himself will be with them and be their God. And the only ones not living in this city will be those who just can't handle having God at the center, who reserve that spot for themselves.

It's hard to imagine, of course. It's hard to imagine keeping the city but losing the rust, keeping the earth but losing the disease and corruption and death and tears that seem so much a part of it. It's really quite a bit easier to have a heaven up there, but God wants a heaven right here. And every day it's a little closer.

That's more true than we think. Paul says, "So if anyone is in Christ, *there* is a new creation; everything old has passed away; see, everything has become new!" (2 Cor. 5:17). Even now, even while the city is still old, you and I who have communion with Christ — *we* are a new creation, a touch of heaven even before the new Jerusalem gets here. There is a touch of heaven wherever God is at the center of a life, whenever you ease the pain or lessen the corruption or put out the fire. In that moment you've

---

21. Frederick Buechner, *Whistling in the Dark: An ABC Theologized* (San Francisco: Harper & Row, 1988), p. 59.

brought the new that much more into the old. You've joined John and gotten a glimpse of the new heaven and the new earth.

And then you can see a day ahead when the pain and death and tears will all be done away with, a day when Jerusalem and Detroit and Las Vegas and Toledo will be completely new. And, on that day, even the buses will show the difference.

Coming to the End

Text: Revelation 22:7-21

And he said to me, "Do not seal up the words of the prophecy of this book, for the time is near. Let the evildoer still do evil, and the filthy still be filthy, and the righteous still do right, and the holy still be holy." . . . The one who testifies to these things says, "Surely I am coming soon." Amen. Come, Lord Jesus! The grace of the Lord Jesus be with all the saints. Amen.
Revelation 22:10-11, 20-21

The last words of the last book. We've come to the end. But what a strange end it is, what a letdown, what an understatement: "The grace of the Lord Jesus be with all the saints. Amen." The Amen fits — we're used to that in these spots — but that prayer for grace seems so oddly placed. After all, for the last nineteen chapters John has been drawing magnificent pictures for us. They're pictures of dragons and angels and infernos and Satan in shackles and a beautifully new heaven and earth. All this time John has been drawing pictures for us that describe only one thing: the transformation of the kingdom of this world into the kingdom of our God and of his Christ. That is John's thesis sentence for the book of Revelation. What John is out to describe is the smashing success of heaven in its battle with sin and evil. His whole message is about the victory of God, the overwhelming presence of his kingdom, the incredible sight of the Lamb who was slain now sitting on the throne, the exciting newness of life with him forever. That's the book of Revelation: the Conqueror has conquered.

Sometimes, right now, sin and evil get in the way of that, of course. But the point is that all those old enemies — death, hell, Satan, suffering — they're not going to win out, they're not going to have any presence at all in eternity. They will be defeated. This book is about resounding victory.

And now, in the last chapter, what do we read? We read that the wonderful victory isn't far off, not at all. "See, I am coming soon! The time is near. . . . Come, Lord Jesus." So we have eighteen chapters of pictures of this grand triumph; and now, at the end, in the last chapter, we hear that it is near, it is soon, it is just seconds away, just a snap of the fingers. "Amen. Come, Lord Jesus. Praise God! Hallelujah!" Those are ways to end this book — in triumph, in confidence, in joy. But that's not what John does. John ends with a prayer. John ends his book of pictures with a strangely quiet and humble word, a word not about victory or salvation or the future, but about grace: "The grace of the Lord Jesus be with all the saints," he says. That is the final word of Revelation.

And we must make sure we hear that word about grace, because it is just as important here, just as much a part of Revelation, as all the pictures and the descriptions in the rest of the book. Maybe it's more important, because without the grace of Jesus Christ being with you, the message of John will not make any difference in your life. Everything John draws for us can be true — the victory can be certain and the new Jerusalem can be glorious and God's people can reign forever and forever — but, if the grace of Jesus Christ hasn't invaded your life, you won't know it.

Let me tell you why. Revelation — most of it, anyway — is a view from above; it functions on a different plane. It tells us not what we're going to see but what we can't see, what we have to imagine. If you want the things that we can see, read Revelation 2 and 3, the letters to the churches. There is the stuff we can see: churches full of division and suffering and sin, a world in which violence reigns and Satan often seems in control, a place in which nice guys often do finish last — if by nice we mean things like patient and honest and full of character. The churches where John was pastor live in this world, and it's just like our world, a world without a lot of hope. That's what you see when you see only with your eyes.

So John shows those churches, and ours, something else — a new vision, beginning at chapter 4. And the biggest mistake the church has ever made with this vision is in thinking that it's about the future, that it's about what's going to happen. This vision is not about what's going to happen; it's about what is happening, even though you and I and some persecuted Christian in the Roman Empire can't see that it's happening, unless the grace of Jesus Christ is with you.

If all we do is live by what we see, if we lose that bigger picture, if we can't see from above as well as from below, then we have no hope and our lives are a waste of time. And that is a lot like Will Barrett's life. In the words of Walker Percy, who created him, Will Barrett "is a talented, agreeable, wealthy man living in as pleasant an environment as one can imagine and yet who is thinking of putting a bullet in his brain."

In Percy's novel *The Second Coming* we have a man, Will Barrett, who has lived the American dream: a successful Wall Street legal career, early retirement on a beautiful southern mountainside, a six-handicap golf game, more money then he'll ever spend. As far as anyone can see, things can't be better. But Will Barrett realizes one day, in the middle of all his achievement and luxury and pleasure and time, that his life has not been such a success after all. For the first time, believes Will Barrett, he can see everything clearly: "Not once in his entire life had he allowed himself to come to rest in the quiet center of himself but had forever cast himself forward from some dark past he could not remember to a future which did not exist. Not once had he been present for his life. So his life had passed like a dream." He was ever reaching to get ahead, to move on, until there was no place left to go. So now Will Barrett asks a devastating question, a question that is as devastating to you and to me as it is to him. "Is it possible," he wonders, "for people to miss their lives in the same way one misses a plane?"[22] Is it possible to miss your life in the same way you miss a plane?

John has an answer for us. And the answer isn't a prediction of the future, it's not a description of Middle East politics, the answer is that yes, you can miss your life, but you don't have to, you won't, not if the grace of Jesus Christ is with you.

Don't these words in Revelation 22 bother you a bit? Don't they put a little sprig of doubt in your heart? I mean, 1,900 years ago John the apostle proclaimed to his world, "The time is near!" And he quoted the Lord as saying, "See, I am coming soon!" And not once, but three times. Don't you wonder about that? Don't you want to say, Okay, so where is he? How soon is *soon?* How *near* could this thing have been?

It's a good question, especially if you've been taught, as we've been taught, that Revelation is about the future. If the book's about the future, then you'd hope John would get it right. You'd hope he'd be careful to choose his words, that he'd get the timing down, that *soon* would mean *soon,* and not two millennia. But we misread John when we heave us and

22. Walker Percy, *The Second Coming* (New York: Washington Square Press, 1980), p. 144.

him into the future; we make the Will Barrett mistake and concentrate so much on what's coming that we miss what's happening. John's not writing to the future — he's writing to seven congregations in the first century. And I doubt he's bothered at all that nineteen centuries have gone by since he wrote, because his message is one for the present. That's why he ends with "The grace of the Lord Jesus be with you."

It's true, of course, that John says in verse 10, "The time is near." Talk like that makes many of us get out our binoculars and our calendars, but that's not the kind of time John's talking about. In Greek there are two words for time: *chronos* and *kairos*. *Chronos* is about schedules and date-books and events. *Chronos* time is measured in hours and months and years. Your watch tells you what *chronos* it is. *Kairos* time is something very different. *Kairos* has to do with meaning and seasons and opportunity. *Kairos* isn't a quantity of time; it's a quality of time. Missing *chronos* makes you late; missing *kairos* makes you empty.

When John says, "The time is near," the word he uses is *kairos*. He's not worried about schedules and timetables and predictions about the Lord's return — that's *chronos* material. John has on his mind not the schedule of it all but the meaning of it all. So when he says, "The time is near," he's saying to his church members living with all their dates and responsibilities and pain that the opportunity for meaning, for understanding, for the coming of Jesus Christ is nearby, it's at your fingertips. May you have the grace to see it.

Chronos time is important, of course. We need our schedule planners — mine's a day planner, two pages per day. When I faithfully record in it and then remember to look at it, my life goes a little more smoothly and I have fewer apologies to make. We need *chronos*. But, as Eugene Peterson says, "only by means of *kairos* can we comprehend and participate in Christ's coming. For the coming of Christ cannot be confined to a date — it is primarily a meeting, an arrival which is already in the process of taking place."[23]

Tomorrow morning you're going to get up at 6:15. You're going to go to work or take the kids to school or try to catch a plane. You'll be back in the world of deadlines and appointments and projects and far more tasks than hours to complete them. Days are measured in what there is to do; the week is something to endure, so that we can get time off in July or have enough money to retire on or be important. And it's all *chronos*. And if that's all there is, if life is just one dumb thing after another, just getting

23. Peterson, *Reversed Thunder*, p. 192.

through to the future, if life is spent building some dream, then we will miss our lives in the same way we miss Flight 1214 to Chicago.

So the last word John has for his readers is not "Wait for the future"; it's not "Here's the date things will really shake up"; it's "The grace of the Lord Jesus be with you." By grace we see that now is the time to live forever in the presence of Jesus Christ. By grace we know that all the *chronos* activities — all the schedules and the deadlines and the routines — are only good if they're part of something better. By grace we live in the present as if it means something for the future, as if how we live matters as much as what we do. By grace we are released from some rat race "out there" and so can value a friendship and have peace in seeming chaos. By grace we can smile at the ironies of life, even if there are more important things waiting for us. By grace we say with the Heidelberg Catechism, "My only comfort in life and in death is that I am not my own but belong to my faithful Savior Jesus Christ."

And so a life of grace is a life that says every day, "Come, Lord Jesus." And a life of grace hears him say, "See, I am coming soon!" and knows that it's true, because he's been coming every day we've known him.

It's a devastating question: "Can you miss your life?" But it's a good one, because it's so easy to get wrapped up in the visible. In some cases it's especially true of Christians, because they're so set on thinking that Christ's return is a matter of chronology that they're staring at the Gaza Strip and the new millennium and trying to get dates and places and times. But his coming isn't a matter of chronology; it's a matter of opportunity. It's a matter of letting that future with him fill up the present and make a real difference at gas stations and family reunions and the times when tears are streaming down your face. That's what John is after, that there will be enough grace in our lives to see the bigger picture, enough grace that we can rest in the quiet center of ourselves. John wants you to know that the kingdom of this world is becoming the kingdom of our God and of his Christ. He wants you to know that the coronation is coming, but you can live with the King even now. You can celebrate today. You can be part of the new Jerusalem even here.

So come, Lord Jesus. Keep on coming. And may your grace allow us to see it. Amen.

TITLE SERMON

Where All Hope Lies

Text: Romans 5:1-11

Therefore, since we are justified by faith, we have peace with God through our Lord Jesus Christ, through whom we have obtained access to this grace in which we stand; and we boast in our hope of sharing the glory of God. And not only that, but we also boast in our sufferings, knowing that suffering produces endurance, and endurance produces character, and character produces hope, and hope does not disappoint us, because God's love has been poured into our hearts through the Holy Spirit that has been given to us. For while we were still weak, at the right time Christ died for the ungodly. Indeed, rarely will anyone die for a righteous person — though perhaps for a good person someone might actually dare to die. But God proves his love for us in that while we still were sinners Christ died for us. Much more surely then, now that we have been justified by his blood, will we be saved through him from the wrath of God. For if while we were enemies, we were reconciled to God through the death of his Son, much more surely, having been reconciled, will we be saved by his life. But more than that, we even boast in God through our Lord Jesus Christ, through whom we have now received reconciliation.

Romans 5:1-11

This is a strange day, for all of us. Some of you may be unaware that today marks my return to this pulpit after seven months during which I've been dealing with a particularly aggressive and deadly form of cancer. Now, with the cancer vacationing for a little while, I am back, and glad for it. But this is a strange day, because I don't really know what to say. I want to ignore the whole thing, pretend everybody's forgotten that I was gone — and why I was gone — but we can't do that.

We can't ignore what's been going on. We can rise above it; we can live through it; but we can't ignore it. If we ignore the threat of death as too terrible to talk about, then the threat wins. Then we are overwhelmed by it, and our faith doesn't apply to it. And then we have no hope.

We want to worship God in this church, and for our worship to be real it doesn't have to be guilt-ridden, or fun, or crowded; but it does have to be honest — honest about faith in a world of violence and pain, a world that decries faith and smashes hope and rebuts love. We must be honest that believing is not always easy and that life is hard.

So we must face the truth here, and the truth is that I was scared. Not of cancer, not really. Not even of death. Dying is another matter — how long it will take and how it may go. That still scares me. But when I say I was scared, it's not those fears that I'm talking about. This fear was something else altogether.

One man has influenced my preaching more than anyone else. His name is John Timmer, and he's a recently retired Christian Reformed minister in Grand Rapids, Michigan. In his working with a text and in his preaching, John Timmer showed me that a sermon that misses or ignores or disowns the scandal of the gospel is no sermon at all. And the scandal of the gospel is grace. The scandal of the gospel is that there is nothing you can do to be made right with God; but God has made himself right with you — through blood, through death. And it's amazing how a man could in one sense preach the same message week after week and still mold my life with what he said. John Timmer taught me that baptizing an infant reminds us that God comes to us before we go to him. John Timmer showed me that God came to Abraham when there was nothing to come to, an old man at a dead end. And that's how God always comes — to infants and old people, to sinners and losers. That is grace. And no sermon can be without it.

So I've tried to fill my sermons with it, faithfully and honestly and even courageously, but always with grace. And it's an amazing thing to do, to proclaim through the poetry and the stories and the letters of the Bible a plan of God that runs contrary to every instinct we have, to every principle of our world. And, you know, I believe it. I believe that God has come to Kevin, this infant baptized here today, long before Kevin can make a move toward him. I believe the words of John Calvin and the Heidelberg Catechism and the New Testament that we have only one comfort, but it is a comfort in life and in death. I do believe that, but I was scared.

We've dealt with a lot of interesting and difficult topics the last three years — war and divorce and homosexuality, *and death*. And I said that the gospel speaks to every one of them — I said that God receives broken people all the time. But that was before I faced death myself.

This is a silly thing to admit. I don't know if I ever realized the absolutely shocking, radical idea that is God's grace. I said those things about it fully believing them, but at the same time fully believing — or at least expecting — that I had a few decades yet before I really needed to count on them. I assumed that I had forty or fifty years yet, years in which I would earn my way, be a kind old man whose sin wasn't so significant anymore, who of course would be received by God because he was good to animals and picked up the mail for his neighbors. Like I say, it's silly thinking.

And scary. Because suddenly I wasn't looking at fifty years but five months, or seven months, probably not two years, almost certainly not more than that. My appointment was moved up — now I would meet my Judge not kind and old but *soon*, with not enough time to undo the wrong, not enough time to straighten out what's been crooked all these years, not enough time to prepare, to clean up. *That's* what I was scared of.

So, for the first time in my life, I had not only to preach this scandalous good news, not only to believe it, but to rest on it, to depend upon it, to stake my life on it. And as I faced all of this and was frightened by it, I remembered one of the simplest, most powerful statements in the entire Bible.

You may have thought that I chose this text because of those wonderful words about suffering producing endurance and endurance character and character hope. Those are beautiful words, true words, but I'm not so sure they apply to me; I'm not so sure I've suffered so much or so faithfully to claim that result. I hope so, but many of you easily outdistance me in those ways. Actually, what drew my attention to Romans 5 was not that beautiful paragraph, but just one little word: *eti*. That's what brought comfort to my soul. *Eti* is a Greek word that means "yet," "still" — as in "while we *still* were sinners Christ died for us" (v. 8); or "while we were *still* weak, at the right time Christ died for the ungodly" (v. 6). What's interesting about verse 6 is that the word is used twice; it's repetitious and ungrammatical, but it's like an additional emphasis, an additional marveling at the glorious goodness of the gospel: "For while we were still weak, at the right time Christ died for the ungodly."

Kevin is weak right now — he's weak in language and intellect and faith. That's why his baptism is a wondrous act; it's a celebration of grace, a celebration of how, when he was still weak, God came to him before he could even know to go to God. I am weak, too — physically, of course, quite profoundly in some ways, but that's not my main weakness, my most debilitating weakness. And if I ever doubted that, it's been proven to me in this last half year. My weakness is more of the soul than of the body, and I've realized that as I've dwelled on thoughts like, "How will I explain myself to my God? How can I ever claim to have been what he called me to be? I can't." That's the kind of weakness Paul's talking about. And that's where *eti* comes in — while we were *still* weak, while we were *still* sinners, while we were *still* enemies of God, we were brought together with him through the death of his Son.

I find it unfathomable that God's love propelled him to reach into our world with such scandalous grace, such a way out, such hope. Let me tell you, there's no hope anywhere else — I looked. There is no hope in this world apart from that scandal. It all lies right here.

You learn that when you face death and think about what it means. It means the same friends you enjoy now will still get together a year and three years and twenty years from now and you will almost never come up in the conversation. It means that your work will be gone — in my case, this church will call a new minister with new gifts and a new future — and you will soon be out of mind as you are out of sight. And don't feel too sorry about that — I would be the same way, I *am* the same way. Hope doesn't lie in your legacy; it doesn't lie in your longevity; and it doesn't lie in your personality or your career or your politics or your children or your goodness. It lies in *eti*.

When I was saying something like this a few months ago to a friend of mine, he reminded me of those poignant words of Psalm 103: "As for mortals, their days are like grass; they flourish like a flower of the field; for the wind passes over it, and it is gone, and its place knows it no more." For the first time I felt those words in my gut; I understood that my place would know me no more.

One of my favorite recent poems — even before the cancer — is from Miller Williams. It's called "Adjusting to the Light." It's about that scene in John 11 in which Jesus raises his friend Lazarus from the dead. For the most part the words of the poem are spoken by Lazarus's friends and neighbors, after they are surprised to see that he really is back among them, back among the living, after four days of being gone. This is what they say:

> Lazarus, listen, we have things to tell you.
> We killed the sheep you meant to take to market.
> We couldn't keep the old dog, either.
> He minded you. The rest of us he barked at.
> Rebecca, who cried two days, has given her hand
> to the sandalmaker's son. Please understand
> we didn't know that Jesus could do this.
> We're glad you're back. But give us time to think.

Imagine our surprise. . . .
        We want to say
we're sorry for all of that. And one thing more.
We threw away the lyre. But listen, we'll pay
whatever the sheep was worth. The dog, too.
And put your room the way it was before.[24]

I love that line. Time goes on, whether we do or not. Miller Williams is right: Lazarus's place knew him no more. I *liked* that poem, but now I've *lived* that poem. And, believe me, don't put your hope in your legacy or your name recognition, in some sermon you wrote or project you accomplished. Even if it allows you to last a little longer, it won't matter, because in the end you'll still be swallowed up, and your place will remember you no more. The story of Lazarus being raised isn't really the story of Lazarus; it's the story of Jesus. Lazarus got a few more years and then he died all over again — he was resuscitated, not resurrected. The story of Lazarus makes for a good film, but it's not much to rest your entire existence on. But this isn't the story of Lazarus; it's the story of Jesus, the story of the one who gives life, even through his death, the story of the one who breathes the breath of God into utterly dead souls.

Our place will know us no more. It's true. All the stuff we think will keep us alive, when we really look at it, it only shows us how little we have to depend on, to stake our lives on, to put all our hopes in. All we really have is the scandalous gospel of grace, that while we were still weak and sinners and even enemies, Christ died for us.

My place will know me no more, but God knows me. The Giver of life, who came to me and kept coming to me before I ever went to him, knows me, and so I have hope, hope on which I can rest all that I am — hope that I believe Kevin will have some day, hope in the story of Jesus.

So don't be surprised that we won't talk about this cancer situation very often. This is not the story of me, it's the story of Jesus. And that story applies to every cancer, every job, every family, every divorce, every sin that belongs to any of us. But to us who believe, it's always Jesus' story, and Jesus' story carries beyond all of it.

I'm dying. Maybe it'll be longer instead of shorter; maybe I'll preach for several months instead of a few weeks. But I am dying. And it's hard and I hate it and I'm frightened by it. But there is hope, an unshakable hope.

24. Reprinted from *Adjusting to the Light: Poems* by Miller Williams, by permission of the University of Missouri Press. Copyright © 1992 by Miller Williams.

That hope is not in something I've done, some purity I've kept, or some sermon I've written. I hope in God, the scandalous God with a plan the world has never heard of — reaching out for an enemy, saving a sinner, dying for the weak. And that I can stake my life on. I must. And so must you.

SERMONS FOR
VARIOUS OCCASIONS

Thanks But No Thanks

Text: Philippians 4:10-20

I rejoice in the Lord greatly that now at last you have revived your concern for me; indeed, you were concerned for me, but had no opportunity to show it. Not that I am referring to being in need; for I have learned to be content with whatever I have. I know what it is to have little, and I know what it is to have plenty. In any and all circumstances I have learned the secret of being well-fed and of going hungry, of having plenty and of being in need. I can do all things through him who strengthens me. In any case, it was kind of you to share my distress.

Philippians 4:10-14

Thank-you notes can play a rather important part in our lives. Thoughtfully and appreciatively written, a thank-you note can liven our spirits and send us off to other kindnesses. But a poorly written one, or a lack of one, can overwhelm whatever gracious act was performed and even create resentment. I'm serious — I know people who twenty years later still remember and complain about a young couple's neglecting to send thank-you notes for their wedding presents. Well, after reading Paul's words in Philippians 4, I hope Epaphroditus isn't somebody like that.

When you read these words of Paul, it seems that Epaphroditus and the rest of the Philippian congregation have been given ample opportunity to be offended. After all, as soon as they heard that Paul was in prison, they put together a care package for him, because they know how bad Roman prisons are; they know the kind of suffering and barrenness he's living with. So they had an offering, they gathered canned goods, they bought him some stationery, they held a clothing drive, and then they asked the deacons to get it to Paul. And Epaphroditus was the one chosen to go all the way to Rome, hundreds of miles, so that Paul's suffering would be relieved and he would feel better.

And this is the letter they receive in return. For three chapters he hardly mentions their gift at all. And when he finally does get around to it, at the very end, does he tell them how grateful he is that they gave him a hand? Does he say how their package made all the difference, how it got him through a long day or a cold night? Does he even say thank-you? No. Not really.

Instead Paul says something like this: "I'm really happy that you thought of me, but I want you to know something: I don't really need you; I don't really need what you send. My life will be more comfortable this way, sure; but to be really honest with you, it doesn't matter whether I have a little or whether I have a lot, whether I'm full or whether I'm hungry. You see, I've learned to be content whatever the circumstances. As far as I'm concerned, Epaphroditus, you might as well have stayed home and watched the Lions and Steelers. Even here in prison I don't live for things like this. Thanks but no thanks." Actually, that's giving Paul a little too much credit, because in these eleven verses, in this thank-you note from Rome, Paul never says the word *thanks* once. You get the idea that maybe Paul doesn't even know how to say thank-you.

I wonder how that note would fly with us today; I wonder if Hallmark has a card for this occasion: "Thanks, but understand, I don't need you. Love, Paul." I think my poor health these last eight months is well known to most of us. What may not be so well known is how much this congregation has blessed me with gifts of all kinds, and continues to do so. Imagine how it would sound if I stood here today and said, I'm glad you took the opportunity to assist me in a hard time, but I want you to know that I don't really need things like that. You see, I can live in a house or an alley; I'm fine with or without health insurance; as far as I'm concerned, having good doctors or no doctors really makes little difference.

It's a strange way of saying thank-you. And it seems strange to a lot of people. Some people think that Paul was struggling with these words because saying thank-you for a very meaningful gift is difficult and humbling, as it can be. Others think that he didn't write it at all, that somebody else wrote this part of the letter, and that's why it's so strange and put way at the end. But there's another answer, a better answer, an answer that may not improve his manners but does display his faith. Paul distances himself from the Philippians' gift because, before they hear how important their giving that gift is, he wants them to know that that's not where his joy comes from — not from blankets or food or money or even freedom. His contentment doesn't come from those things; it comes from Christ.

Paul wants the Philippians to know that his ability to make it through the day, the reason he can praise God and have peace in his soul, doesn't depend on anything that they do for him, or even anything that happens to him. He tells them something like this: I appreciate your gift because it is a sign of your love for me, but I don't need your gift to have joy in my heart, because over the years I've learned something. I've learned the secret of being content in every situation. I've learned to be content in a prison cell in Rome with a piece of bread just as much as at the emperor's table with all the trimmings of a Thanksgiving dinner.

"I have learned to be content with whatever I have." Paul has *learned*. Apparently there was a time when he was different, when his contentment depended on his well-being, on his comfort, on his family, on his job, on his prosperity, on his health. But somewhere along the way there's been a change in Paul. Paul learned to be content even with a thorn in his flesh that God says is going to stay there. He learned that his life, his outlook, is not determined by thorns or beatings or arrests, or awards or popularity or wealth. Paul learned to let his life be determined not by the outside but by the inside, by Jesus Christ, who gives him strength for every situation. So Paul says, I have joy in my heart not because of any package Epaphroditus brought; I have joy in my heart because Jesus Christ is there. It may be kind of rude, but you get the idea that for Paul there's no other way it can be.

The emphasis today is on adding up, taking inventory, counting our toys, evaluating our dreams, looking at all the things we have to make us content: the new cars and the remodeled houses and the lots of money and the food, of course. For most people that's where this holiday lands, if it lands anywhere: counting up what we've got, and, if it's a good amount, finding joy in it.

But it cannot be that way for us who have Jesus Christ. In one sense this could not be a more Christian day; praising God for his goodness is fitting and proper. But that goodness doesn't come by way of cars and toys and European vacations, not first off. That goodness comes by way of Jesus Christ, dying for us, living in us. So our praise today, our joy tomorrow, our thanksgiving always is dependent not on our salaries or even our health; it's dependent on our Savior, whose strength allows us to survive all things.

And that's why what Epaphroditus did is so important. It's important, not because without it Paul will be miserable and with it he'll be fine, but because it displays that the God who lives in Paul is the God who lives in Epaphroditus as well. The Savior in Paul means that he doesn't need a care package to survive his prison, to rejoice even in chains; the Savior in the Philippians means that they send it anyway. And when they do it, they are saying thank-you, not to Paul, but to Christ. What they did is a sacrifice to God that he finds very pleasing. And that matters so much more than the right kind of thank-you card.

"In any and all circumstances I have learned the secret," says Paul, "of being well-fed and of going hungry, of having plenty and of being in need." The secret is Jesus Christ — saving, sanctifying, strengthening. That's how a person can be content — even in prison, even in sickness, even in death. Even right now among us today, with whatever has gone wrong for this group, whatever has brought tears to our eyes, whatever has bound us up in some personal prison — the bad relationships, the poor health, the loss of a spouse or a friend or a job, whatever it is — we can bring our thanksgiving, because we know the secret, because we can do all things through him who strengthens us.

"I know what it is to have little, and I know what it is to have plenty"; "I have learned to be content with whatever I have." Whether in a Roman prison or a Philippian church, the person who says that is a person in whom Jesus Christ lives, and she knows exactly how to say thank-you.

Meditation

Text: Galatians 4:1-7

My point is this: heirs, as long as they are minors, are no better than slaves, though they are the owners of all the property; but they remain under guardians and trustees until the date set by the father. So with us; while we were minors, we were enslaved to the elemental spirits of the world. But when the fullness of time had come, God sent his Son, born of a woman, born under the law, in order to redeem those who were under the law, so that we might receive adoption as children. And because you are children, God has sent the Spirit of his Son into our hearts, crying, "Abba! Father!"

Preached December 31, 1999.

So you are no longer a slave but a child, and if a child then also an heir, through God.

Galatians 4:1-7

I have to admit it — I'm a Y2K atheist. All my money's still in the bank. Apart from some Christmas leftovers, there's no extra food in the refrigerator. And if my credit cards stop working tomorrow, I'm going to be in trouble. If the Y2K problem is real, then it's going to be a big problem for me. And this may turn out to be not the smartest thing I've ever done, because — as we all know too well — some of the world's important computer systems may be facing some pretty serious problems with the change from the nineteen-hundreds to the two-thousands. So there may be pretty good reasons to wonder about bank accounts and credit cards and grocery store scanners, I guess. And I may be sorry three days from now for not believing a little more sincerely in this Y2K stuff, because technologically there's probably some issue for concern.

But I think my technological perspective has gotten confused with my theological perspective. As you know, a lot of people — a lot of Christians — think that this day is a vital one not only for IBM and Microsoft and Wegman's but for God, too. And the believers in that kind of Y2K problem talk about things like the end of the world and big cataclysmic events and other divine indications that in 2000 God's really going to start getting involved — Y2K theology, not technology. And one thing we need to remember as the digits change tonight is that the theology is misguided; it's so misguided that, for me, it's been awfully easy to dismiss all the other Y2K issues as well, and tomorrow maybe I'll be wishing I'd stocked up on milk this morning.

But let's go back to that theology, to the idea that we can determine some crucial things for the course of history in the change of the calendar, or that the Bible is to be used for dates and times and predictions, or that somehow we know that for God the — or at least *a* — big moment in time is upon us at the end of this millennium. As I say, that idea is misguided, it's wrong, and there are lots of reasons why we know that.

Some of them are simple, like Jesus himself saying that we shouldn't try to figure out God's timetable, because nobody knows the day or the hour. God's ways are not our ways, and therefore we should not expect our dates to be God's dates, either. As John Calvin said, "It is a . . . vanity to seek and enclose Christ's kingdom within the elements of this world." Too much of such vanity is going around these days.

But we also shouldn't pursue such millennial theology because that's not what the Bible is about. Sadly, in our time, the Bible has become not so much good news to a sad and fallen world as a codebook to be cracked, and once we crack it we'll have all the answers. That's not how the Bible is to be read. It's not about the magic of God; it's about the grace of God. It's the Word of God in the words of human beings. And the Word of God isn't prediction; it's good news.

But there's an even bigger reason, I think, a fundamental reason, why we know that this is not the big moment in history dawning upon us. And that reason is that that moment has already dawned, and that moment actually defines who we are. That's the moment Paul talks about in the words we read from Galatians 4: "when the fullness of time had come, God sent his Son, born of a woman, born under the law, in order to redeem those who were under the law, so that we might receive adoption as children."

It's funny in a way that so many think the fullness of time is a night like tonight, when the world's odometer turns over, when in fact the fullness of time came when nobody had any inkling about it. As Matthew tells us, the important people didn't even bother with it. For God the fullness of time was a time nobody else saw as all that full. And the year wasn't "round" at all, by the way, because, due to some later miscalculations, Jesus Christ was actually born in 5 B.C., which means that it wasn't two thousand years ago, but two thousand four years ago. That's when the fullness of time was, in a quiet place, with nobody looking for it, on an odd year.

And that's why we shouldn't look for it now — not only because God is less enamored of our dates and calculations and decipherings than we usually think, but because it's already happened. The big moment in time has already dawned, God has already made his statement, and that's the event that must carry us, certainly those of us who are not atheists, through every year and every date and every millennium.

For us, celebrating the big moment in history came last week, not this week. The big moment was when God sent his only begotten Son, when the time was full, to come here, to be born of one of us, and to give himself up, so that we might have hope, we might have confidence, we might be able to face new centuries without fear of the great unknown before us. In that act of God at the true crux of history, we became children of God — heirs even, as Paul says — through him.

That is the identity we have as those who know Jesus Christ, those who know that the fullness of time has already come and what happened then. God has sent the Spirit of his Son into our hearts so that we call him Father.

Now, of course, that's not the end of the story. There are events still to take place in order to complete the transformation of the kingdom of this world into the kingdom of our God and of his Christ, and they may even be cataclysmic events. But we await them not as people trying to decode the Bible, not as people who think we can get a handle on God because of what day we call it or because Israelis and Arabs aren't getting along; we await those events knowing that our Father knows when the time is full. Our Father always knows the right time to send his Son, and our Father always has before him the needs of his children.

I hope my credit card works tomorrow and I don't have to borrow any cash in the council room Sunday morning, because that would be a real nuisance. And my computer has to function, because I still have work to do on Sunday's sermon. But let us watch the passing of this age, and the passing of every age, not with fear or panic or attempts to crack the codebook to find out what's going to happen; let's watch the ages pass knowing that God knows, so much better than we, what time it is. And at the fullness of time, he sent a Son born of a woman in order to make us his daughters and sons. Everything else that happens takes place in a world whose Master is our Father, and he is not about to be pushed around. Even death would not stop him from having us as his children. So don't think anything in Y2K — or any other time — is going to, either.

"So you are no longer a slave but a child," says Paul. We're not slaves — to dates or computers or bank accounts or disease or death. We are children, we are even heirs of God, because in the fullness of time he sent his Son. Tonight, if we are wise, we will remember that day in time with much more faith, much more gravity, than we will this one. We will remember that, not once every millennium but once for all, Christ gave his body, his blood, for us, to become children of God — for all time.

Meditation

Text: Mark 14:43-46, 50-52

Immediately, while he was still speaking, Judas, one of the twelve, arrived; and with him there was a crowd with swords and clubs, from the chief priests, the scribes, and the elders. Now the betrayer had given them a sign, saying, "The one I will kiss is the man; arrest him and lead him away under guard." So when he came, he went up to him at once and said, "Rabbi!" and kissed him. Then they laid hands on him and arrested him. . . . All of them deserted him and fled. A certain young man was following him, wearing nothing but a linen cloth. They caught hold of him, but he left the linen cloth and ran off naked.

Mark 14:43-46, 50-52

According to the experts, the cross is in. And I'm not talking about the theologians here, I'm talking about the fashion experts. The cross is a fashion statement. A while back, *Vogue* magazine declared that "both as streetwise pendants and as couture pieces, crosses have had a popular revival. . . . With medieval-inspired fashion making its mark, a cross worn at the neck or pinned to a jacket will continue to be the definitive accessory of the moment — whether a simple wooden piece . . . or Verdura's extravagant aquamarine-and-yellow-sapphire cross."[1] So the cross in *our* culture is something that healthy and beautiful and "with it" men and women want to attach themselves to.

Well, how things have changed, at least since the days of the Gospel of Mark. If there's one thing Mark definitely did not consider the cross, it's fashionable. If there's one way Mark would never describe the cross, it's as a "definitive accessory of the moment." And if there's one way Mark could never picture the cross, it's in extravagant aquamarine and yellow sapphire.

In Mark we notice that things have been building up toward Jesus' capture for a long time already. Way back in chapter 8 we read that Jesus "began to teach them that the Son of Man must suffer many things, and be rejected by the elders, chief priests, and teachers of the law, and that he

---

1. Quoted by Richard John Neuhaus in *First Things* 40 (February 1994).

must be killed." And then we read that Peter refused to listen to Jesus say such things, and that Peter actually took Jesus aside and rebuked him. And that becomes sort of a pattern in Mark: Jesus' describing a time when he will be struck down, and the disciples' refusing to hear it, because what Jesus is predicting is not fashionable or attractive; it is ugly, it is unspeakable, it is something from which to flee.

And when the time comes, flee from it is exactly what the disciples do. For them the cross never stops being something ugly, something horrendous, something awful. So, to avoid facing it, these best friends of Jesus are willing to do something awful themselves. In a few verses Peter is going to scream "I don't know this man!" to steer away from the ugliness of his cross. Mark tells us that all of the disciples deserted him at his arrest; all of them fled because of the terrible idea that, if they didn't, they would end up at the cross, too. In the Gospel of Mark — only in Mark — we read of one more person, an unknown young man, who came out in his underwear to follow Jesus that night. But this last disciple, this last one following the Lord, also ends up high-tailing it out of there. They grab his cloth, and he runs off naked, willing to humiliate himself, willing to suffer disgrace — just to stay away from that cross.

So, you see, if there's one thing clear in the Gospel of Mark, it's that Jesus is going to an ugly, ugly place and a terrible, terrible death — so terrible that those who know him as Lord and left everything to follow him now leave everything they have to get away from him, to distance themselves from him, to keep away from the cross. The disciples all flee. "I don't know this man!" says Peter. "But [the young man] left the linen cloth and ran off naked."

So who is this fellow who tried to follow Jesus when it mattered but ended up running away like the others? Is he Mark himself? That's what some people think. But we don't know that. All we know is what Mark tells us: there was a young man walking with the Lord that night, and the word Mark uses for this person suggests that he was "exceptionally strong and valiant, or faithful and wise."[2] This is a person of courage and health, someone who climbs mountains and plays chess with equal aplomb, someone who would never run out on his Lord. So the death of Jesus on that cross is such an ugly, horrible event that even society's best run from it like scared rabbits, disgraced and humiliated. Amos put it like this:

2. William L. Lane, *Mark*, New International Commentary on the New Testament (Grand Rapids: Eerdmans, 1974), p. 527.

"And those who are stout of heart among the mighty shall flee away naked in that day, says the Lord" (Amos 2:16).

So one thing we must remember from this night is that we who follow Jesus have chosen a difficult thing. Bearing his name produces comfort, but it does not produce ease, and we must not mix up the two, if we want to stay faithful to him and truly have communion with him. Earlier in Mark, Jesus says, "If anyone would come after me, he must deny himself and take up his cross and follow me" (8:34). And that is a hard thing to do, an ugly thing to do. May the ugliness of taking up a cross not turn us away from following Jesus.

It was ugly for him, too, of course. Perhaps it is easy to forget that. Jesus wanted out of there as much as Peter, as much as John or James, as much as that anonymous young man. "Remove this cup from me," he prays just a little while earlier (14:36) — don't make me face the horror of that death, the ugliness of the cross. But, unlike the ones who were with him, Jesus was faithful; he kept going toward that cross. While his disciples are turning and fleeing, or joining the enemy, or denying that they know him, or running off naked, Jesus keeps going toward that ugly cross.

The darkness of this day in the church is not that Jesus lost this battle, because of course we know better; we know that on Sunday he will be the victor, his name lifted above every name. The darkness of this day is not that he lost but that, while every disciple was busy betraying him or denying him or deserting him, for their sake, for *our* sake, he went forward to hang on a cross.

And in that cross there is nothing fashionable, nothing romantic or stylish, nothing aquamarine and yellow; there is only agony, the agony of the one who died for the sins of the world.

So let us not forget that the Christ went to an ugly cross; he went to a place his followers couldn't even look at, couldn't even consider. He went anyway, for them, for *us*, for weak and scared and disgraced disciples. He went so that we wouldn't have to, so that the ugliness would be all his and we would escape. Let us remember that when we remember the cross.

The Waters of Israel

Text: 2 Kings 5:1-14

But Naaman became angry and went away, saying, "I thought that for me [the prophet] would surely come out. . . . Are not Abana and Pharpar, the rivers of Damascus, better than all the waters of Israel? Could I not wash in them and be clean?" He turned and went away in a rage. But his servants approached him and said to him, "Father, if the prophet had commanded you to do something difficult, would you not have done it? How much more, when all he said to you was, 'Wash, and be clean'?" So he went down and immersed himself seven times in the Jordan, according to the word of the man of God; his flesh was restored like the flesh of a young boy, and he was clean.

2 Kings 5:11-14

The church I used to serve in California sits on a busy intersection. Across one street is a popular gas station–mini-mart; across the other is a major bus stop. People come around that corner and by the church all the time. And, for various reasons, with various questions and requests and troubles, they stop in. Since I was the only real employee and my office door faced the intersection, I was usually the one who would greet them. Amid all of the different and sometimes strange things people came there for, one young woman stood out, for her politeness and her innocence and her expectation. She had a baby with her and one question on her mind. She asked it as soon as I opened the door: "When do you do your baptisms?"

That was all she wanted to know — when we scheduled baptisms, what arrangements had to be made to have a baby baptized. I'm pretty certain that, had I mentioned a dollar amount that covered our baptism package, she wouldn't have blinked an eye, and probably would have gotten out her checkbook. And since I was alone in the building, and could probably have taken care of the whole transaction in about fifteen minutes, it was tempting. Baptism for this person, in all her innocence, was something you arrange.

Naaman thought just the same way. Naaman, we are told, was a great man. He was chairman of the joint chiefs of staff for the king of Aram.

And he was good at it, too. Naaman had the king's respect and the people's trust and admiration. That's the kind of unsurpassed power and influence Naaman possessed in his world — he was a hero, a star, a ruler, a mighty warrior. But he was also a leper.

Fortunately for Naaman, the leprous superhero, serving in his house is a young, insignificant girl, a slave, someone his troops had picked up on one of their jaunts through Israel. And this girl remembers a man in Israel — a prophet — who knows a thing or two about leprosy. Now Naaman has the line on a cure.

So Naaman does what any general, any great man, would do: he gets his credentials in order and puts together some things that show what kind of man he is — a letter of reference from the king, a suitcase full of cash, ten tailor-made suits — and he heads off to Israel, in all his innocence, ready to arrange a healing. But, as the king of Israel already knows and is afraid to tell Naaman, it doesn't work that way. You can't just make an appointment for this sort of thing. What this mighty warrior has to learn is that he can have wealth and power and status and rulers and victories on his side, and he still won't be able to arrange his healing. All the king's horses and all the king's men aren't going to be able to save Naaman from leprosy.

Fortunately for Naaman the power-broker, not everyone in Israel is a king, and not everything happens by royal decree. So the prophet Elisha sends a message, "Let him come to me and he'll learn that there is a *prophet* in Israel." So Naaman lugs his suitcases and his garment bags and his royal letters and his entourage over to Elisha's place. The great man is ready to arrange this great healing event once more. But before the chauffeur can even get out of the chariot, there's a servant standing there with a message for Naaman: "Go, wash in the Jordan seven times, and your flesh shall be restored and you shall be clean."

Naaman didn't come all this way to be treated like some commoner, to be met by some prophet's messenger as if he were a nobody, to be told that his cure lies in making a fool out of himself in some scummy little river. If it's a river he needs, the ones at home are certainly as good as anything they've got in Israel. Naaman is a great man, and great men don't take baths in the Jordan, and they don't take orders from the servants of prophets.

And that's the problem with Naaman. He'll play along with a little of this Israelite religion, but he's not going to bend too far to do it. "But Naaman became angry and went away saying, 'I thought that for me he would surely come out, and stand and call on the name of the Lord his

God.'" That's what is keeping Naaman from receiving his salvation, from being healed of his leprosy. Naaman wants to arrange his healing — he wants to pay for it or contract for it or make an appointment for it — but he wants to do it all along as Naaman the great, Naaman the powerful, Naaman the mighty warrior. Naaman wants attention and admiration and ceremony from Elisha; all he gets is, "Go wash up in the Jordan."

Fortunately for Naaman, he took a few servants with him to Israel, and his servants are willing to speak up: If he asked some hard thing from you, you'd have done that, right? they say. So then, why not do this little thing? Why let your pride get in the way of your life? Why let your status come between you and being made well? And their words work. So Naaman, the great man, the mighty warrior, goes down and washes seven times in the Jordan River, and when he comes out his leprosy is gone, and his skin is like that of a young boy. Or, in another way to translate it, his skin is like that of a small servant. When Naaman becomes like a servant, he is made well.

And that's how God's grace works. It's not something you can arrange. It's not something you can purchase. It's not something you can have and keep your dignity at the same time. As John Timmer says, that's just God's way. That's how he gives his grace, so that we have to bend to receive it.

Bending is not something we like to do. And that is why we need to protect this font. That is why we need to make sure that it keeps its place, that it's visible, that it's important. That is why we even need to make sure that we use enough water. Because this font, this activity of baptism, is a bending to receive the grace of God. And as long as we try to keep our dignity while we do it, as long as we try not to spill or muss or embarrass or bend, we're not doing it right and we're not recipients of grace.

I worry about our practice of baptism today sometimes. I worry because it's not just people knocking on the door from outside the church that think it can be arranged. I worry because some of us think of baptism as only an honor or a blessing and we don't remember that it's a bending, a humbling, a dying. We who were baptized into Christ Jesus were baptized into his death, says Paul.

If baptism's not a bending, if it's only a ceremony or a good-luck charm or a superstition, then it's nothing. Then we may as well use the water of Damascus. Don't forget what this font is all about, and as you raise your children, do it as humble servants. Do it as those who listen to the Word of God, and train them to do the same. That's when God's grace takes effect — when we bend to receive it.

The font needs to be here, whether we happen to be using it or not, to remind us that God's grace means giving up our dignity and our importance and our status and becoming servants. That is the only time we are healed — when we respond to God's Word, even when it comes from someone beneath us. Notice that in the story of Naaman the words of the kings come to nothing. The king of Aram writes a letter, but it doesn't do any good, because the king of Israel isn't able to do anything about leprosy. Naaman the general, with all of his money and status and importance, has to give it all up and dive into a muddy river. It's the servants that speak the truth, the lowliest people in this story. The slave-girl in the house, the messenger of Elisha, the servants of Naaman — their words are the ones to listen to.

And that is the hard thing about this passage, and about baptism, and about the gospel of Jesus Christ. In spite of all our efforts, it will never be "seeker friendly." As Timmer says, Elisha telling Naaman to go wash himself in the Jordan River was not a seeker-friendly thing to do. And neither is Christ's command that those who enter the church should do something similar, should be baptized. These things are humbling experiences, but we will not be made whole unless first we take off our medals and get off our horse and wash ourselves in the waters of Israel.

You know, Naaman's right: there's nothing special about the Jordan River. And I wouldn't be surprised if those two rivers in Damascus are significantly better than this one — they're probably much more attractive, nicer color, better temperature, much more conducive to healing, much more therapeutic. There's just one thing wrong with them: they're not in Israel. And whether Naaman likes it or not, the God who has brought him victory after victory, the God who has given him the highest place in the kingdom of Syria, the God who will heal his leprosy is the God of Israel. Only when Naaman recognizes that and obeys is he made whole.

And the same is true of baptism. There's nothing special about the water. The rituals of other religions may be more impressive or more powerful or more beautiful. But like it or not, the God who brings us life, the God who allows us whatever status or importance or wealth we possess, the God who heals us is the God of Israel, the God of the church, the God of Jesus Christ. And only when we recognize that and humble ourselves before him are we made whole.

Do come here to worship. Do come to Jesus Christ. If you're wandering, if you're looking to be made whole, I hope you keep coming, and I hope you know that this is the place to be, this is the Savior you need. But don't expect to stay who you are, don't expect to hold on to your dignity.

The healing, restoring grace of God is here for you, but you're going to have to bend to receive it.

I guess it would be nice if Naaman could just stop by Israel, write his check, and receive his cure, without even having to get out of his chariot, without even having to get his feet wet. It would be nice, maybe, if we could just stop by some church and find out the baptism schedule, hand over the Visa card, and have everything taken care of. The grace of God from the drive-through window.

But, whether we want it so or not, whether it would be friendlier or not, that's not how it works. There's nothing to purchase, nothing to earn, nothing you get because of who you are or what you have. It can't be arranged. The grace of God can only be received by those who have given up all of that and become servants. And that is good news, that is the good news of the gospel. This good news is for all of us who don't have life by the tail like Naaman the Great. The good news is that a child may receive God's grace, even if a Syrian commander may not. The good news is that God lifts up the humble, but he opposes the proud, and the waters of Israel are here to remind us of that.

The Man Behind the Sermons

When the idea for this book first came up, Jim was nearing the end of his battle with cancer. He was pleased that people wanted to remember him this way. I, too, was touched that the thing in life that Jim did best would be a part of the people he was leaving behind for a very long time. When I first began to consider what I wanted to write about Jim, I knew that I wanted to give a small glimpse of the man behind the sermons, who was far more than just a young minister struck in his prime by cancer. He was a unique individual who touched many people's lives, more so than, I think, even he realized.

I met Jim when he was a seminary student doing his internship at Third Christian Reformed Church in Denver, Colorado. Already then, people could tell that this man had a gift for preaching, even though he often questioned his decision to become a minister. But anyone who heard Jim preach knew he had a gift, and as you read this book that will be obvious. However, Jim was more than a preacher — he was an avid sports fan, an animal lover, and a bookworm. He spent his days off walking the dog, catching up on the latest sports trivia from either ESPN or *Sports Illustrated*, or simply reading a good novel. All of these activities impacted his preaching and found their way into sermon illustrations, which helped make him the talented preacher that he was.

Jim was the youngest of five children and was born and raised in Chicago, Illinois. After attending Timothy Christian School he went on to Calvin College. Throughout his college career, he continued to debate the merits of entering seminary versus law school. Finally, after graduating from Calvin in 1987 with a degree in Greek, he decided to give seminary a try and entered Calvin Seminary. Jim grew both spiritually and emotionally in seminary. He often commented on the fine instruction and mentors there who helped shape his strong beliefs and develop his preaching style. He did a one-year internship at Third Christian Reformed Church in Denver, Colorado, in 1988-89 and then finished his Master of Divinity degree in May of 1991. He stayed on at Calvin Seminary for one more year to study under some of his favorite professors and work on his Master's of Theology.

Jim and I were married in June of 1992, and he accepted his first call to Sacramento Christian Reformed Church. He served this small congregation for three and a half years and for the most part truly enjoyed being a full-time pastor. He grew both as a pastor and as a church leader those three years, and I was privileged to see this transformation.

After three years and with prayerful consideration, Jim accepted a call to Rochester Christian Reformed Church, and we moved to New York in January of 1996. Not only did we have to acclimate ourselves to winter again, but Jim also had to adjust to being senior pastor of a much larger church. Once again, Jim's gift for preaching is what attracted people to his ministry. Our time in Rochester proved to be both challenging and exciting, and once again Jim grew in his creative preaching style and ministry gifts.

In March of 1998, two years into his Rochester ministry, Jim was diagnosed with a rare and aggressive form of cancer. We were fortunate to be in Rochester where he was able to receive excellent medical care, including some experimental treatments in Boston. Although the last three and a half years of Jim's life focused a great deal on various treatments and surgeries, he still was able to continue doing what he loved best — preaching. He preached his last sermon on December 31, 2000, and died peacefully at home on January 22, 2001.

Even though it was the cancer that brought about this book and certainly occupied a great deal of Jim's life the last few years, cancer never killed Jim's spirit or ability to preach. It affected his life but did not consume it, and I hope that when you read this book it becomes clear that Jim was not first a cancer patient, but a committed and faithful child of God secure in the knowledge that God's grace was all-sufficient. In fact, cancer was only a small part of his life.

This book is published to honor Jim and to preserve some of his sermons that touched the lives of people in his congregation. So when reading through these sermons, remember that they were written by a man who loved creatively delving into Scripture. Even though his time on earth was far too brief, he lived life to the fullest and set a fine example for his family, friends, and congregation of living a faithful, committed life in spite of difficult circumstances. That is how Jim should be remembered, not as a cancer patient or a tragic figure struck in his prime, but as a gifted preacher who faithfully lived the life God laid out for him.

Rachel Payne Van Tholen